Remembering James Agee

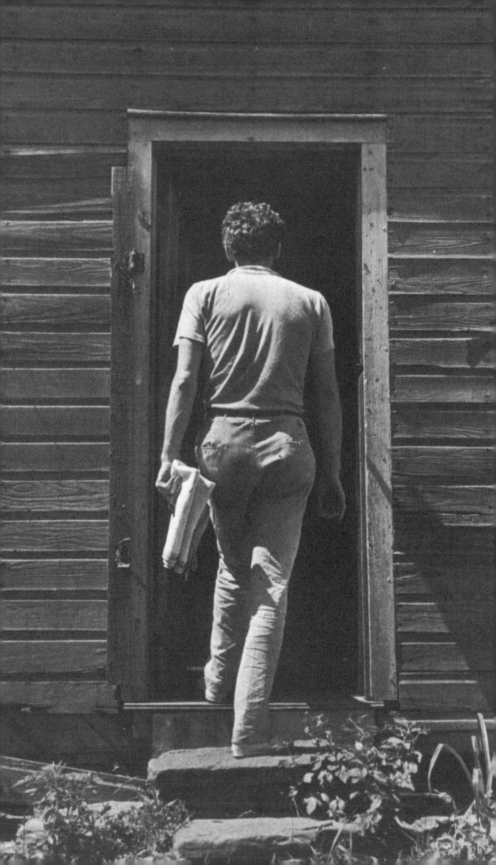

EDITED BY DAVID MADDEN
AND JEFFREY J. FOLKS

Remembering
James Agee

Second Edition

The University of Georgia Press

Athens and London

© 1997 by the University of Georgia Press

Athens, Georgia 30602

All rights reserved

Designed by Erin Kirk New

Set in 10 on 13 Electra by G & S Typesetters, Inc.

Printed and bound by Braun-Brumfield, Inc.

The paper in this book meets the guidelines for
permanence and durability of the Committee on
Production Guidelines for Book Longevity of the
Council on Library Resources.

Printed in the United States of America

01 00 99 98 97 C 5 4 3 2 1

Library of Congress Cataloging in Publication Data

Remembering James Agee / edited by David Madden and Jeffrey J. Folks.

— 2nd ed.

    p.   cm.

Papers originally presented at the James Agee Week Conference, held at
St. Andrew's Episcopal School, Sewanee, Tenn. in October 1972.

Includes index.

ISBN 0-8203-1913-9 (alk. paper)

1. Agee, James, 1909–1955 — Biography — Congresses.   2. Authors,
American — 20th century — Biography — Congresses.   I. Madden, David,
1933–   .   II. Folks, Jeffrey J. (Jeffrey Jay), 1948–   .   III. James Agee Week
Conference (1972 : Sewanee, Tenn.)

PS3501.G35Z86   1997

818'.5209 — dc21   97-8507

[B]

British Library Cataloging in Publication Data available

Contents

Illustrations

Acknowledgments

The editors would like to thank the late Reverend William S. Wade, headmaster of St. Andrew's–Sewanee School, for permission to publish panels from the Agee Week Conference. Fred Guyette, formerly librarian at St. Andrew's–Sewanee School, was especially helpful in locating and providing the editors with copies of audio-tapes of the Agee Week panels. We are thankful for permission to publish photographs by Helen Levitt, and we are grateful to the Metropolitan Museum of Art and the National Portrait Gallery, Smithsonian Institution, for permission and prints of Walker Evans's portrait of Agee. We acknowledge the kind permission of many Agee Week participants or of their executors in publishing material from the conference: Scott Bates, Edward Carlos, Arthur Ben Chitty, Mrs. Robert Daniel, Warren Eyster, Mrs. Robert S. Fitzgerald, the Estate of Father James H. Flye, the Estate of Louis Kronenberger, James Ward Lee, Andrew Lytle, the Estate of Dwight Macdonald and Yale

University Library, Frederick Manfred, Mrs. Franklin Martin, the Estate of David McDowell, the family of Walker Percy, John Reishman, Mrs. Edwin M. Stirling, and William Stott. We also appreciate permission to reprint essays from the first edition of *Remembering James Agee* from Robert Saudek and Gerald Locklin and from the estates or executors of Father James H. Flye, Robert Fitzgerald, David McDowell, Walker Evans, Louis Kronenberger, T. S. Matthews, Dwight Macdonald, John Huston, and Whittaker Chambers. We acknowledge permission from the James Agee Trust for quotations from *The Collected Poems of James Agee*, and from Grosset & Dunlap, Inc., to quote from *A Death in the Family*.

"James Agee in 1936" by Walker Evans, from *Let Us Now Praise Famous Men* by James Agee and Walker Evans. © 1960 by Walker Evans. Reprinted by permission of Houghton Mifflin Company. All rights reserved. From *A Death in the Family* by James Agee, © 1957 by The James Agee Trust, © renewed 1985 by Mia Agee. Reprinted by permission of Grosset & Dunlap, Inc. Excerpts from *Let Us Now Praise Famous Men*. © 1939 and 1940 by James Agee. © 1941 by James Agee and Walker Evans. © renewed 1969 by Mia Fritsch Agee and Walker Evans. Reprinted by permission of Houghton Mifflin Company. All rights reserved. We also acknowledge excerpts from *Letters of James Agee to Father Flye*. © 1962 by James Harold Flye and The James Agee Trust. © 1971 by James Harold Flye. Reprinted by permission of Houghton Mifflin Company. All rights reserved. British Commonwealth rights granted by Peter Owen Publishers, London.

Malcolm Call, senior editor at the University of Georgia Press, has encouraged and coordinated this project through several stages of development. Nancy Summers Folks contributed editorial assistance without which completion of the manuscript would have been impossible.

Jeffrey J. Folks

Preface to the Second Edition

The panels recorded at the Agee Week Conference at St. Andrew's School in October 1972 chronicle the responses of James Agee's contemporaries and near contemporaries, his personal friends and literary acquaintances, as well as the scholarly evaluations of literary and cultural critics such as James Ward Lee and William Stott. In bringing together a cross section of Agee's contemporaries, a representative group of Agee critics, and a selection of younger writers and teachers interested in Agee's work, Agee Week clearly contributed to the development of Agee's reputation in the two decades following the conference. The conference panels, carefully edited and published here for the first time, register the spontaneous discussions, as well as the prepared remarks, of a wide range of participants.

As the response of James Agee's contemporaries and near contemporaries, the Agee Week panels are a unique record of the development of a major writer's reputation at a critical transition point. The panels afford us a vivid sense of the strong impression that Agee made on his contemporaries; what is more, they indicate precisely in what terms he was appreciated: *why* for some contemporaries he became an admired writer, for others a major cult figure compared at times with James Dean and with J. D. Salinger.

Bordering at times on intense debate, the Agee Week panels foreshadow the terms in which Agee would come to be discussed in later decades. In the panels included in this second edition, major contemporaries such as Robert Fitzgerald, Andrew Lytle, Dwight Macdonald, Frederick Manfred, and Walker Percy discuss Agee's impact on their generation. The panels are therefore of interest not only for those studying Agee but also for those interested in Agee's circle — in Lytle, Macdonald, Percy, and the other panelists: a cross section of American writing from the thirties through the seventies. In addition, Father James H. Flye, Agee's lifelong friend, describes his early impressions of Agee and their growing friendship. Younger writers and critics such as Scott Bates, Edward Carlos, James Ward Lee, David Madden, Edwin M. Stirling, and William Stott interpret Agee's works; their discussions, valuable in their own right, also document the perspectives from which Agee's work was read a quarter century ago.

Published here alongside the more formal essays and memoirs that comprise the first edition of *Remembering James Agee*, the Agee Week panels capture vividly the excited spirit of discovery and debate that characterized Agee Week at St. Andrew's School in October 1972. By printing the panels for the first time, the editors of the second edition hope to convey something of the enthusiastic atmosphere out of which much of the later critical writing on Agee evolved.

The present collection reflects the continuing interest in Agee's work suggested by recent books such as *James Agee: Reconsiderations* (1992), edited by Michael A. Lofaro, and Laurence Bergreen's *James Agee: A Life* (1985) and the success of the James Agee Film Project. Equally important is that Agee's major works remain in print and that new editions, including his *Selected Journalism*, continue to appear.

Agee's continuing importance is related to the sense that he was a precursor in so many ways: as a sensitive, poetic novelist exploring cinematic and surrealistic techniques; as an innovative journalistic writer anticipating the New Journalism of the sixties; as a screenwriter whose scripts satisfied the requirements of limited commercial formats but who also experimented with outlandish dadaist and expressionistic images and techniques; as the first major American film critic, developing the film review far beyond the often quirky efforts of Vachel Lindsay and others into a canon-building exercise in which he ferreted out unappreciated B-films and defended masterpieces such as *Monsieur Verdoux*; as a cultural critic, whose commentary in his *Nation* film column and in his *Time* articles ranged from dissections of American social classes to apocalyptic predictions concerning world politics (precursor to cultural critics fifty years later, Agee adopted a "cool," satiric tone vis-à-vis the dominant commercial art intended primarily for consumption by the American middle class); as a poet, who, like W. H. Auden, employed conventional forms to relate new and often frightening psychological discoveries. Agee's ideas for multimedia, his elaborately detailed experimental film scripts, his suggestions regarding the direction of mass culture and its importance in America — these aspects of his work alone should earn Agee recognition as an important innovator.

Not least in importance in our time of academic specialization is Agee's faith in communicability. The stance that Agee adopts of speaking *with* his reader, perhaps derived in part from his formidable conversational gifts, is utterly incapable of patronizing or lecturing. As the aspiring writer who, according to Bergreen, could be "savagely critical" of his own writing (*James Agee: A Life*, 73), Agee displayed a rare concern for the reader: the reader was an equal participant in a democratic culture, a colleague possessed of the same passionate mental and emotional commitment to truth as the writer himself. Agee believed in the ability of language and art to convey the problems of ordinary citizens and to improve society. In the context of our post-poststructuralist culture, now as weary of linguistic indeterminacy as of doctrinaire ideological approaches to criticism, Agee's humanistic assumptions about art and society seem old-fashioned but also oddly relevant and original.

Writing without pedantry and without jargon, Agee continually adapted his prose style to his ever-fresh understanding of truth. In its sincerity and accessibility, his prose continues to attract new readers. Agee grasped intuitively, even before his fourteen years of labor at Luce publications, the transcendent value of human existence beyond commerce and what he, in *Let Us Now Praise Famous Men*, labeled simply "MONEY." Readers have recognized the universality of Agee's longing for freedom, an impulse that he shared with his cultural idols Beethoven, Blake, Dostoyevsky, Chaplin, even Christ. Agee always insisted on the artist's independence, even at the cost, in his own case, of long periods of poverty and exclusion.

For our own culture, Agee's defense of individualism and his assertion of individual moral conscience as a primary obligation seem crucial. Bergreen notes that, working during the Second World War at the *Nation* in an atmosphere of enforced patriotism, "Agee's refusal to reveal a distinct political leaning isolated him from his peers" (276). Earlier still, Agee had avoided the faddish radicalism of the thirties, finding it impossible to endorse the left-wing sympathies of most of his colleagues at *Fortune*, but even more strenuously, he resisted the pseudo-religious and conservative drift of American culture after the war. Agee felt more genuine compassion for the disadvantaged than many who proclaimed their ideological sympathies at the convenient moment, and his deeply spiritual nature, while skeptical of the institutional dogma of the church, never discarded the teachings of his religious upbringing. In the universalist sense of his beliefs, Agee's faith in mankind connects with a philosophical tradition in American and European writing extending back through Whitman and Stephen Crane to Emerson and Thoreau, and beyond that to Coleridge and European romanticism.

Sympathy for the world's downtrodden was not, in Agee's case, a posture that he adopted for expedient ends but a deep emotional response originating undoubtedly in the class tension of his parents' marriage and in the conflicts inherent in his relatively privileged childhood amidst a background of glaring poverty. Like George Orwell's excursions at "tramping," Agee's attempts to connect with a broader democratic people — his decision to work the wheat harvest in the summer of 1929, his research for *Fortune* articles on the Tennessee Valley Authority or the "Great American Roadside," and his two challenging months living among Alabama sharecroppers in the late summer of 1936 — anticipated periods of very real hardship in Agee's own life and fused his sympathies with the poor.

The Agee Week Conference occurred at a critical moment of reevaluation of James Agee's reputation. Moving beyond the "cult" response of the fifties and sixties, decades in which Agee's romantic personal life was often the underlying focus of interpretation, the conference set out to study Agee's writing in a serious critical manner. In this way, the panels reflect the same transition that was occurring in Agee criticism generally: from the early impressionistic reviews, including insightful analyses by W. H. Auden, Dwight Macdonald, and Lionel Trilling and through that criticism published after his early death and in the wake of the success of *A Death in the Family* (and its Broadway and filmed versions, *All the Way Home*), Agee's reputation all too often reflected the growing legend of a rebellious saint, an innocent, if impractical, idealist martyred by society because of his unwillingness to compromise his principles.

The image of James Agee as a cult figure could hardly bear up under serious critical examination by book-length studies such as Kenneth Seib's *James Agee: Promise and Fulfillment* (1968). While only intended as a general introduction, Seib's book does accomplish a critical reading of Agee's major works and challenges the uncritical acceptance of the Agee legend. Of *Let Us Now Praise Famous Men*, for example, Seib argues that Agee "eventually came to realize his mistaken judgment . . . and, for that reason, soon turned to fiction" (57). Judging *A Death in the Family* to be Agee's major accomplishment, Seib approaches the novel in an eclectic fashion, partly as an innovative work of "cinematic" fiction, partly as a nostalgic tribute to marital love and "American culture." Seib interprets the development of maturity and "manhood" in Rufus as the central action in the novel.

Other early books include Peter H. Ohlin's valuable study, *Agee* (1966), a critical work that has held up well and been often echoed by later books, and Erling Larsen's concise but insightful introduction, published by University of Minnesota Pamphlets on American Writers in 1971. Larsen, who summarizes Agee's major works and offers brief commentaries, is among the first to focus on the problem of identity as the central theme in Agee's writing. With its brief format, however, Larsen's pamphlet does not deal with several central problems that have occupied later critics: among them, Agee's "failure" to produce a large canon of work or the relationship of his journalism and film writing to his literary works.

Following these early studies, Victor Kramer, Alfred T. Barson, and Mark Allen Doty published important critical evaluations that, for the first time, presented a detailed rationale for the enduring value of Agee's writing. Kramer's work on Agee, which includes his volume in the Twayne series and numerous critical articles, has advanced the critical assessment of Agee's reputation and in doing so has provided a more solid foundation for further study. In his sympathetic and perceptive book, *James Agee* (1975), Kramer argues that Agee's major works are linked by Agee's central attitude of "selflessness": "Being able to put himself into the frame of mind of another was his fundamental characteristic as critic and person" (25). Agee's commitment to "honoring reality" and to validating everyday experience runs through his work in different media. Kramer is one of the very few critics to analyze Agee's early poetry fully and to suggest its relationship to the later work. Focused on Agee's realism, Kramer judges *Let Us Now Praise Famous Men* to be his "masterwork" (75).

Two of the finest books devoted to Agee are Barson's *A Way of Seeing: A Critical Study of James Agee* (1972) and Doty's *Tell Me Who I Am: James Agee's Search for Selfhood* (1981). Doty studies the problem of identity and Agee's relationship to his father as central themes. He makes a convincing case for the personal quest for identity as the central thematic structure in all of Agee's writing, and he presents insightful readings that support the centrality of the autobiographical emphasis in Agee's fiction and journalism.

In contrast to Doty's focus on the autobiographical, Barson locates Agee's writing within the cultural milieu of his time, particularly in that of the forties, a decade that Barson considers crucial in influencing Agee's fiction. Agee's attitudes of antiauthoritarianism and anarchism, originating in his negative reaction to his sense of having failed a demanding father and his aversion to a God-centered church, were fully confirmed in the culture of the forties, which, to Agee and to many of his contemporaries, seemed to be verging toward authoritarian forms of social and technological order. Barson shows that *A Death in the Family* was drafted largely in 1947–48 and was heavily influenced by Agee's commentaries on world politics, written for *Time*. *A Death in the Family* culminated the frustrating tension between art and life that Barson traces in Agee's early poetry and in *Famous Men* — a work that was "revolutionary" not in its political doctrine but in its aesthetic approach of including both the "thing itself," the subject of sharecropping, and the emotion in the perceiver, the seemingly intrusive persona of "Agee" as *Fortune* reporter.

Agee's writing in the forties was equally revolutionary in its effort to bring to consciousness the present moment in which he lived as well as the historical past out of which the present had evolved. In describing this aesthetic, much influenced by James Joyce, Barson writes that for Agee, "the artist's task" is "to arrange or produce that which already existed" (105). Barson's study is a compelling and thoughtful analysis of Agee's "way of seeing" and of Agee's moral intentions, although its focus on the culture of the forties does lead to somewhat limited interpretation, such as the assertion that *A Death in the Family* "grew out of his reaction to the Bomb and the latent despair of the cold-war era" (142).

Books and essays published more recently have adopted equally specialized approaches. A chapter in Robert Coles's *Irony in the Mind's Life* (1974) focuses on the complexity and unresolved tensions of Agee's sensibility. A chapter by Louis D. Rubin Jr. entitled "Trouble on the Land: Southern Literature and the Great Depression" in *Literature at the Barricades: The American Writer in the 1930s* (1982) characterizes *Let Us Now Praise Famous Men* as "more imposing" than Erskine Caldwell's work and "pivotal" to Agee's career. While "ineffective as a work of political and social reportage," Agee's book is imaginatively intricate. William Stott's chapter on Agee in *Documentary Expression and Thirties America* (1973) expands remarks that he first presented at Agee Week and that are printed here. F. Garvin Davenport's "Machines and Sexual Ambiance in James Agee's *A Death in the Family*," collected in *Beyond the Two Cultures: Essays on Science, Technology, and Literature* (1990), discovers technological motifs connected with the masculine world from which Rufus feels excluded, particularly following the death of his father in an automobile accident. J. A. Ward's *American Silences: The Realism of James Agee, Walker Evans, and Edward Hopper* (1985) finds versions of silence in Agee's writing as an aesthetic response to his conclusion that naturalism was ineffective in embodying the lived experience of ordinary human beings. Like Walker Evans and Edward Hopper, Agee attempted to distill the "beauty" of ordinary moments of existence without violating his subject with obtrusive techniques of art.

The essays collected in *James Agee: Reconsiderations* (1992), edited by Michael A. Lofaro, are confirmation of the continuing impact of Agee's writing on a new generation of readers. While the range of approaches in this collection reflects the breadth of Agee's own interests, the relative emphasis on *Let Us Now Praise Famous Men* and on Agee's journalism highlights the significance of Agee's social vision for the present generation. An essay by George Brown Tindall, an eminent southern historian, confirms the importance of Agee's journalistic prose in relationship to southern history. Linda Wagner-Martin's "*Let Us Now Praise Famous Men* — and Women: Agee's Absorption in the Sexual" focuses on Agee's sexual metaphors and his imagined relationships of conquest and seduction in relation to sharecropper women. Paul Ashdown traces a prophetic stance in Agee's journalism; essentially reading Agee's *Fortune* pieces as cultural criticism, Ashdown discusses Agee's sense of his own role as a social visionary. Eugene T. Carroll's "Mood and Music: Landscape and Artistry in *A Death in the Family*" offers convincing support for the "sense of symphonic form" and the use of musical techniques in Agee's posthumous novel. New essays by Victor Kramer and David Madden substantially advance the earlier work of each on Agee. This valuable collection also includes a complete bibliography of secondary sources compiled by Mary Moss.

Although several recently published biographies and memoirs significantly enlarge our knowledge of Agee's life and the conditions under which he wrote, they also raise troubling questions about his often obsessive, self-destructive personality. In addition to these biographical works, the documentary films on Agee produced by Ross Spears at the James Agee Film Project have served as a valuable resource for the study of Agee. Spears's full-length documentary film *Agee* relies on interviews with contemporaries and readings from Agee's works. The short documentary *An Afternoon with Father Flye* was recorded over a period of years starting when Father Flye was ninety years old. *To Render a Life: "Let Us Now Praise Famous Men" and the Documentary Vision* explores the making of a documentary dealing with a contemporary sharecropper family in Alabama.

It is understandable that any writer who so frequently turned to autobiographical expression should be the object of intensive biographical research. Laurence Bergreen's *James Agee: A Life* is a vivid and sympathetic account, based on access to unpublished materials in the James Agee Trust, on letters and interviews, as well as on a careful reading of Agee's published works. Along with Genevieve Moreau's *The Restless Journey of James Agee* (1977), Bergreen's book is valuable in placing Agee's writing against the backdrop of his life; it is impressive in its knowledge not just of Agee but of his entire circle, of his milieu at Time, Inc., and of the historical and literary backgrounds for his work. Like others who adopt a largely biographical approach to Agee's writing, Bergreen perhaps too readily accepts Agee's fiction as a factual record, and his biography contains a measure of speculative interpretation that is open to reevaluation. Nonetheless, it remains the most detailed and illuminating biographical work on Agee.

Reminiscences of Agee also abound. Alma Neuman's *Always Straight Ahead* is an autobiography of Agee's second wife. As with Joel Agee's *Twelve Years: An American Boyhood in East Germany* (1981), Neuman's autobiography is an interesting sidelight, revealing little, if anything, new about Agee. More closely related to Agee as a writer are the literary reminiscences collected in the present volume, especially the indispensable remembrances by Robert Fitzgerald, Dwight Macdonald, and T. S. Matthews.

If the present volume contributes in some measure to a critical reevaluation of Agee's writing, it should do so without glossing over many disturbing elements in his life and work. Agee's personal faults were all too numerous, and his critics have perhaps not looked closely enough at the extent to which psychological duplicities entered his writing. By any objective measure, Agee's conduct as a husband was, to use one of his own favorite words, "lousy." His disdain for conventional morality, reflecting his generation's reaction against the puritanical ethos of nineteenth-century America, was extreme even for his time. His bohemian ideal envisioned the artist's necessary independence from bourgeois society. Agee's penchant for narcissistic self-analysis was not limited to sessions with Jungian analyst Frances Wickes; it also entered into passages of *Let Us Now Praise Famous Men* and *A Death in the Family*. Even Agee's phenomenal compassion for defenseless human beings — for children and for the economically disenfranchised — may be more problematic than it seems, for somewhere connected with his defense of the weak, one senses Agee's potential for fury and unbending judgment. These qualities in themselves, however, merely confirm the need for further study and understanding of Agee as a singular and powerful sensibility.

The second edition of *Remembering James Agee* intends to bring James Agee's legacy to the attention of the general reader and to serve as a resource for scholars. The Agee Week materials published here were originally addressed to a bright high school audience prepared for the conference by an intensive full semester of Agee study. One can imagine that Agee himself would have been pleased with the sincerity and straightforward language employed by his critics at Agee Week in 1972 — if not by the excessively reverential tone that almost invariably accompanies such occasions. It is to the credit of all who participated at the Agee Week Conference that an atmosphere of open discussion, lively debate, and intellectual skepticism informed the panels and presentations. It is hoped that an accurate sense of that week's excitement and debate is communicated in this volume.

In compiling this edition, the editors have worked from copies of audiotapes of the Agee Week panels and an unedited transcript of the tapes, graciously supplied by the staff of the James Agee Memorial Library at St. Andrew's School. We have adhered closely to the language and intent of the recorded panels, while deleting some passages that were not closely related to Agee's life or work. We have made only minor corrections of wording, when the language of the panels became overly repetitious or seemed unclear. One panel session of St. Andrew's alumni devoted to reminiscences of the school itself seemed largely unrelated to Agee and was deleted entirely.

DAVID MADDEN

Introduction:
On the Mountain with Agee

In October 1972, St. Andrew's Episcopal School in Tennessee held a commemorative gathering for the dedication of its James Agee Memorial Library. People who had known Agee personally or who had been interested in or influenced by his work were invited to the school. The man who arranged this confluence of novelists, critics, scholars, clergymen, and students was David McDowell, Agee's biographer, custodian of the Agee Trust, and editor-publisher of *A Death in the Family*. Book review editors from the *Nashville Tennessean* and the *Louisville Courier-Journal* came, though none came from Knoxville. Scholars and writers came from universities in Texas, from Sewanee, Kenyon College, Vanderbilt, Harvard, Louisiana State University—though there were none from the University of Tennessee. Novelists whom McDowell had published came: Brainard Cheney,

Frederick Manfred, Margaret Long, Madison Jones, Andrew Lytle, Warren Eyster, Bowen Ingram — few of whom ever met Agee in the flesh but in whom his spirit now abides. Walker Percy came. Friends of Agee came: Father Flye, eighty-eight that week, Dwight Macdonald, and Robert Fitzgerald. And Mia Agee came, with her son John.

Skimming back through Agee's work before leaving Louisiana to participate in that weeklong tribute to Agee at his boyhood school in Tennessee, I said to my wife: "You know, I really don't like Agee very much." I was reluctant to stop work on my own fiction to drive four hundred miles to struggle with ambivalent feelings about Agee. When A Death in the Family came out in 1957 and won the Pulitzer Prize, I was still a student, living a block away from Agee's childhood home, the locale of the novel. I was writing a novel set in Knoxville, which would be published a decade later by David McDowell. That Agee should be then the famous Knoxville writer I dreamed of becoming made me hellishly jealous. For if Dublin was Joyce's city, Knoxville was mine.

Over the years I had become convinced that the Agee legend, enhanced by publication of his letters to Father Flye, had inspired a sentimentality that beclouded his actual achievement as a writer. The romantic isn't-it-a-shame-he-died-before-he-could attitude was appealing, but I resisted it. When I first read Agee, especially Let Us Now Praise Famous Men, some passages struck me as precious, mannered, pompous. Though there were fine moments in A Death in the Family, Agee's poetry was pretentious and archaic. The Morning Watch, for me, was tedious and self-indulgent. I had to acknowledge that Agee was a superb movie critic and that his own movies, The African Queen and The Night of the Hunter, were wonderful. But his letters to Father Flye made me feel so queasy I couldn't read very far into them.

In that week of communion with Agee through his friends and admirers, and afterwards during months alone with Agee in his work, I was slowly converted to new attitudes about him. Many of us rediscovered Agee that week. But for me, as a writer and a teacher, something more than a rediscovery happened. A regenerative process began — a process that moved me to collect these previously published memoirs and to request new ones.

Trying to describe that experience, I feel as Agee must have felt when he began Famous Men: "If I could do it, I'd do no writing at all here. It would be photographs; the rest would be fragments of cloth, bits of cotton, lumps of earth, records of speech, pieces of wood and iron, phials of odors." At St. Andrew's I touched no such talismanic objects inhabited by the spirits of those who had used them; rather, I was taken by an aura, an atmosphere, a mood such as Agee caught in *The Morning Watch*, which is set at the school: "As if the whole air and sky were one mild supernal breath. . . ." This air became charged with an energy made manifest in what I must call signs, parallels to Agee's work, even symbols. Everything seemed runic to us. Like Good Friday in the novella, that week was one of those occasions when everything seems related, significant; coincidences were more strikingly coincidental than they normally are. A mystical note reverberated throughout that weeklong ceremony of meditation that preceded the formal dedication of the library. Through his work and through the informal reminiscences of his friends, Agee's presence was most profoundly felt during that uncannily felicitous time on the mountain.

Watching the students at St. Andrew's experience Agee through these men and women who either had known him or felt that he had affected their lives or work, my own ambivalent feelings surfaced initially. The students, seventh- through twelfth-graders, had spent the entire semester with coordinated assignments in English classes, dealing with the range of Agee's work — short stories, a novella, a novel, poetry, personal journalism, movie criticism, television and movie scripts. Then for a full week, all classes were suspended to allow a massive immersion in Agee's work — discussion groups, movies, and panels conducted by the novelists, critics, and scholars. I sensed that some of the students were feeling as Rufus had felt in *A Death in the Family* when he was taken to visit his great-great-grandmother in the country: "It seemed to Rufus like a long walk over to the old woman because they were all moving so carefully and shyly; it was almost like church."

Like Agee in Alabama, we aliens risked being regarded as invaders, imposing a saint on the students, forcing their participation, exacting their admiration and respect. I didn't want to contribute to a ritual in which students might be bored, bewildered, resentful, or even apathetic. When James Lee, editor of *Studies in the Novel*, disrupted the churchlike atmosphere with a blast at *Let Us Now Praise Famous Men*, I knew the students were as relieved as I was. As an Alabamian, Lee had resented Agee's romanticization of the suffering he knew as a country boy in the thirties. When the students applauded Lee's comments, I could only think that Agee himself would have appreciated such a clearing of the air.

When an English class met in the chemistry lab to discuss *A Death in the Family*, the teacher slumped between two Bunsen burners and confessed to being sick to death of talking about Agee. During the discussion that followed, the students and I began to share both our positive and negative feelings about Agee and his work. As I dealt with the various shifting literary and human contexts enacted at St. Andrew's — with my own sometimes virulent objections and reservations — I realized that my responses to Agee's work were changing and my enthusiasm was growing.

Agee himself would, I think, have been entranced by the strategies some of the students used for defeating boredom and by the grace with which they responded to particular moments in which insight, intellect, and emotion fused. I experienced some of those moments myself at a premier screening of a movie about St. Andrew's, *School on the Mountain* by Charles Angermeyer, a young alumnus. In many ways, its images evoked several of Agee's works. In the film Father Flye reminisced about Agee and read from his writing. He also talked about teaching: "Not *I* against them, but they and I against the problem." Some students were beginning to respond to Agee as if he were such a teacher, and their "problem" was this week devoted to Agee. What an incredible teacher Agee would have been — a combination of Father Flye and Agee's other great teacher, I. A. Richards. In 1931, Agee had told Father Flye, "I am attracted to teaching almost enough to dread it . . . it would be very bad for me." He would have put all his intellect and emotion into it as he did with every job he ever had. In his writings, Agee did in fact presume to teach, and he was very conscious of the responsibilities.

This formal ceremony was now becoming not simply a structure in which normal breathing was difficult but one in which a rarer kind of breathing had become possible. The already exhausted students endured the tedium of *All the Way Home*, the movie adaptation of *A Death in the Family*. Although I had been deeply moved when I first saw the film with my son, then Rufus's age, I disliked it intensely this time. Even so, I was profoundly affected by some of the parallels to my own life; I felt a compulsion to tell about those feelings in the discussion I led afterward. The movie theater scene was filmed in the Bijou, the setting of the novel I had put aside to come to St. Andrew's. My father was living in the old L&N Hotel seen in the background as Rufus and his father walked home. John Cullum, who had acted in plays with me at the University of Tennessee, portrayed the agnostic uncle, Andrew.

Later, in my motel room, with the door open to let in the mountain mist, I returned to *Famous Men*. Now Agee as a man and a writer began to affect me as a reader and a writer. Agee's compulsion to transcend mere description moved him to devote four pages to overalls: "[T]hey are a map of a working man." In "new work-clothes a man has the shy and silly formal charm of a mail-order-catalogue engraving." Agee sees "wild fugues and floods of grain" in old wood, "the patternings and constellations of the heads of the driven nails . . . shadows strong as knives and India ink." I reread "Knoxville: Summer 1915": "*On the rough wet grass of the back yard my father and mother have spread quilts. We all lie there . . . and I too am lying there.*" Recalling a similar passage in *Famous Men* — Agee and Walker Evans lying on the porch of the Gudger house — I felt, in that midnight mountain air, that such a mood of felicity was what we all were beginning to create among ourselves and that it was beginning to flow like a current between the increasingly faithful adults and the still somewhat skeptical students.

Just before the showing of Helen Levitt and Agee's documentary, *The Quiet One*, Father Flye talked about Agee's religious life at St. Andrew's. Father Flye is himself a quiet one; he hates microphones but knows he speaks softly and so uses his cupped hands as an amplifier. The restless kids stilled themselves in attentiveness. "Did Mr. Agee really believe his father's ghost was in the room?" one asked. The question transfixed Father Flye in contemplation; his eyes were wide in wonder, his mouth an O of awe; it seemed his very body was thinking. "What matters is not whether Agee himself believed in ghosts but that the people in the novel were convinced they felt the father's presence in the house." The tone of the students' feelings began to change now. I began to see that Agee, with lasting awe more than with clever paradox, regarded life and death as one unbroken process. More important than the effect of the father's death upon each member of the family was Agee's use of that death as an occasion to celebrate life in its everyday context of death.

Helen Levitt had sent us the original print of *The Quiet One*, with Agee's voice narrating. The movie opens with an Ageean dedication: "To all children who need help and to everyone who tries to help them." Then, through the leaves, we see boys running in the country. Hearing Agee's slow, quiet, natural, meditative voice with its slight Harvard accent just after Father Flye, the students became very still, respectful, and soon were deeply moved. We were beginning to reach out, less and less reluctantly, to touch Agee, as Rufus had reached for his father and as Richard in *The Morning Watch* had reached for Christ.

Later there was an unscheduled showing of Agee's adaptation of Crane's story "The Bride Comes to Yellow Sky." In the opening scene, the town drunk stands in the window of the jail saying good-bye to the marshal. The marshal has given the drunk the jail key so that he can go over to the saloon for a drink and then lock himself back up. When the students in the audience suddenly realized that it was Jim Agee playing the drunk — moving, speaking, as if alive on the screen — they cheered. Seeing his own father for the first time in a movie, hearing him speak from the upper window of the jail as the town drunk, John Agee, Jim's nineteen-year-old son, seemed to experience an epiphany such as Richard had wanted. John's face, startlingly like his father's, lit by the reflections from the screen, had a similar effect, perhaps, on others in the audience.

John Agee had seemed rather aloof at first, a gangly young man striding slowly about the campus in a big grey hat he never removed, long hair bouncing on his shoulders. I was glad later to see John with Charles Angermeyer, the man who had filmed *School on the Mountain*, taking a long walk in the woods where Richard had walked after his morning watch. It seemed particularly appropriate that a young filmmaker should be the first person to put John at ease in what must have been for him a claustrophobic atmosphere of adulation for a father he never knew.

The spirit of Agee had become embodied in us all, but it was most visible during the final panel discussion by men who had known him at different stages in his life or whose lives had been touched by his writings, many of whom have contributed to this collection of reminiscences: Robert Daniel, Robert Fitzgerald, Father Flye, Andrew Lytle, Dwight Macdonald, David McDowell, and Walker Percy. At first the panelists enacted a complex series of attitudes like the boys in *The Morning Watch* who undressed in front of each other to dive into the cold pond, but McDowell as moderator was so in tune with these men of very different sensibilities that he got from them the most remarkably amiable and productive public conversation among writers I ever expect to hear.

My own attitudes were affected by the comments of Walker Percy, himself a lover of movies, even bad ones. "I never knew Agee," he said. "I wish I had. I can only speak about his influence on me as a writer. I can best describe this influence as being technical. I do not think of Agee in connection with southern writers but in connection with Englishmen and Irishmen, like Hopkins and Joyce — the early Joyce. His influence on me has been technical, simply, in the way that he crafts an English sentence and uses poetic devices, metaphors, and sentence structure within a single paragraph."

McDowell talked about Agee's approach to the *craft* of writing: "Agee welcomed criticism more than any writer I've ever known, and I've been working with them most of my life. He loved to read whatever he was working on to friends or to any group." To this Robert Fitzgerald added, "Jim was secure in that he knew that he was a decent writer. He could listen to the worst criticism, and he was generous and open about it. After all, what he was about was making something that was good. Whether or not this came about in an untouched singular effort or with a few touches of assistance doesn't matter at all. The important thing was to get it right and accurate with the words in the correct order. He was selfless in this area in many, many instances. What he wanted was good writing. If it was his, fine. If it was yours, equally fine — better, in fact."

St. Andrew's became for me James Agee's cenotaph. The ceremony dedicating the library was short, hollow compared with, though indispensable to, the informal ceremonies that had by now become unforgettable. The Agee Memorial Library contains all of his works, memorabilia, photographs, the uncut *Omnibus* film about Lincoln. There are videotapes of guest novelists reading from Agee's work and of all the sessions of that week, with facilities for showing them. Signed books by friends and admirers are there. The library houses research material that scholars will not find elsewhere.

After leaving the mountain, I struggled to achieve some balance between skepticism and adulation. Reading and knowing Agee, many people have come to sense a saintly quality, but Agee must also have felt possessed of a devil sometimes. His obsession with original sin and the mortal sin of pride helps to explain his avocation of failure. The subtle dialectics of sin and guilt pervade his life and work. In *Famous Men* he apologizes for calling the tenant farmer's shack beautiful, then in a footnote he calls his apology the real sin. The very things before which they stand in awe, in fear, or in ecstasy, Agee's autobiographical characters Rufus and Richard feel they eventually betray. Somewhere in the tension between self-destructive guilt and creative overreaching, Agee expressed his finest moments of mental and emotional consciousness. He seemed to need some form of punishment simultaneous with joy — as when he lay on Gudger's mattress, vermin biting his flesh, his spirit perfectly attuned to the lives of the sharecroppers.

Byronic in life and art, Agee was always keenly, often cripplingly, aware of the opposite possible truth to whatever he was passionately analyzing and advocating at the moment. Knowing the nature of things as they are, he looked at both sides. Like F. Scott Fitzgerald, Agee seemed to write out of a "dark night of the soul," where "it is always three o'clock in the morning, day after day." He seemed to struggle as actively and consciously as Fitzgerald to pass Fitzgerald's test of a first-rate intelligence: "the ability to hold two opposed ideas in the mind at the same time, and still retain the ability to function."

Although he was one of the most intellectual and analytical of modern American writers, Agee denied on every theoretical occasion that he was intellectualizing; he advocated constantly, in abstract terms, the necessity to rely mainly on the senses, instinct. Hypnotized by his own rhetoric in some passages of almost everything he wrote, Agee could make some irrevocably contradictory, even silly statements. His proclaimed antipathy to art was always expressed in the most artistic context, concepts, and diction. He even tried to subvert whatever medium he was working in. "You should so far as possible forget that this is a book." But even as he jeeringly cautions his readers not to call his book a work of art, every page bears witness to his struggle to achieve nothing less. And a few pages after he laments his lack of imagination, he expresses a resentment of the "deifying of the imagination." His insights are forged in the crucible of the moment, and the medium of their expression ought, appropriately, to suffer the same time-fate; he wanted *Famous Men* printed on newsprint so that in fifty years it would crumble to dust.

Few writers have been as obsessed as Agee was with analyzing the difficulties of the creative process, and in the works of few writers has the suffering of the artist's vision been so much the subject of the work. On the Caedmon recording Agee recited a long list of possible jobs: "I simply have *got* to make a choice and — I can't." He describes the jobs in detail. "Right now I am in such a perplexity that my stomach is like a fist. I really cannot make up my mind to anything." One of the many jobs Agee described was writing the movie script about Paul Gauguin, in which the artist is presented "not as the criminal romantic but as a man whose vocation was like a lure set out by God." He would find after many years that "it was not the real thing even but only the lure and that all it was trying to teach him was to be as absolutely faithful to his own soul and his own being as he could, and that he find out the price of that as he went along." The script offers yet another autobiographical perspective on Agee.

Agee's achievement as an innovator and a forerunner in several media astonishes me. Along with Wright Morris, he was among the first imaginative writers to experiment seriously with phototext techniques. His work suggests the possibilities of imaginative nonfiction and anticipates, as McDowell has suggested, the personal journalism we find in Truman Capote and Norman Mailer in the sixties. Anticipating the current study of popular culture, he preached to the editors of the *Partisan Review* that "you learn as much out of corruption and confusion and more, than out of the best work that has ever been done." Agee was the first film reviewer to write of movies with personal commitment and a high seriousness. His descriptions of inanimate objects anticipate the experimental techniques of Robbe-Grillet's objectivism. I don't think he was deliberately innovative; rather, his innovations seem to come out of a necessity implicit in the force of his temperament upon his material. Few American writers have been as responsive to media, high and low, as Agee, and that tendency attracts me to him because of my own compulsion to explore the possibilities of expression in all media.

Since the publication in 1957 of *A Death in the Family*, James

Agee's reputation has remained strong among general readers and critics. All of his major works are in print, several of them in paperback. His innovative approach to movie reviewing and personal journalism partly explains our interest in him today, forty years after his death; respect for the artistry of his fiction remains high, and a reevaluation of his poetry seems imminent. But it is the legend of James Agee that has remained most consistently fascinating. He is with us now almost as a mythic presence.

With the mobility of the camera eye that so impressed him early in his life, Agee's omniscient vision moved among us on the mountain. We all seemed to move that week as if through "a ceremony of innocence" — no drowning as in Yeats's poem, but an emergence, as in *The Morning Watch*. Richard, too long submerged in his dive: "*Here I am!* his enchanted body sang.*" Many of us experienced a moment like Andrew's in *A Death in the Family:* "Andrew glanced quickly down upon a horned, bruised anvil; and laid his hand flat against the cold, wheemed iron; and it was as if its forehead gave his hand the stunning shadow of every blow it had ever received." So it was, for a moment, to touch Agee. Or to feel as Jay Follet's family did that someone other than visible company is present in a room. With us, Agee finally achieved Richard's wish, to see mirrors face to face, endlessly reflecting each other. Agee lamented the inability of words to "communicate simultaneity with any immediacy." He exhorted the reader to collaborate imaginatively with him in *Let Us Now Praise Famous Men:* "Whence let me hope the whole of that landscape we shall essay to travel in is visible and may be known as there all at once." By the end of the week, all we knew and had felt about Agee many of us knew and felt together in an intuitive simultaneity. Implicit in the letters of gratitude that participants sent to McDowell is a sense of communion. And through Agee, we all, as Macdonald testified, made lifelong friends. Like the multiconsciousness that resurrects Jay Follet's spirit even as his body is being buried, we achieved in our communion there on the mountain nothing less than a resurrection.

I

Agee's Early Life and Writing

An Article of Faith

In 1905, on the Cumberland plateau in Middle Tennessee, two miles from Sewanee, some members of the Order of the Holy Cross, a monastic order of the Episcopal Church, started a little mission center, and for some young boys who were put under their care and a few others from the neighborhood, they provided teaching in school subjects and religion. From this developed St. Andrew's School, which in a dozen years had come to have some seventy-five boarding boys and a few day students, with grades of instruction from primary up through high school.

It was a rural setting, a property of perhaps two hundred acres, some wooded, some under cultivation as a farm; a few dwellings, the school buildings, and the small monastery or priory where members of the order lived.

My connection with the place began in September 1918, when I went there to teach in the school and be of assistance in some religious services and ministrations. My wife and I lived in a cottage on the school grounds. After the end of the school year, I stayed on there through the summer, as did some other persons of the staff and a few of the boys.

Mrs. Agee, whose home was in Knoxville, had friends at St. Andrew's and in 1918, two years after the death of her husband, she with her two children had spent the summer there, living in one of the cottages. In 1919 they came again, and it was thus that I came to know them. James (or Rufus, as he was then called, using his middle name which he came to dislike and later dropped entirely) was then in his tenth year, and Emma was two years younger. And so began one of the most cherished and rewarding relationships of my life.

Many factors act as deterrents to rapport between individuals, but a difference of chronological age is not necessarily such, as Rufus and I soon discovered. Here was a friendly, intelligent boy, of active mind, fond of reading, with a good store of knowledge and eager for more. There was no lack of things for us to talk about. He was interested in fossils and shells, knowing many by their scientific names, which he used fluently and naturally. Then there was the subject of possible pets, and we discussed monkeys, ponies, elephants, rabbits, pigeons, and kangaroos, with citations from pet books and books of natural history. Then foreign countries, and Indian life, and Scout lore and woodcraft. He wanted a bow and arrows, and we made a bow which he used some. Later he wanted a .22 rifle. It wasn't considered advisable to buy him one, but we borrowed one and did some target shooting. He wouldn't have thought of shooting at birds or rabbits or other living things.

But besides talk and doings such as just mentioned, there were real bonds between us in spirit, feelings, and instincts. He was very tenderhearted, touched to quick sympathy and pity at the sight or thought of suffering, human or other, and incapable of willingly causing it. He had a keen sense of humor and comedy, but was never comfortable with teasing or banter. He was by nature affectionate and trustful, with many endearing traits, and I felt deep tenderness and affection for him at this lovely age.

It may not be out of place here to include something told me years later by his mother of an incident in his childhood in Knoxville. "A friend of mine," she said, "was interested in a Settlement School out

at the woolen mills. The women brought their children and they had
to have people there in the nursery with them all day long while they
worked in the mills. And she was taking Rufus in a little pony-cart or
something. She had him with her to ride around to some of those
places and she was telling him about those children. And Rufus said,
'Well, why do they have to stay in such a place? What are they there
for?' She explained that they were very, very poor, which they were.
And she said, 'You know, some of them don't even have shoes and
stockings to wear.' And Rufus's eyes commenced to fill up and he was
taking his shoes and stockings off then and there to give to whoever
would need them. And that was like him, too. That continued to be
like him, you know."

Some have felt James Agee saw in me something of a surrogate for
his father, but I do not think this was the case. Our friendship and
association and feeling toward each other were such, it seems to me,

as we might equally well have had if his father had been living. As to the word *Father*, by the way, used by James Agee, that was simply standard usage at St. Andrew's in addressing or speaking of any priest.

With the passing of summer, I had assumed that Mrs. Agee would be returning to Knoxville, but she decided that as the cottage where they were living could still be had, she would stay on through the winter and have the children attend St. Andrew's School. This arrangement was made and continued for the next four years, with visits in vacations at the home of Mrs. Agee's parents. In late February 1924, when her father was not well, she left St. Andrew's, and in 1924–25 Rufus attended high school in Knoxville.

I was glad that our association was not to be broken off, but I could not help wondering how things would be with a boy like that in the regimen and surroundings to which he would have to adjust, with few of the boys of anything like his type or background. And he would undoubtedly be in trouble in the matter of some school rules and requirements: not by his intentionally breaking them, for he was not of defiant or uncooperative spirit, but because, though he meant well, he was absentminded, forgetful of details, absorbed in what he was doing, and not sufficiently conscious of time.

Life at St. Andrew's School at that time was of rather plain and simple type. Most of the boys had very little money, and some really none. The charge for tuition and board was extremely low, and the school could not have carried on without the contributions sent in for its support. It was quite different from places modeled after English schools. There was no system of rank and status within the student body, or between "old" and "new" boys, but general free choice of association and personal relations. Most of the boys were from rural or small-town background. The range in age was from a few very young boys to those in their upper teens, and three or four who after service in the First World War had come back to school for more education. The boys for the most part got on with each other very well, and the general spirit was friendly and pleasant. The boys took care of their own living quarters (with regular inspections) and each had some assigned job (changed every two weeks) — cleaning, waiting on table, pantry duty, or other inside or outside work about the place. As to scholastic aptitude and ability, the range was from boys who would never make any progress with "book learning" to those who would go to college and do well.

The religious commitment of St. Andrew's was definite and strong. The head person there was the prior, appointed by and responsible to the father superior of the Order of the Holy Cross at West Park, New York, who would from time to time come for a visit. At the time of which we are writing, the prior was also headmaster of the school, and he taught one or two classes. The members of the order were not aloof but were friendly men and held in warm regard.

The aim and hope of the Holy Cross fathers at St. Andrew's was to be of service in promoting Christian faith and practice in the form called Anglo-Catholic, a term designating the religious position of those in the Episcopal Church (or the Anglican Communion) who emphasize the organic historic continuity of the church and the teachings, rites, and practices that bear witness to this. Some other places then or later with that same religious alignment would be the Church of the Advent and the Church of St. John the Evangelist in Boston and the monastery of the Cowley fathers in Cambridge.

In the school, attendance was required at daily chapel service and on Sundays at the sung mass and at evensong; grace was said at meals in the school dining room, and religious instruction was a required course in the curriculum. There was due observance of Lent, Holy Week, and other special seasons and days of the Christian year, and church boys were encouraged to go to Confession and Holy Communion. Many of the boys were acolytes and liked to take part thus in the church services. And each year would see a number of boys from other backgrounds coming into the church. It should be said here that what was emphasized in the religious teaching given at St. Andrew's, whether in sermons or group instruction or personally, was not mere externals, though these had their place, but real Christian faith and devotion.

In this setting, then, James Agee spent the years of his school life from the age of ten to fourteen. For most of that time he had quarters in a dormitory, it being felt that this was better for him than living at home. Our friendship continued and developed, but not in any exclusive way. I was on very good terms with all the boys and we had many very pleasant associations, but with him there was a special fullness of understanding and communication. When he was eleven, just for fun, outside of school hours, I started him with French, in which he did well; and somewhat later, with another boy four years older who had had some French, we continued and read *Tartarin de Tarascon*, which they greatly enjoyed. When he reached the ninth grade (high school) he was for the first time in one of my classes (English history), in which he was an excellent student.

After his return with his mother to Knoxville in the spring of 1924 I saw him occasionally, and in the summer of 1925 we spent two months in France and England, traveling mostly by bicycle. That fall he entered Phillips Exeter Academy, and during the next several years we met very seldom but kept such contact as we might by writing. From 1941 to 1954 I took parish duty each summer in New York, and we would see each other often.

When he first began to think of creative writing, or make any attempts at it in prose or verse, is not certain, but this does not seem to have been while he was at St. Andrew's. On our trip abroad he spoke sometimes of wishing he could write something about things we had seen, but such feeling and such writing are not unusual. After getting to Exeter, however, that fall, his first letter to me spoke of his keen interest in writing and of his having written a story and two or three poems for publication in the *Monthly*.

A rich store of memories, impressions, and no doubt influences remained with James Agee from those years at St. Andrew's: that Cumberland country of Middle Tennessee and its people; persons of all ages whom he had known — boys, teachers, and others; and that school life in its various aspects and relations. I remember seeing pages of penciled jottings by him — single words, phrases, idioms, proper names — recalling persons, places, incidents, or experiences, unintelligible except to himself or perhaps someone in whom these might also stir recall. He made use of memories of this sort in his writings and would have liked to use more. The scene of *The Morning Watch* — the dormitory, the Maundy Thursday Watch in relays through the night before the Blessed Sacrament — is unmistakably St. Andrew's, and the originals of probably all the characters in that story would be easily recognizable by anyone familiar with that place in the early 1920s. He had a deeply perceptive understanding of his fellow human beings in their individual lives and would have liked to write more about them and also to write some form of autobiography. *A Death in the Family* (which though called fiction is largely factual) shows what could be done with one episode in a life narrative.

Mrs. Agee was a devout and faithful church member of Anglo-Catholic convictions to whom the religious faith and practice at St. Andrew's meant a great deal, and Rufus grew up well grounded in this teaching and practice and familiar with the language of the Bible and Book of Common Prayer. He was an acolyte and used to serve often at the altar. In later years he felt unable to commit himself to full acceptance of some doctrinal statements of the church, but he had not abjured religion or Christian faith. He had a humble sense of wonder and reverence before the mysteries of the universe, of existence, of life, of human lives — a religious sense. There were many things about which he felt simply that he did not know, but he was not one of those who sit in the seat of the scornful. I remember his declaring his belief in "a divine or supernatural consciousness, power and love." As between the essentially religious and the non- or anti-religious, there is no doubt whatever in which category James Agee belongs. Read "Dedication" in the book of his poems.

He often had difficulties in regard to commitments, for he could not pledge himself to full support of or membership in an organization of any kind — political, social, economic, religious, or other — some of whose principles or policies he could not accept. He knew very well, however, the problems and difficulties of anyone considering this matter and what he should do.

He was truly humble, very conscious of weakness, shortcomings, and failures; a kind and loving person with great capacity for understanding and compassion, he will continue to speak through his writings. And to many there will be communicated thus the realization that here was one who had desires, hopes, uncertainties, moods, and emotions similar to theirs, one who would understand how they feel. For he did understand, and perhaps hoped that through something he had been able to put into writing some might come to feel more deeply the bond of our common humanity.

ROBERT SAUDEK

J. R. Agee '32:
A Snapshot Album, 1928–1932

When Jim died they took him to the tiny chapel of St. Luke's in Greenwich Village where his oldest friend, Father James Harold Flye, having finished the service, stepped to the head of Jim's coffin. "It is not the custom of this church to eulogize its departed," he said. "I want to say only that anyone who ever met Rufus Agee will never forget him."

September 1928. George Smith B-41

The door burst open and in strode the roommate—tall, shy, strong long arms and legs, a small head, curly dark hair, a spring in his heels as he bounded past with a wicker country suitcase in one hand and an enormous, raw pine box on his shoulder. He turned his head suddenly, squinted his eyes in an apologetic smile, said softly, "Hello, Agee's my name," swept through to an empty bedroom and deposited

his belongings, bounded back through the gabled maroon-and-white study, murmured, "See you all later," waved an awkward farewell, and didn't show up again for several days. Such was the magnetic field that had rushed through the room that I didn't even think to introduce myself. Now that I had at last seen him, heard him, and learned to pronounce his name, he was more of a stranger than before.

A week later Jim returned from his first morning of classes looking like a volcano. He went over to the fireplace, turned and announced that he hated the place and hated a system that would seat "Agee" next to "Alsop" since that fat sonovabitch, not yet having bought himself a Latin textbook, picked up Agee's new book, opened it up and broke its spine, then clearing a great hock out of his throat, spat it on the open page. Jim swung his fist against the stucco wall above the fireplace with all his might, abrading his knuckles, and he felt so ashamed of this display that he then struck the bleeding fist against his own temple and leaned spent against the wall. He would not have said anything to Alsop; instead, he took it out on himself. He always did. That kind of eruption was awesome, for Jim was the most compassionate person and the least able to cope with insensitivity in others. The fact that he was a little older than some of us — and inexperience was full grown — left me with the feeling that this was the way all the rest of us would react some day.

Jim did not especially love Harvard as he loved Exeter, but he did appreciate its people and its atmosphere of personal freedom. He could come and go at will. He could increasingly satisfy his need to feel secure with the styles, forms, and conceits of written English, and in a sense it would be the only kind of security he ever felt. But it was his comprehension of human behavior and a great fear of his own behavior that set him apart. For it was Jim who, coming back weak and sick from Stillman Infirmary to the Yard one midwinter's night, could smash his fist into the glass door of a moving streetcar on the Mt. Auburn Street line when the conductor closed the door in his face; who could rise at 4:30 on Sunday mornings to walk up the river and help the Cowley fathers serve communion at their Episcopal monastery; who would proudly struggle into white tie and tails in order to sing Bach in the Glee Club; who so adored Helen Hayes in *Coquette* that he saw it seven times in a week; who would spend a whole New York weekend in an all-night movie; who would mimic Lee and Grant at Appomattox ("Mah sword, Suh!" with an elaborate bow. "Drink to that!" replies General Grant, sliding out of his chair onto the floor); who could sit up all night writing a poem or talking and smoking so that his fingers were stained to the color of a horse chestnut. The radius of his friendships extended beyond Harvard contemporaries, into the faculty, other colleagues, and out to his fellow workers in the summer wheat harvest. Jim listened carefully to each one of them.

September 1930. Thayer 45

As junior year was about to start, a young man named Tom showed up — the kind of debonair outsider that Harvard always seems to attract: he was never enrolled as a student, yet he was completely at ease in the setting, alive with college gossip and stocked with faculty anecdotes. He would give a spellbinding account of a Broadway torch singer tangling with a big-name bootlegger; he dressed with casual correctness, spoke with the right accent, and in the long run became a very bothersome freeloader at mealtime and a tiresome schizophrenic, drunk by 9 and knocking at your door by 3 A.M. in search of somebody to tell funny stories to.

Whole entries would conspire elaborately against Tom, but not Agee. Jim would answer the door, greet Tom with a low "Hello, Tom," take him out to the entry's steps, and talk quietly until dawn, when Tom would either depart in peace or fall asleep in the stairwell. Whatever it was they found to talk about, Jim had a way of understanding it. He would frown, drop his head in staccato jerks, and say quietly, "Sure, I know. . . . It's lousy. . . . Jesus knows it's lousy." Nothing could be more reassuring than when he went into that kind of litany.

By the time classes began we lost Tom in the reality of the business at hand, and so he sadly turned himself in to a mental institution for help, whence, for a few weeks, little mocking sparks flickered back to Cambridge. Most of us felt guilty for having done nothing, but Jim felt worst of all for not doing enough for Tom, whatever on earth that could possibly have been.

March 1931. Thayer 45

In college one learns the significance of privacy. Anyone who, in high school, had been led to believe that privacy was antisocial if not unmanly came to discover that in this college being by yourself was both respected and respectable.

In this discovery, Jim was a good preceptor, for he thought and wrote in private, and when he was elated at his results he would ask quietly if I, or another friend, would mind listening to what he had just finished.

Once he wanted to talk about an idea loosely drawing on his interest in demonology. The idea was that a pair of adoring parents would have a beautiful baby who was perfect in every way but one: he was a cross between Don Juan and the Devil. Thus, as parents cooed over the cradle and sent out little blue-ribbon announcements, the dear little nipper would privately embarrass its mom by drawing blood like a vampire as it suckled and by so titillating her in the process that she was driven close to madness in her attempts to put up a bold front, as it were. The precocity of her offspring was, to her, a total embarrassment which would have delighted Jim, for he believed in sentiment but deplored sentimentality.

I don't know where that poem is, but years later his long and marvelous poem *John Carter* would state some such proposition without the mysticism and with great wit:

> Like Byron, I'll begin at the beginning.
> Unlike that better bard, my lad's a new one,
> Expert in charm, supremely so in sinning,
> Nevertheless he differs from Don Juan
> In ways enough to set your brain to spinning.

Then, with Chaucer's sense of weaving into wondrous tales the poet's own yarns, scruples, and distractions, Agee (stanzas later) reports on the progress of the devilish Leonard:

> It flurried Leonard frightfully at times.
> At night he thought of one thing and another,
> Of sweet-fleshed maidens bred in palmier climes,
> Also of Jesus, Hubert, and his mother.
> So finally when he'd hoarded enough dimes,
> He snuk to Boston. . . . Well, I guess I'll smother
> That little incident (which nearly threw him):
> A friend has come, I want to read this to him.

The poem, wandering all over in time and space, finally treated events of the year 1935 as Agee writes resentfully of Tory England:

> We wish you folks homesteading in the States
> Would realize once for all that time and tide
> Sooner or later make the earth our onion.
> So won't you join the English Speaking Union?
> . . . .
> And thanks to British pluck and the Almighty dollar,
> We'll fit the whole world round to a Rhodes collar.

But his desperate side, which Agee turned most often to the world, watching life corrode into death, x-rayed a lover's lips and saw a skull. Once during junior year Jim emerged from days and nights within himself and asked if he might read aloud an "Epithalamium" he had just completed. He first defined it as a poem to celebrate the joining of bride and bridegroom as they approach their marriage bed. Jim, who often formalized nature, explained that he thought of this marriage bed as the grave and its canopy as the night sky; the bridegroom as destroyer; the bride as the destroyed; the bed as tombstone; the lovers as skeletons beneath their wedding raiments.

The private thoughts that had been working in his mind were transformed into words and rhythms written in a minor key, and his relief in beginning to read them aloud was very great.

> Now day departs: upreared the darkness climbs
> The breathless sky, leans wide above the fields,
> And snows its silence round the muttering chimes:
> The night is come that bride to bridegroom yields.

And eleven verses later he closed it:

> Quiet, forever free from all alarms,
> They lie where light is strengthless to descend.
> The night is come, that hollows as it harms;
> The night is come that day may never end.

January 1932. Eliot G-52

As president of the *Advocate* Jim produced a parody issue, something I think this magazine had never done before, and it was a huge success. With his sense of containment within a form, Jim never let this caricature of *Time* magazine get out of hand and become a burlesque. The cover-picture had elegance: set within *Time*'s red-bordered cover was a fine photograph of a bronze Mercury poised lightly on one foot.

Jim had been so involved in writing, editing, picture-selecting, captioning, and layout that when the issue finally went to press, on a Saturday night, Jim went out to celebrate.

The next morning there was a note in the study asking me to wake him up as usual, since several of us had Sunday jobs in the First Church octet. Beside the note was a large, sealed manila envelope marked: "Metropolitan District Police, Defendant's Belongings."

I went in to wake him. His clothes were bloody, his sleeping face bruised, puffy, and cut.

On Saturday night Jim and his girl had gone out to Revere Beach for a winter's evening hike along the deserted boardwalk. Pretty much alone, they were singing, laughing, and drinking from a bottle of boot-leg gin when two policemen came up and ordered them to pipe down. As the peace of that snowswept beach was in no way being disturbed, Jim apparently reacted strongly enough that the two policemen, leav-ing Jim's girl behind, took him protesting, under each arm, lifted him in the air and gave him a bum's rush to precinct headquarters where he was booked, ceremoniously relieved of his belongings which were neatly sealed in an envelope, and then beaten up.

By dawn, Jim had managed to make bail through a Boston bail bond commissioner, picked up his envelope, called his girl, then struck out for Harvard Square. He felt no shame. He thought of him-self as independent and responsible. He believed that the city of Revere should have wanted him to have a good time that night in their silent, snow-covered amusement park. That they did not want him to — that instead of protecting him they should have pummeled him — was beyond Jim's comprehension, and he was more confused than outraged by that brutal assault.

June 1932. *Class Day*

As class poet, Jim had sat up all night on the last possible night, composing the class ode in pencil on coarse, unlined yellow sheets he purchased by the pound. It made the printer's at the last pos-sible hour.

Class Day might not have concerned Jim but for the fact that as odeist he was expected to appear in bachelor's gown with white frogs and the special cap marked by the muted crimson tassel of a Harvard class officeholder.

The co-op being closed, Jim hustled a knee-length choir robe from the First Church and, from a Radcliffe senior, a girls' style mortar board that sat primly on his head like a coronet with a long, red Rad-cliffe tassel draped over his shoulders.

As the officers mounted the Sanders Theater stage, I think Jim really felt proud, for he was that day accepted into the elite band of classmates plucked from the ranks of football, polo, and the Banjo Club.

The ode was meant to be singable (though never sung) to the melody of "Fair Harvard," and Jim had tried desperately to commit it to memory and had pocketed his draft.

When his turn came, he sprang to the lectern and began to recite: "Now the winter is past and the storms of our youth, / We who gather to part in our power."

The lines rolled in that low, soft, somewhat monotone Tennessee cadence with its distinctive sibilance. But somewhere along the way he lost a word, and then a thought, and his eyes began to show terror, and he froze the audience of seniors with his helpless expression. Nobody laughed. Jim fished for a way into his gown to fetch the yellow sheets, but without success. Like a slow-motion film the pantomime seemed endless, until someone handed Jim the program which contained the printed text. He found his place, recovered, and went on to the end:

And all wisdom we wring from our pain and desire
　On this field between devil and God,
Shall resolve to a white and unquenchable fire
　That shall cleanse the dark clay we have trod.

Jim went to commencement, but early that afternoon he was ready to hitchhike to New York to start his *Fortune* job. We stood among the half-packed trunks, textbooks, poems, unfinished stories, letters, term papers, prayer books, sheet music, photographs, and diplomas, and Jim and I shook hands, and we said so long and good luck and write. Four years were all over almost before they started. Then he lifted to his shoulder the raw pine box that held his phonograph, picked up his old wicker suitcase, and opened the door. I remember looking down from the window as he emerged five stories below and hiked across Eliot quadrangle with the heel-lifting stride he had brought with him four years before. The heavy pine box rested as lightly as a parrot on his shoulder.

He still seemed like Rufus or Jim, and we wanted to cling to that, but soon thereafter and forever, the world would know him only as James Agee.

During October a visit to the University of Tennessee gave me a chance to find Jim's childhood neighborhood, which is the setting for A *Death in the Family* and some early short stories.

Like other Appalachian Mountain communities, Knoxville rises in steep waves of mined-out earth, so that every street seems to run uphill. Architecturally, his neighborhood is much the way he remembered it: *"It was a little bit mixed sort of block, fairly solidly lower middle class, with one or two juts apiece on either side of that."* The frame houses still line up in white, gray, or yellow. An occasional brick house of the twenties is soot-red. *"The houses corresponded: middle-sized gracefully fretted wood houses built in the late nineties and early nineteen hundreds, with small front and side and more spacious back yards, and trees in the yards, and porches. . . . There were fences around one or two of the houses."*

There is an old cast-iron picket fence next door to Rufus's front yard, but now its black spearheads are rusty and pockmarked and droop to left and right. The fence must once have been a low hurdle inviting small boys to clear it easily on the way home from school.

The sounds of a half century ago are gone: the old West Knoxville Fire Hall, which was built down the block in 1906 for one horse-drawn pumper-engine, is gone, so the cobblestone racket of its fire horses and fire bells is gone.

The tracks of the Highland Avenue streetcar line that used to run in front of Rufus's house are interred in asphalt. *"A street car raising its iron moan; stopping, belling and starting; stertorous; rousing and raising again its iron increasing moan and swimming its gold windows and straw seats on past and past and past . . . still fainter, fainting, lifting, lifts, faints forgone: forgotten."*

Rufus spent his childhood in the second house from the corner, with a front porch that was garlanded with vines, at 1505 Highland Avenue in West Knoxville, Tennessee. That house and the corner house, 1503, were both razed in 1963. In their place has been erected the James Agee Apartments, three middlebrow stories of acne-colored brick, with outside galleries that stretch back from the street like cellblocks. A tiny pool, coffin-shaped, skinny and dry, sits beneath the cellblocks. *"On the rough wet grass of the back yard my father and mother have spread quilts. We all lie there, my mother, my father, my uncle, my aunt, and I too am lying there. First we were sitting up, then one of us lay down, and then we all lay down, on our stomachs, or on our sides, or on our backs, and they have kept on talking."*

The alley that runs behind the houses of the 1500 block, and was Rufus's alley, gave access to all the backyards, which are still wide and deep but turned to weeds. The trees are out of hand and choking with nondescript vines. The back fences along the alley have been replaced, but their heavy old iron bolts remain. The neighbors still hang their wash out back from clotheslines strung between T-poles. A few small barns, windowless, paintless, and exhausted, have been padlocked for years.

The backyard of 1505 is no longer rough, wet grass. It is concrete clear out to the alley, and beyond it is a tenants' parking lot for the James Agee Apartments. *"[W]ho shall ever tell the sorrow of being on this earth, lying, on quilts, on the grass, in a summer evening, among the sounds of night."*

The apartments, like the older dwellings along Highland Avenue, are occupied by students of the neighboring University of Tennessee.

A pleasant young man emerged and began to climb into his green VW.

Q: Do you know the name James Agee?

A: I don't, but there's a directory of everybody who lives in the building right inside.

Q: Well, James Agee has been dead for some years.

A: Oh, I'm sorry.

I knocked at the door of 1507, a gray frame house of the vintage, and a very frail old lady answered the door.

A: Yes, I remember when the Agee family lived there. . . . I think I do. . . . I've been here quite awhile.

Q: Since the twenties?

A: (Pause) I'd have to look it up. I know I've lived here quite awhile.

"There were few good friends among the grown people, and they were not poor enough for the other sort of intimate acquaintance."

Jim's memory of Highland Avenue, Forest, 15th Street, the nearby viaduct, and the L&N Depot below it was long and vivid. But living inhabitants did not remember. There was no evidence of curiosity about the black-and-white sign out front, JAMES AGEE APARTMENTS.

Town and Country Construction Co. Agents. Phone 572-2083. Two English department professors at the university had no notion where it was that Agee had lived and written of, although they were sitting three blocks away from that sign. It seemed odd. Yet we, as students, had never given a thought to who either Thayer or George Smith was. That's the way it is.

Around three o'clock a boy about eight years old came walking along the old iron fence. He was carrying home from school a folded sling, pasted with paper handles and filled with several sheets of lined tablet paper covered with the painful handwriting of a beginner. That is the closest I came to a living memory of Jim.

Participants:

WARREN EYSTER

FATHER FLYE

DAVID MCDOWELL

DAVID MADDEN

FREDERICK MANFRED

FATHER MARTIN

CYNTHIA O'FLAHERTY

Panel on Agee's Poetry

FATHER MARTIN: First of all, we shall be looking at Agee's poetry and then at some of the work he did in the area of documentaries, both written and on film. Tomorrow we will look at his great novel, *A Death in the Family.*

This particular panel will consider some aspects of James Agee's poetry. We have two persons very familiar to you here — to my right, Cynthia O'Flaherty of our English Department; to my left, Father Flye. I am going to ask David McDowell, also very well known to you, to introduce the three distinguished writers and scholars who have joined us on our panel.

MCDOWELL: I couldn't be happier to introduce to you, on my right, Mr. Warren Eyster — director of creative writing at Louisiana State University, a novelist, and a friend of mine for many, many years. On your right, Frederick Manfred, author of more than twenty books — a distinguished novelist, poet, and critic — who is director of the creative writing program and writer-in-residence at the University of South Dakota. And another good friend of mine, a great writer, David Madden, who is writer-in-residence at Louisiana State. He's written several novels and a book of criticism and is going to be adopting a column for the *Saturday Review* beginning in December. All of these gentlemen whom I have mentioned are not only novelists, critics, teachers, and friends of the young, but they have written poetry themselves. I think it's very important for all of us to remember that if one had to say anything basic about Agee, he was essentially a poet, even though most of his writing was in the field of fiction or nonfiction or criticism. Basically, however, he was a poet. I am delighted to have such a distinguished group of people here, and I am sure that this is going to be one of the most fascinating of all the programs.

O'FLAHERTY: I would like to ask you a question, which sounds like an "English teacher" question, but it really does have relevance because of the nature of our discussion. How is our response to poetry different than our response to prose?

McDOWELL: Could I pass that question on to Mr. Madden? What about the difficulty of modern poetry?

MADDEN: Literature is language charged with meaning, and by that Agee meant meaning fused with emotion. There was a period when there was a great effort to make the language really charged by leaving so much out, by making what you put in a whole rich context. This is what some people mean when they say they are coming to poetry with a feeling of resistance to the words, even though the words are familiar. You know that they are going to be put into a new, strong, powerful context and that you're going to have to work to respond to all of the echoes and reverberations that are there. In the last five or six years, another kind of poetry was introduced that goes back to Wordsworth's contention of simplicity: poetry that is like the spoken language that everybody speaks. It's poetry that is immediately understandable on one level but that retains the subtlety and theater. You want to stay with it awhile, and you want to come back to it. There's a kind of poetry of everyday speech. I can't think immediately of examples, but there is a tendency to return to simplicity in poetry.

The interesting thing about Agee's poetry is that you can find characteristics in his collected poems of almost every type of poem you could want to talk about—narrative poetry, lyrical poetry, complex language, simple language, slang, the use of dialect, mountain dialect, satire, polemic. We have a lot of poems that rail against the injustices in the world, usually on behalf of something that women and children suffer from social structures. You have long narrative poems, sonnet sequences. Think of Donne: he was a very different poet but not so different in the use of language.

In many ways, the poems that Agee published in 1934 already began to anticipate a lot of the trends and characteristics, especially of American poetry, right up to the present day. I almost feel as if you couldn't pick any good poet, from now on back to Agee's time, whom he doesn't in some way anticipate. It is fascinating to study him in this light. He was reaching out all the time for new ways in poetry to express the experiences he was having.

The other thing that I would like to stress right away that is also in his poetry: I see his reaching out for different forms and different kinds of language, using artificial language as well as simple spoken language. I think he reached out for every kind of media with which to express his stories and his emotions, which makes him really a child of this age, makes him a lot like a young person in many ways. We speak of you as being "children of television." Agee was obviously a child of the movies long before you could recognize this in other writers of his time or even of the last two decades. He was constantly looking for new ways and new forms in poetry. He was very serious and cared about the movies and opera—a very unusual thing for a writer in his time—and he got into Broadway musicals. He just couldn't be satisfied with any one form. When David McDowell said that he was essentially a poet, everybody agreed. Agee was a poet trying to find other ways to express his poetic sensibility. He was not content with poems themselves, with poetry as a form, nor with any particular kind of poetry within the genre of poetry.

AUDIENCE: Tell us what you mean by "artificial language." Do you think Agee wrote in artificial language?

MADDEN: A lot of the poems are far from the way that James Agee would talk. I never met him. I never listened to him talk, but I asked the people who knew him about this specifically. How did he talk? Did he talk the way he wrote? In the finest artistic sense, Agee made up the language to express what he wanted to say, rather than saying it very simply and very straightforwardly, and this is fine.

MCDOWELL: Could I add something to that? Basically art is artifice. If one did tape recordings of the way you speak, it would not work as a story or novel or poem. One has to take it and shape it and make it clear in order to achieve something that is an ideal of what language is really like.

EYSTER: I'd like to go back to a few things that Mr. Madden said regarding the definition of poetry. The thing that I felt most strongly in all of Agee's works was his really reaching out and trying to get to you, to communicate to you. This is one of the reasons that no single form, that no single technique, would satisfy him. When poetry works for me, it's the closest another human being can come to me without actually touching me. When it really works, I feel closer, I feel a kinship and understanding. I always become the person who wrote it. When it doesn't work and it gets into this sort of artificial language, then I feel put off and distant more than in any other form of communication. One of the problems in reading poetry is that it either really hits you or you are really alienated from it; the very medium sets you off from it.

I came from a background where it was very "sissy" to read poetry. I came to poetry very hard. The question was whether or not I would give poetry what it needed. If a poet takes time to write, to think, to get to his higher concentration, then I, as a reader, have to try to give it that time. I always ask myself when a poem doesn't communicate: "Is that failure the poem's fault, or is it my fault?" When I feel it's the poem's fault, then I go to another poem. When I feel that it is my fault, I try harder to reach an understanding of the poem, which comes back to what I feel so strongly about Agee. In all of his works, and especially in his poetry, there is a real effort to communicate. And also the beauty. . . . The thing that stands out for me in all his poetry is the beauty he gives the simple things—to the quiet moments of life, to the falling of a leaf, to the shape of a horse's head. He is trying to give you an image and an understanding with it.

MADDEN: Most of you have probably studied the "The Rime of the Ancient Mariner," where he grabs people on the street and tries to tell them a story. Agee didn't necessarily want to tell you a story. He wanted to share some subtle insight about the way a guy looks standing on a street corner, the way the earth looks as day comes on (Sonnet 2), the way he relates that to his relationship with his loved one. I have a feeling when I read Agee that he is grabbing me as I'm walking by and looking into my eyes and saying, "I want to tell you something," in a very quiet voice, not like some drunk at a cocktail party. He is like some guy standing casually on the street corner in Tennessee, and you walk past and catch him in the middle of his train of thought, and he mumbles a few words. You wonder if he said something to you, and you wonder if you should respond or not. You are slightly embarrassed, but it sounds kind of interesting, so you stop and listen to what he says. You're drawn physically as well to his voice and his eyes, and you listen, and you're caught. It's as if in the poetry he says, "Let me tell you just a few words; let me tell you what it is that I want you to see and feel." Your eyes get big and you say, "Yes, Yes!" I know that these words are there in Agee's poetry, but they're in this strange new context, and this is wonderful, and I'd better hear it before it's over.

In *The Morning Watch* it's like: "Sit down, you're on a curb with me and I want to tell you this story about the time I was at St. Andrew's. There was this religious festival, and I want to tell you all the thoughts that went through my head." In *Let Us Now Praise Famous Men*, he wants to say, "We went down into the South, and we saw this and we saw that, and here are some statistics that aren't important, but here they are. What I really want to tell you is how Mr. Gudger looked."

With his movies, he said, "Stop. I just want to show you this right here on the screen. It won't take long. Look!" And then you settle into it. Very few writers give you the feeling that you are being accosted. It's also like *Kubla Khan*, where Coleridge said, "Weave a circle round him thrice, for he hath drunk the milk of paradise." James Agee, I believe, stands within this magic zone that he has created around him. If you step one little tiptoe into that magic zone, you become affected for the rest of your life, even if you have strong qualifications about his work.

O'FLAHERTY: I wonder if someone would like to talk about his language.

MANFRED: I had the same trouble Warren [Eyster] had. When I was your age and before, I couldn't get into poetry. I couldn't read it, and I didn't know what it was about. I did read a little of Shakespeare in high school, but it wasn't until I was in college and in danger of flunking out of my freshman year that I caught on to a secret of how to survive college. One of the profs I liked best seemed to be striving toward a main point that he wished to express in his course. Once I caught hold of what he was driving at, all the notes I had taken up to that point fell into place and had some meaning. It was at that point in freshman English that I caught on to what a poem was about. At first I resisted words, and I would become angry at the page because I couldn't get at what was there. I then learned to look at the poem and sit in the seat of the original to see how he felt at the time he wrote.

EYSTER: I was thinking about this artificiality in language. When I was first starting out with poetry, I was not willing to go with anything that did not sound like voices that I heard in my everyday life. This is one of the problems. The styles and the modes change. I think that Agee, in his poetry, was constantly reaching to do two things. One, he was aware of trying to reach you to communicate, and I think he also had a value for language itself where he felt that the selection and the arrangement of the words contributed to that. What I am trying to say, for example, is in one of Agee's poems — the words "I know you." You can turn the words around six different ways. You suddenly realize what the words, each part of the words, are — I know you, you know I, know I you. If you really go at them, you realize how each of them has a little different feeling or meaning. This kind of thing in that first poem of his is the very simplicity of things that you feel so strongly. "Now I know you do not love,/ Now you know I do not love,/ Now we know we do not love,/ No more doubt, no more deceiving." The thing that strikes me is that this is in everyone's language. There is not a word in that first stanza that isn't in the language of every single person here. Maybe the word *deceiving* is not common, but it's not, in this case, hunting for the "high-flown" word but for the word to communicate. Agee would go for the high-flown word and for the very simple word. Finding both qualities in him is one of the most remarkable things about him. Most poets either go one way or another. They're trying to be the voice of every day, or they become extremely artificial. I feel that Jim was much more mobile, and he was constantly searching to communicate his feelings.

MANFRED: I'd like to say something about finding the right word. Assuming that you have this powerful feeling, it's an operation from the inside out, rather than from the outside in. One of the reasons that poetry looks artificial to many people is that the writer originally wrote from the outside in. Workmen come up with wonderful bits of poetry, although they don't continue it. For example, the fellow who first thought of the phrase "rat-tail file." What a marvelous observation. He was probably the head carpenter and was trying to tell his helper: "Listen, I want that file, that round one, for making the holes through the doors so I can put the doorknobs in. You know, the one that looks like a rat's tail." This is the way that the poet operates. He's very much like that carpenter. "I want that file, and I want it now. How can I tell that dumb kid what it looks like?" He's seen a rat scurrying away from him. He's probably been trying to shoot a rat for months in the barn. Every time he has missed it, and this is why he thought of a rat-tail file. That one word came out of a long period of devotion to hunting rats. [Laughter from audience]

MADDEN: Looking at that from a reader's point of view, I can imagine that carpenter's apprentice saying for the rest of the day, "Hey, don't you need that rat-tail file again?" And then the next day, "Do you want me to get that rat-tail file for you?" Just so he can say the word.

What I am eager to hear is more questions because, looking at it from a human standpoint, this room cannot possibly be full of James Agee devotees. There are bound to be some people who have been reading his poetry whose reactions are somewhat like Mr. Eyster's were when he was a kid and like Mr. Manfred's. Maybe if you struggle with this to express your reactions to him, we can talk about it, maybe negative reactions, too. I don't see how there's too much to be gained by an awful lot of praise, because if you struggle with some of your reservations, you may end up liking him better or at least knowing why you don't like him.

AUDIENCE: Could you comment on the passage in *A Death in the Family* with Rufus at night? What happens in his bedroom?

EYSTER: There are many other things going on in it, but I think it's a very strong attempt at making you feel what it's like for a child to be alone: to have to find his way in the dark or to make his peace with the dark; to communicate all those things that, as we get older, we wouldn't admit anymore. Outside on a cold night, a tree slumps against the side of the house and a kind of creepy feeling goes through you, and you're suddenly alone. It's not quite like a Frankenstein movie, but suddenly you realize that your mother and father, or whomever you feel close to, are separated from you. Suddenly there is a wall. A door means real separation. I feel that it's just an endless desperate attempt to get the full feeling of what a child obviously feels many a night.

I originally came from coal country. I am living in Louisiana now, so Pennsylvania seems like a contrast. I always remember the coldness associated with the nights. I didn't like to wake up. If I felt cold, I would feel very much alone. It's really not fair to say that that's the only thing he's doing. Instead of recounting what happened over many nights, he's trying to set down this one time, one place, and all the feelings that he had toward that.

Let me ask a question. Did you feel the kid's loneliness at any place in that? Did you feel that at some times you lost it, that you didn't follow it? With all writers, there comes the problem that part of it catches, and sometimes you lose it for a while, and sometimes you pick it up again. That's when you say, "Why did you put that in?"

MADDEN: [to student] You really felt that it went on too long in that particular scene? Although you liked part of it, maybe? I think that there's an interesting contradiction in what we've been saying. Agee's basically a poet, and if poets are basically economical in their language, why is he extravagant? Why does he go on spending words there? I think that it goes back to the problem that I was talking about before — this sense of dissatisfaction with what he was doing. He senses that he hadn't really said it after all. Since he was writing prose rather than a poem, he felt more of a sense of space in which to operate. So he could keep on talking about it, trying with the next sentence to express the essence of this emotion that he was having. Although he knew he was lonely, he felt that there was something more to it. He kept reaching for it, grabbing for it, and starting again; he backtracked and repeated. I think that sometimes some readers don't want to go through that whole process with him on the page. They wish that he had resolved it before he came to the page and that he had given them only a few lines that would evoke all that process.

Agee somehow felt that it was a greater honesty to take the reader through the whole process — a false start, half successes — straining to achieve the impossible. Some of the dissatisfaction on the reader's part may be, "I realize you tried very hard, but you didn't quite make what *you* wanted to achieve." Some readers like that. Some readers think the effort was beautiful. It was beautiful to watch him try. It was beautiful to struggle with him. "It's very exciting to see you try so very hard." Other readers say, "Come and see me when you've got it." It's a difference in this sensibility, both on the part of the reader and the writer. Now in other parts of the book, he does achieve in a few words what he wants to express.

There are those moments, especially in *Let Us Now Praise Famous Men,* where the length of it is partly due to his constantly reaching and his sense of dissatisfaction and overreaching.

AUDIENCE: I wonder if this might be related to the sheer pleasure in words that southern writers such as Wolfe and Faulkner take. In the prologue, there is this pleasure in the words.

MADDEN: Southern writers don't write to communicate; they write to hear the sound of their own voice. To me, that's not a negative statement. When they write to hear the sound of their own voice, they want to hear echoes of the voices of all their people, living and dead. They want you to listen with them. This is the beautiful thing about southern speech. We don't say simply, "Go down to the store and get me a bottle of milk." We embroider it with all kinds of language and we go on and on about it. It's really marvelous! I think southerners and Jews are the same way. They love to "do" the language. One contrast is that the Jewish people love to embroider it with the gestures. The southerner stands still, and all these words come pouring out. That's an interesting thing, too — stand still and let it all come out.

MANFRED: I know one northern writer who had that same fault. There's one word in that first poem that you have in front of you, somewhat related to that rat-tail file. That's the word *morsel.* When I read that, I felt this was where he was standing when this emotion hit him and he wanted to reach out and tell us about it. He was feeling something giving way beneath him. The wedding or the marriage of these two people on the edge of a precipice — the precipice slowly frittered away by the wind. And to me, the word *morsel* would be the remark of my father saying that we don't have much food today, only a morsel of this or that. It would be the remark of someone really poor. And also someone who goes to communion and receives the bread broken by the priest, morsel by morsel. This is the way, not only a literal straight remark but also a remark loaded with all these religious moments that Jim Agee felt. It is really a loaded word like a *rat-tail file*. Only much more so.

McDOWELL: I'd like to ask Father Flye to say something about the simple language . . . how the language of simple people can become poetry.

FATHER FLYE: When we would get started on some topic and start discussing it, there would be a fine quality of verbal expression. Jim could speak casually and in very ordinary terms. Whatever he was saying, you never had the feeling, listening to him, that he was talking in some artificial way; he was trying very simply and sincerely to communicate with you. It might be very simple language, or — he had a wide vocabulary — he could use any word that would suit his purpose. His speech was easy to follow. I don't think I can say much more than that.

O'FLAHERTY: What did you think when his first book, *Permit Me Voyage*, was published?

FATHER FLYE: I had read a few of the poems in there that he would send me or show me. I don't know what to say about how I felt when I first read the book. Not only did I have this dear friendship with Jim as a person but I had a great regard and admiration for his writing. As soon as I began to read some of his poetry, his writings, and his letters to me, or he began to open up and do some reading, I thought, "That's a fine quality of verbal expression." In his letters to me, for example, the passages of excellent English — whether it was a simple discussion like that or poetry, I would feel certainly that he was essentially a poet. Some of his prose I would say is exquisite poetry, not in stanza or meter, something that I could quote, but just beautiful, lovely prose.

I wonder if I could read one or two of his poems. These are simple things. Any of you can follow this. I used to go to New York and take some church duty. I'd been out there one summer, and he and I got together, as would always be the case. I'd not much more than gotten back here than I received a letter from him. This was the letter.

Thursday, September 8, Dear Father
(That's the first line), if you'd rather,
Next time I will write in prose,
In the meantime, anything goes.

Even if it doesn't scan
I will rhyme it if I can;
Though my penciled emendations
Are guaranteed to try your patience,
I am bound to pull some boner
Working on a Smith-Corona . . .
    Well, now what? So work begins.
Pedagogy barks its shins
Once more and yet again once more
(As Lord knows many times before)
On every gradus ad Parnassum;
Well we can't teach 'em, better pass 'em.
Let those eradicate who can
Man's inhumanity to man
Through teaching boys to kiss the Flag,
Keep their rooms tidy, kick a fag,
Follow the leader, mind the rules,
Blunt and ignore the only tools
That interest the half mature
Enough to make some learning sure
If only people didn't refuse them
The right to feel the right to use them . . .
That which Authority thinks good
Turns into just that much dead wood:
And so perhaps it's just as well
They outlaw Heaven and in-law Hell.
That way, a fighting chance remains
For the boy with heart, and blood, and brains.
    So much for that. Too much, in fact.
I'm rather weary of this act.
I really should abstain from rhyme
And so I will, until next time.
Much love to you and Mrs. Flye,
And pardon this abortive try —
What comes of acting on whim,
You see.
    Affectionately,
                Jim.

He gave me a copy of this next poem just after he'd written it. I'm not dealing here with some of the higher poetry, sonnets, beautiful specimens of Agee's poetry. This is called "A Lullaby."

Sleep child, lie quiet, let be:
Now like a still wind, a great tree,
Night upon this city moves
Like leaves, our hungers and our loves.
    Sleep, rest easy, while you may.
    Soon it is day.
    And elsewhere likewise love is stirred;
Elsewhere the speechless song is heard:
Wherever children sleep or wake,
Souls are lifted, hearts break.
    Sleep, be careless while you can.
    Soon you are man.
    And everywhere good men contrive
Good reasons not to be alive.
And even should they build their best
No man could bear tell you the rest.
    Sleep child, for your parents' sake.
    Soon you must awake.

There's one more perhaps you'll like. This was on a sheet of paper among his things we found after his death. The title of it is "Delinquent."

Neat in their niches with retrousse faces
The choir boys chant the chorale of the mass,
Suspicious sopranos and imminent basses,
Molding their mouths as a blower of glass.
Hymning the high gods with oscillations,
As pliable lips adapt to the air,
Distracting the flock from divine occupations
By singing so loudly and looking so fair.
Limp in their linen that glistens and grates,
They ogle an octave with unctuous eyes,
Or lower shy lids as the organ abates,
Demure as a demon in cherub disguise,

Till troubled parishioners cannot be sure
So much naïveté's utterly pure.

EYSTER: I might add, since the young man has asked me the question about the boy sleeping in the dark in A *Death in the Family,* I really think that this poem, "A Lullaby," retains a little of the same sort of thing James Agee felt of a very curious experience at the time of sleep, at the time of waking from sleep, and a child and the relationship with the world and with his parents. Dealt with a little differently, but the same sort of thing . . . much more compacted.

II

Agee at *Fortune* and *Time*

ROBERT FITZGERALD

A Memoir

The office building where we worked presented on the ground floor one of the first of those showrooms, enclosed in convex, non-reflecting plate glass, in which a new automobile revolved slowly on a turntable. On Sunday a vacant stillness overcame this exhibition. The building bore the same name as the automobile. It had been erected in the late twenties as a monument to the car, the engineer, and the company, and for a time it held the altitude record until the Empire State Building went higher. It terminated aloft in a glittering spear point of metal sheathing. From the fifty-second and fiftieth floors where Agee and I, respectively, had offices, you looked down on the narrow cleft of Lexington Avenue and across at the Grand

Central Building, or you looked north or south over the city or across the East River toward Queens. As a boom-time skyscraper it had more generous stories than later structures of the kind — higher ceilings, an airier interior. Office doors were frosted in the old-fashioned way prevalent when natural daylight still had value with designers. In a high wind at our altitude you could feel the sway of the building, a calculated yielding of structural steel. Thus contact of a sort was maintained with weather and the physical world. In our relationship to this building there were moments of great simplicity, moments when we felt like tearing it down with our bare hands. We would have had to work our way from interior partitions to plaster shell to exterior facing, ripping it away, girder after girder, until the whole thing made rubble and jackstraws in 43rd Street. Jim was vivid in this mood, being very powerful and long boned, with long strong hands and fingers, and having in him likewise great powers of visualization and haptic imagination, so that you could almost hear the building cracking up under his grip.

He was visited on at least one occasion by a fantasy of shooting our employer. This was no less knowingly histrionic and hyperbolic than the other. Our employer, the Founder, was a poker-faced, strong man with a dented nose, well-modeled lips, and distant gray-blue eyes under bushy brows; from his boyhood in China he retained something, a trace of facial mannerism, that suggested the Oriental. His family name was a New England and rather a seafaring name; you can find it on slate headstones in the burial grounds of New Bedford and Nantucket and Martha's Vineyard. These headstones in the middle years of the last century were fitted with tintypes of the dead as living reminders on the spot of what form they were to reassume on the Last Day, provided that the day should occur before the tintypes utterly faded, as now seems not altogether unlikely. The Founder had that seacoast somewhere in him behind his mask, and he had a Yankee voice rather abrupt and twangy, undeterred by an occasional stammer. A Bones man at Yale, a driving man and civilized as well, quick and quizzical, interested and shrewd, he had a fast sure script on memoranda and as much ability as anyone in the place. He had nothing to fear from the likes of us. Jim imagined himself laying the barrel of the pistol at chest level on the Founder's desk and making a great bang. I imagine he imagined himself assuming the memorable look of the avenger whom John Ford photographed behind a blazing pistol in *The Informer*. It is conceivable that the Founder on occasion, and after his own fashion, returned the compliment.

The period I am thinking of covers 1936 and 1937, but now let me narrow it to late spring or early summer of 1936. Roosevelt was about to run for a second term against Alf Landon, and in Spain we were soon to understand that a legitimate republic had been attacked by a military and Fascist uprising. One day Jim appeared in my office unusually tall and quiet and swallowing with excitement (did I have a moment?) to tell me something in confidence. It appeared very likely, though not yet dead sure, that they were going to let him go out on a story, a story of tenant farming in the Deep South, and even that they would let him have as his photographer the only one in the world really fit for the job: Walker Evans. It was pretty well beyond anything he had hoped for from *Fortune*. He was stunned, exalted, scared clean through, and felt like impregnating every woman on the fifty-second floor. So we went over to a bar on Third Avenue. Here I heard, not really for the first time and certainly not for the last, a good deal of what might be called the theory of *Let Us Now Praise Famous Men*, a book that was conceived that day, occupied him for the next three years, and is the centerpiece in the life and writing of my friend. It may occur to you that if he had not been employed in our building and by our employer (though upon both at times he would gladly have attracted besides his own the wrath of God), he would never have had the opportunity of writing it. That is true; and it is also true that if he had not been so employed the challenge and the necessity of writing it might never have pressed upon him so gravely as for some years to displace motives for writing, other ends to be achieved by writing, including those of which the present book is a reminder.[1]

2

The native ground and landscape of his work, of his memory, was Knoxville and the Cumberland Plateau, but his professional or vocational school was one that for a couple of years I shared. You entered it from shabby Cambridge by brick portals on which were carven stone tablets showing an open book and the word *veritas*, a word — not that we paid it then the slightest attention — destined to haunt us like a Fury. The time I am thinking of now is February of 1930 in the Yard of that college where the stripped elms barely shadowed the colonial brickwork, and planks on the paths bore our feet amid clotted snow. On a Wednesday afternoon in the dust of a classroom I became sharply aware for the first time of Mr. Agee, pronounced quickly *Aygee*. We had been asked each to prepare a lyric for reading aloud. The figure in the front row on my right, looming and brooding and clutching his book, his voice very low, almost inaudible, but deliberate and distinct, as though ground fine by great interior pressure, went through that poem of Donne's that has the line "A bracelet of bright hair about the bone." It was clear that the brainy and great versing moved him as he read. So here, in the front row, were shyness and power and imagination, and here, moreover, was an edge of assertion, very soft, in the choice and reading of this poem, because the instructor for whom he was reading did not belong to the new School of Donne.

After this, Agee and I would sometimes have a Lucky together and talk for a few minutes outside Seaver Hall in the bitter or sweet New England weather. Seniority was his, then and for that matter forever, since he was a year older and a class ahead. He lived in the Yard and we had no friends in common. Older, darker, larger than I, a rangy boy, alert and gentle, but sardonic, with something of the frontiersman or hillman about him — a hard guy in more than the fashion of the time — wearing always a man's clothes, a dark suit and vest, old and uncared for, but clothes. His manner, too, was undergraduate with discrimination. He was reading Virgil that year under a professor whose middle initial had drawn down upon him the name of Pea Green William; Agee grimly referred to him strictly as Green. In the Seaver classroom with a handful of others we gave our attention to English metrics as expounded by our instructor, the Boylston Professor, who had set his face against Eliot and Pound. Faintly graying, faintly blurred, boyish and cheerful, mannerly and mild, he turned back to us each week our weekly sets of verses with marginal scrawls both respectful and pertinent. He was also good at reading aloud. Our metrical sense was educated by such things as the hovering beat of "Hark All You Ladies," and we heard the heroic couplet doomed by Romantic orchestration in "Whether on Ida's Shady Brow."

Far away from college, in the realm where great things could happen, great things had in fact happened that year: works of imagination and art in newly printed books, and these we pored and rejoiced and smarted over: *A Farewell to Arms*, most cleanly written of elegies to love in war, in the Great War whose shallow helmets, goggled masks, and khaki puttees were familiar to our boyhood; *Look Homeward, Angel,* the only work by an American that could stand with *A Portrait of the Artist as a Young Man;* and *The Innocent Voyage,* from which we learned a new style of conceiving childhood. Agee and I were very fond of these books. We were also devoted to Ring Lardner and to all the Joyce that we knew. But "The Waste Land," which had made my foundations shift, had not affected him in the same way, nor did "Ash Wednesday" seem to him as uncanny and *cantabile* and beyond literature as it did to me. Here we diverged, and would remain divided in some degree, as he desired in poetry something both more and less than I did, who chiefly wanted it to be hair-raising.

In the *Harvard Advocate* that year there were poems by J. R. Agee, but to my intolerant eye they seemed turgid and technically flawed. I did not see until several years later the highly mannered and rather beautiful "Epithalamium" that he wrote in the spring. "Ann Garner" was a more complicated matter. This longish poem appeared in the quarterly *Hound & Horn,* still known that year by the subtitle *A Harvard Miscellany* and edited by the princely Lincoln Kirstein, then in his last year as an undergraduate. Kirstein had known James Rufus Agee as a new boy at Exeter four or five years before, and there is a passage on Jim in his book, *Poems of a Pfc.,* finally published in 1964. "Ann Garner" had been written, in fact, while Jim was still at Exeter in 1928. Boys in prep school do not often write anything so sustained, and it is clear from one of Jim's letters what an effort it had been. In the first year of our friendship it impressed me more than any of his other verse for the ambition of the attempt at narrative with variations, not really like Jeffers but reaching like him toward myth, a vision of elemental life in the American earth.

What brought me fully awake to Agee as a writer was not this poem, callow even in its power, but a short story in the April *Advocate.* Two boys hunting with a BB gun in the outskirts of Knoxville got some infant robins out of a nest and decided they must be "put out of their misery," so while the mother bird flew shrill and helpless overhead they did the deed with stones. In puzzlement, in awe, in fascination, in boastful excitement — in shame, in revulsion. The younger boy threw up; the boys went home. That was about all, but the writer fully realized and commanded his little event. When I reread this story after thirty-three years I saw that he had put into it some of the skills and passions of his life: sympathy with innocent living nature, and love of it; understanding of congested stupidity and cruelty, and hatred of it; a stethoscopic ear for mutations of feeling; an ironic ear for idiom; a descriptive gift. No other contributor to the *Advocate* that year (in what other year?) wrote with ease, and repeatedly, prose like this: "The birds were very young. A mildew fuzz covered their heads and backs, along their wings lay little white spikes, like hair-fine fishbones. Through the membrane globing their monstrous bellies the children could see a mass of oystery colours, throbbing faintly. The birds kicked, and gaped, and clenched their wings." Significantly, too, the story intimated a pained interest in the relation between the actuality of birds and boys — kicking and gaping — and the American institution of "Church" or weekly Christian observance. The two hunters, parting uneasily after their crime, agreed to meet at Sunday school.

3

By simply descending a flight of steps and pushing through a turnstile for a nickel you could leave the university behind and set off for the big-city mystery of Boston, where wine in coffee cups could be drunk at the Olympia or *arak* at the Ararat on Atlantic Avenue; then other adventures would follow. If the Yard was our dooryard, Boston and neighborhood were the backyard we explored, and Jim later wrote a short catalog of attractions that he liked:

> Window table in Tremont St. Childs, brilliant Sunday mid-morning; the New England Boxing Tournament, for steady unsparing (if unskillful) ferocity; Boston Common with an actor and hangover and peanuts and pigeons, midafternoon; the Common on a rainy afternoon or night; on a snowy night; on a Sailor's night; the Fenway at about dusk, fair weather; for good movie stuff: the Arlington Theatre and lampposts from just beyond the level bridge; the debouchment of the Forest Hills subway . . . Revere Beach in midwinter, for sea sounds and pure ghoulishness; East Boston for swell houses, stunted trees struck through with mordant street lamps, and general dilapidation; the Arnold Arboretum in October or May; up the Charles at midnight, down at dawn; the fishboats unloading before dawn.

We lacked neither opportunity nor time for excursions like these and for a good deal of what we had to concede was Young Love. As for the university, it could be contented with a few classes a week and a few sleepless nights before exams. Considering human bondage in general and the demands of any other mode of life, it is remarkable that Agee and I both talked of breaking for freedom from this one, but we did, and he even had a plan of bumming to the Coast that spring on the chance of getting a movie job. If he had, the American cinema might have felt his impact twenty years before it took place. I reconcile myself to things having turned out as they did. He waited until summer and went west to work as a harvest hand and day laborer in Oklahoma, Kansas, and Nebraska.

Jim had been briefly in England and France in the summer of his sixteenth year, on a bicycle trip with his boyhood and lifelong friend, Father James Flye. Although he never returned to Europe, he had absorbed enough to sharpen his eye and ear for his own country. It can be said of him that he was American to the marrow, in every obvious way and in some not so obvious, not at all inconsistent with the kind of interest that some years later kept us both up until three in the morning looking through drawings by Cocteau, or some years later still enabled him to correct for me a mistranslation of Rimbaud. He took Patrick Henry's alternatives very seriously. Deep in him there was a streak of Whitman, including a fondness for the barbaric yawp, and a streak of Twain, the riverman and Romantic democrat. What being an American meant for an imaginative writer was very much on his mind. His summer wandering fell in, so to speak, with his plans.

Two short stories written out of his working summers appeared in the next year's *Advocate*. They are the last fiction Jim published as a young man, the last he would publish until *The Morning Watch* in 1950. In both stories you may feel the satisfaction of the narrator in being disencumbered of his baggage, intellectual or cultural, urban and familiar and social, and enabled to focus on the naked adventure at hand. The adventure in each case partly happened and was partly made up; the stories are pure fiction in the usual way of pure fiction, as much so as stories by Hemingway, their godfather. My point is that to conceive and feel them on his skin he had deprived himself of all the distraction that he liked — company, music, movies, and books — and had lived in lean poverty like a lens. To write them, and almost everything else that he had to work on for any length of time, he took on destitution by removing himself from class-bells, Thayer Hall, and his roommates, and holing up in the *Advocate* office for days and nights until the job was done. Advocate House at that time was a small frame building up an alley, containing a few tables and chairs and an old leather-covered couch, all pleasantly filthy; and there were, of course, places round about where you could get coffee and hamburgers or western sandwiches at any hour of the night. A boardinghouse bedroom or an empty boxcar might have been still better.

Did he ever draw any conclusions from all this? He certainly did. He never forgot what it meant to him to be on the bum, and he managed it or something like it when he could. His talent for accumulating baggage of all the kinds I have mentioned was very great, as it was very endearing, and he spent much of his life trying to clear elbowroom for himself amid the clutter. But on the question as to whether he had any business coming back to college that year, his third and my second, the answer is yes, and the best reason was Ivor Armstrong Richards.

In the second semester, on his way back to Magdalene, Cambridge, from a lectureship at Tsing Hua University in Peking, Richards paused at Harvard and gave two courses, one on modern English literature and the other carrying on those experiments in the actual effects of poetry that he had begun at Cambridge and had written up in his book, *Practical Criticism* (1929). Jim and I attended both courses and found ourselves at full stretch. Though he appeared shy and donnish, Richards was in fact intrepid and visionary beyond anyone then teaching literature at Harvard; when he talked about our papers he sometimes gave me the impression that he had spent the night thinking out what he would say in the morning. By pure analysis he used to create an effect like that produced by turning up an old-fashioned kerosene lamp, and he himself would be so warmed and illuminated that he would turn into a spellbinder, gently holding sway, fixing with his glinting gray eyes first one quarter and then another of the lecture room. When he spoke of the splendors of Henry James's style or of Conrad facing the storm of the universe, we felt that he was their companion and ours in the enterprise of art.

Richards's exacting lucidity and Jim's interest in the "Metaphysicals" are reflected in a poem in octosyllabics called "The Truce," printed in the *Advocate* for May 1931, the first poem of Jim Agee's that seemed to me as fully disciplined and professional as his prose. I not only admired but envied it and tried to do as well. The image of the facing mirrors fascinated him and made its last appearance in his work twenty years later, in *The Morning Watch* and in his commentary for the film *The Quiet One*. There is an echo in "The Truce," as there is also in one of the sonnets, of a great choral passage ("Behold All Flesh Is as the Grass") in the Brahms *Requiem*, which he sang that spring in the Harvard Glee Club; the surging and falling theme stayed in our heads for years.

Along with his stories, "The Truce" would be evidence enough — though there is explicit evidence in one of his letters — that in the spring of 1931 Jim held the English poetic tradition and the American scene in a kind of equilibrium under the spell of Richards, and lived at a higher pitch, but at the same time more at ease with his own powers, than in any other college year. He was elected president of the *Advocate* and thus became the remote Harvard equivalent of a big man on campus. We still saw one another rarely aside from class meetings, but had now one or two friends in common including Kirstein and a superb girl at Radcliffe, a dark-eyed delicately scornful being who troubled him before she troubled me; I can still see his grin of commiseration and tribute.

4

In the world at large where the beautiful books had happened, something else had begun to happen that in the next few years fixed the channel of Jim Agee's life. I was in England in 1931–1932 and saw nothing of him that year, when he got his degree, nor in the next year when I was back at Harvard to get mine. What gradually swam over everyone in the meantime was an ominous and astringent shadow already named by one cold intellect as the economic consequences of the peace. Worse evils and terrors were coming, but at the time this one seemed bad enough, simple as it was. People had less and less money and less and less choice of how to earn it, if they could earn any at all. Under a reasonable dispensation a man who had proved himself a born writer before he left the university could go ahead in that profession, but this did not seem to be the case in the United States in 1932. Neither in Boston nor New York nor elsewhere did there appear any livelihood appropriate for a brilliant president

of the *Harvard Advocate,* nor any mode of life resembling that freedom of research that I have sketched as ours at Harvard. In the
shrunken market the services of an original artist were not in demand. Hart Crane and Vachel Lindsay took their lives that spring.
Great gifts always set their possessors apart, but not necessarily apart
from any chance to exercise them; this gift at that time pretty well
did. If a freshman in 1929 could feel confined by the university, in
1932 it seemed a confinement all too desirable by contrast with what
lay ahead—either work of the limited kinds that worried people
would pay for, or bumming in earnest, winter-bumming, so to say.
Agee thankfully took the first job he could get and joined the staff of
Fortune a month after graduation.

During the next winter, back in Cambridge, where my Senior English tutor was studying *Das Kapital* and referred to capitalist society
as a sick cat, we heard of Jim working at night in a skyscraper with a
phonograph going full blast. Thus a writer of fiction and verse became a shop-member on a magazine dedicated by the Founder to
American business, considered as the heart of the American scene. It
is odd and, I think, suspicious that even at that point in the Great
Depression Jim did not live for a while on his family and take the
summer to look around. Dwight Macdonald, then on the staff of *Fortune,* had been in correspondence with Jim for a year or two and had
bespoken a job for him on the strength of his writing—which incidentally included a parody of *Time,* done as one entire issue of the
Advocate. The man who was then managing editor of *Fortune* was
clever enough to recognize in Agee abilities that *Fortune* would be
lucky to employ, and he would have had it in him to make Jim think
he might lose the job if he did not take it at once. I do not know,
however, that this occurred. What else Jim could have done I don't
know either; but again at this time there was the alternative of Hollywood, and there might have been other jobs, like that of forest
ranger, which would have given him a healthy life and a living and
left his writing alone. Now and again during the next few years he
would wonder about things like that.

At all events, he hadn't been on *Fortune* three months before
he applied for a Guggenheim Fellowship in October 1932. Nothing
came of this application, as nothing came of another one five years
later. In the 1932 application (of which he kept a carbon copy among
his papers) he proposed as his chief labor the continuation of a long

satirical poem, *John Carter*, which he had begun at Harvard, and said he would also perhaps finish a long short story containing a "verse passacaglia." The title of the story was to be "Let Us Now Praise Famous Men"; I never saw and have not recovered his draft of it. For opinions of his previous writing he referred the judging committee to Myron Williams, an English teacher at Exeter, Conrad Aiken, and I. A. Richards. For opinions of *John Carter* he referred them to Archibald MacLeish, Stephen Vincent Benét, Robert Hillyer, Theodore Spencer, and Bernard DeVoto. Phelps Putnam, he said, would also be willing to give an opinion. If awarded a fellowship he would work mainly on the poem, "which shall attempt a diversified and comprehensive reflection and appraisal of contemporary American civilization and which ultimately, it is hoped, will hold water as an 'Anatomy of Evil.'" He would work on it "as long as the money held out," and he thought he could make it last at least two years. "I don't think I would spend much time about any university," he said. "I expect I would live in France, in some town both cheap and within reach of Paris." It is a fair inference from this that in October 1932 he did not yet know that he would marry Olivia Saunders in the following January. Both in October and January he must have considered that he had a good chance of a Guggenheim. On his record he was justified in thinking so. Yet in the last sentence of his "project" for *John Carter* his offhand honesty about the prospect of never finishing it may have handed the Guggenheim committee a reason for turning him down.

The two long sections that he got written, with some unplaced fragments, have been printed in *The Collected Poems of James Agee*. His hero, never developed beyond conception in the poem as it stands, would have owed something not only to Byron's Don Juan but, I think, to the Nihilist superman Stavrogin in *The Possessed* of Dostoyevsky, a novel we were studying with Richards in the spring of 1931 — greatly to the increase of hyperconsciousness in us both. Jim's fairly savage examination of certain Episcopalian attitudes and decor — and even more, the sheer amount of this — indicates quite adequately how "Church" and "organized religion" in relation to awe and vision bothered his mind. Another value, almost another faith, emerges in the profound respect (as well as disrespect) accorded to the happy completion of love. When Jim spoke of "joy" he most often meant this, or meant this as his criterion.

5

Moderate ambitions may be the thing for some people at some ages, but they were not for James Agee, and certainly not at twenty-three. To make "a complete appraisal of contemporary civilization," no less, was what he hoped to do with his long poem. Now the Founder, Henry Luce, with his magazines, actually held a quite similar ambition, and this accounts for the mixture of attraction and repulsion in Agee's feeling for his job. Attraction because *Fortune* took the world for its province and because the standard of workmanship on the magazine was high. Also because economic reality, the magazine's primary field, appeared grim and large in everyone's life at that time, and because by courtesy of *Fortune* the world lay open to its editors and they were made free of anything that in fact or art or thought had bearing on their work. Repulsion because that freedom in truth was so qualified, because the ponderous and technically classy magazine identified itself from the start, and so compromised itself (not dishonestly, but by the nature of things), with one face of the civilization it meant to appraise; whatever it might incidentally value, it was concerned with power and practical intelligence, not with the adventurous, the beautiful, and the profound — words we avoided in those days but for which referents nonetheless existed. At heart Agee knew his vocation to be in mortal competition, if I may put it so, with the Founder's enterprise. For *Fortune* to enlist Agee was like Germany enlisting France.

Nevertheless he had now three uninterrupted years of it. One blessing was the presence on *Fortune* of Archibald MacLeish, a Yaleman like the Founder and one of the original editors, but also a fine artist who knew Jim for another, respected him and helped him. MacLeish in 1932 was forty and had published his big poem, *Conquistador.* Being experienced and distinguished, he could pick the subjects that appealed to him, and being a clearheaded lawyer-turned-poet, he wrote both well and efficiently. His efficiency was a byword on *Fortune.* Requiring all research material on cards in orderly sequence, he merely flipped through his cards and wrote in longhand until five o'clock, when he left the office. Often enough other people, including Jim, would be there most of the night.

I had a brief glimpse of the scene when I got to New York in the summer of 1933. The city lay weary and frowsy in a stench of Depres-

48 REMEMBERING JAMES AGEE

sion through which I walked for many days, many miles up and down town, answering ads, seeing doubtful men in dusty offices, looking for a job. MacLeish got me an interview with a rather knifelike *Fortune* editor who read what writing I had to show and clearly sized me up as a second but possibly even more difficult Agee, where one was already enough. Staring out of the window reflectively at Long Island he told me in fact that the Founder had taken a good deal from Agee, allowing for Agee's talent, but that there were limits. Back in MacLeish's office I waited while he, the old backfield man, warm and charming as ever, called up Jim. So Jim came in and we poets talked. One subject was the current plight of Kenneth Patchen, a poet dogged by misfortune. Archie also mentioned Hart Crane, whom he had once persuaded *Fortune* to take on for a trial. Hart had been completely unable to do it. It did not cross my mind that this had any relevance to me. I felt elated over my visit, and Jim took me home to dinner.

The basement apartment on Perry Street had a backyard where grew an ailanthus tree, and there under the slim leaves we sat until dark, he and Via and I, drinking I don't remember what but I imagine Manhattans, a fashion of the period. After dinner we went to the piano and sang some of the Brahms *Requiem.* Then he got out his manuscripts, read from *John Carter,* and read a new poem, a beauty, "Theme with Variations" (later he called it "Night Piece"). *Fortune,* I suppose at MacLeish's suggestion, had assigned him an article on the Tennessee Valley Authority, and in the course of preparing it he had gone back that summer to the countryside of his boyhood: hence, I think, this poem. In that evening's dusk and lamplight neither of us had any doubt that we shared a vocation and would pursue it, come what might. We were to have a good many evenings like it during the next three years while that particular *modus vivendi* lasted for Jim Agee as office worker and husband.

Jim must have thought *Fortune* would have me (*Time,* instead, had me, but not until February of 1936), because at the end of August when I was temporarily out of town I had a letter from him that concluded: "I'm wondering what you'll think of a job on *Fortune,* if you take it. It varies with me from a sort of hard, masochistic liking without enthusiasm or trust, to direct nausea at the sight of this symbol $ and this % and this *biggest* and this some blank billion. At times I'd as soon work on *Babies Just Babies.* But in the long run I suspect the fault, dear *Fortune*, is in me: that I hate any job on earth, as a job and hindrance and semisuicide."

His TVA article appeared in *Fortune* for October. It opened:

> The Tennessee River system begins on the worn magnificent crests of the southern Appalachians, among the earth's older mountains, and the Tennessee River shapes its valley into the form of a boomerang, bowing to its sweep through seven states. Near Knoxville the streams still fresh from the mountains are linked and thence the master stream spreads the valley most richly southward, swims past Chattanooga and bends down into Alabama to roar like blown smoke through the floodgates of Wilson Dam, to slide becalmed along the crop-cleansed fields of Shiloh, to march due north across the high diminished plains of Tennessee and through Kentucky spreading marshes toward the valley's end where, finally, at the toes of Paducah, in one wide glassy golden swarm the water stoops forward and continuously dies into the Ohio.

Soon after this Luce called him in and told him that he had written one of the best things ever printed in *Fortune*. It was characteristic of the Founder to acknowledge this; it was also characteristic of him to indicate, as Agee's reward, the opportunity to write a number of straight "business stories" whereby to strengthen his supposed weak side. The first of these concerned the Steel Rail, and according to Dwight Macdonald, the Founder himself buckled down to coach Agee in how to write good hard sense about the steel business. A story later got around that the Founder for a time considered sending Agee to the Harvard Business School. "That story," Luce wrote to me in 1964, "is quite plausible — though I do not actually recall it. A problem in journalism that interested me then — and still does — is to combine good writing and 'human understanding' with familiarity with business." Eventually Luce gave up and the job went to someone else, but the article as it appeared in December retained traces of Jim's hand: "Caught across the green breadth of America like snail paths on a monstrous plantain leaf are 400,000 . . . steel miles. If, under the maleficent influence of that disorderly phosphorus which all steel contains, every inch of this bright mileage were suddenly to thaw into thin air . . ."

6

During that fall and winter and the following year we pretty often had lunch or dinner together. I would call for him in his lofty office, or I would look up over my typewriter in the newspaper city room where by that time I worked and see him coming down the aisle from the elevator. He would come at his fast, loose, long-legged walk, springy on the balls of his feet, with his open overcoat flapping. We would go to a saloon for beer and roast beef sandwiches. I wish very badly that I could recall the conversations of those times, because in them we found our particular kind of brotherhood. Both of us had been deeply enchanted and instructed, and were both skilled, in an art remote from news writing, an art that we were not getting time or breath to practice much. You would underestimate us if you supposed that we met to exchange grievances, for of these in the ordinary sense we had none. We met to exchange perceptions, and I had then and later the sense that neither of us felt himself more fully engaged than in talk with the other. My own childhood enabled me to understand his, in particular his schooling at the monastery school of St. Andrew's in Tennessee. We were both in the habit of looking into the shadow of Death. Although we came of different stock and from different regions, we were both Catholic (he, to be precise, Anglo-Catholic) by bringing-up and metaphysical formation; both dubious not to say distressed about "Church"; both inclined to the "religion of art," meaning that no other purpose, as we would have put it, seemed worth a damn in comparison with making good poems. Movies, of course, we talked about a good deal. My experience was not as wide as his, my passion less, but we admired certain things in common: Zasu Pitts in *Greed* and the beautiful sordidness of that film; the classic flight down the flights of steps in *Potemkin*; Keaton; Chaplin. We saw, sometimes together, and "hashed over," as Jim would say, the offerings of that period: the René Clairs, the Ernst Lubitsches; *The Informer*; *Man of Aran*; *Grand Illusion*; *Mayerling*; *The Blue Angel*; *Mädchen in Uniform*; *Zwei Herzen*.

The various attitudes covered by "taking care of yourself" interested Jim Agee, but rarely to the point of making him experiment with any. Rubbers, for example, he probably thought shameful and never wore in his adult life; on the contrary, in that period, his shoes both winter and summer were often worn through, with cracked uppers. But he had some conventional habits and impulses. He wore a hat, a small one that rode high on his shock of dark hair. For several entire weeks in 1934 he gave up cigarettes for a pipe. The episode of the pipe was the last effort of that kind that he would make until many years later when he cut down smoking after his first heart attack.

Another thing he did with Via was to keep a catboat at City Island and go out there to sail and swim on Sundays in summer. I think he had been on the swimming team at Exeter; at any rate he had an enviable backstroke. On one of these Sunday excursions when I went along I remember that we amused ourselves during the long black blowy subway ride by playing the metaphor game: by turns each describing an inanimate object in such a way as to portray without naming a public figure. Jim developed a secondhand silver flute into Leslie Howard and a Grand Rapids easy chair into Carl Sandburg. Later that evening we had a memorable and I suppose comic conversation about whether or not the Artist should Keep in Shape. In the course of this I quoted Rémy de Gourmont to the effect that a writer writes with his whole body, bringing immediate and delighted assent from Jim, but not to the inference I myself would draw. His own body seemed so rugged and his stamina so great that I thought he could overlook his health and get away with it. The truth is that he was not as rugged as he looked. He had an inclination to hemophilia that had nearly cost him his life when he had his tonsils out in 1928, and at Exeter, too, he had first hurt his heart trying to run the mile. He never mentioned any of this.

Many-tiered and mysterious, the life of the great city submerged us now, me rather more, since I had no eyrie like his, but all day long spanieled back and forth in it and at night battered at my deadlines; and I think Jim envied me the unpretentious but hard craft I had got into. Whatever other interests we had, one became fairly constant and in time inveterate: the precise relation between any given real situation or event and the versions of it presented in print, that is, after a number of accidents, processes, and conventions had come into play. The quite complicated question of "how it really was" came before us all the time, along with our resources and abilities for making any part of that actuality known in the frames our employers gave us. Of those frames we were acutely aware, being acutely aware of others more adequate. Against believing most of what I read I am armored to this day with defenses worked out in those years and the years to follow. Styles, of course, endlessly interested us, and one of Jim's notions was that of writing an entire false issue of the *World-Telegram* deadpan, with every news item and ad heightened in its own style to the point of parody. He could easily have done it. Neither of us felt snide about eyewitness writing in itself or as practiced by Lardner or Hemingway; how could we? We simply mistrusted the journalistic apparatus as a mirror of the world, and we didn't like being consumed by it. Neither of us ever acquired a professional and equable willingness to work in that harness. For him to do so would have been more difficult than for me, since he had a great talent for prose fiction and I had not. After being turned down for the Guggenheim, in fact, he thought of trying to publish a book of his stories, and went so far as to write a preface for it.

"I shall do my best to stick to people in this book," he wrote. "That may seem to you the least I could do; but the fact is, I'm so tied up with symbols and half-abstractions and many issues about poetry which we'd better steer clear of now, that it is very hard for me to see people clearly as people. . . . Someday, if my life is worth anything, I shall hope to give people clearly in clear poetry, and to make them not real in the usual senses of real, but more than that: full of vitality and of the ardor of their own truth."

But he dropped the idea of publishing any stories at that point. Instead, with MacLeish's encouragement, he gathered the best of his old poems together with some new ones to make a book, and in October 1934, in the Yale Younger Poets series, in which MacLeish and Stephen Vincent Benét were then interested, the Yale Press published *Permit Me Voyage*.

7

Of how I felt about Jim's book then, it is perhaps enough to say that at bad times in the next year or two I found some comfort in being named in it. So far as I can discover, none of the contemporary comments on it, including the foreword by MacLeish, took much notice of what principally distinguished it at the time: the religious terms and passion of several pieces, rising at times to the grand manner. In two of his three pages MacLeish did not refer to the book at all, being engaged in arguing that neither of the current literary "programs," America Rediscovered and Capitalism Be Damned, mattered in comparison with *work* done. As to Agee, "Obviously he has a deep love of the land. Equally obviously he has a considerable contempt for the dying civilization in which he has spent twenty-four years." But he said nothing of the fact that Agee's book appeared to be the work of a desperate Christian; in fact, he rather insisted on saying nothing, for he concluded that by virtue of the poet's gift, especially his ear, and his labor at his art, "the work achieves an integral and inward importance altogether independent of the opinions and purposes of its author."

This was true enough, but some of the poems were so unusual in what they suggested as to call, you might think, for a word of recognition. One gusty day years later, as we were crossing 49th Street, Jim and I halted in the Radio City wind and sunlight to agree with solemnity on a point of mutual and long-standing wonderment, not to say consternation: how rarely people seem to believe that a serious writer means it; he means what he says or what he discloses. Love for the land certainly entered into *Permit Me Voyage*; contempt for a dying civilization much less, and contempt here was not quite the word. It could even be said, on the contrary, that a sequence of twenty-five regular and in some cases truly metaphysical sonnets rather honored that civilization, insofar as a traditional verse form could represent it. The most impressive things in the book were the "Dedication" and the "Chorale," and what were these but strenuous prayers? They could have no importance, because no existence, independent of the opinions and purposes of the author.

A sense of the breathing community immersed in mystery, exposed to a range of experience from what can only be called the divine to what can only be called the diabolical, most intelligent in awe and most needful of mercy — a religious sense of life, in short — moved James Agee in his best work. If in introducing that work the sensitive and well-disposed MacLeish could treat this motive as unmentionable, that may give some idea of where Agee stood amid the interests and pressures of the time. It must be added that those interests were also Agee's and that those pressures he not only profoundly felt but himself could bring to bear.

Four years at Harvard had complicated out of recognition his youthful Episcopalianism (he preferred to say Catholicism), but he hated polite academic agnosticism to the bone. In one *Advocate* editorial as a senior he had even proposed Catholicism as desirable for undergraduates. The poem *John Carter*, which he had begun there and would have carried on if he could, was to be an "anatomy of evil" wrought, he said, by an agent of evil in the "orthodox Roman Catholic" sense. At twenty-five, after two years in New York, he published an openly religious book of poems. MacLeish was not alone in ignoring what it said; the reviewers also ignored it. It was as if the interests and pressures of the time made it inaudible. Inaudible? Since I still find it difficult to read the "Dedication" and the "Chorale" without feeling a lump in my throat, I do not understand this even now. If he had been heard, surely a twinge of compunction would have crossed the hearts of thousands. But the book itself, Jim's poems in general, remained very little known or remarked during his lifetime, and for that matter are little known even now. One reason for this, I am well aware, is that in the present century the rhymed lyric and the sonnet for a time seemed disqualified as "modern poetry." Jim was aware of it, too; so aware that his sequence ended with a farewell to his masters, the English poets: "My sovereign souls, God grant my sometime brothers, I must desert your ways now if I can."

The concluding poem in the book, the title poem, was indeed a conclusion, but it enfolded a purpose. "My heart and mind discharted lie — " with reference, that is, to the compass points, religious, literary, and other, within which at St. Andrew's, at Exeter, at Harvard, and in New York he had by and large lived and worked. This was more than the usual boredom of the artist with work that is over and done with. He turned away now from Christian thought and observance, and began to turn away from the art of verse. Yet his purpose was to rechart, to reorient himself, by reference to the compass needle itself, his own independent power of perception, his own soul.

8

Therein such strong increase to find
In truth as is my fate to know.

Everyone who knew Jim Agee will remember that in these years there grew upon him what became habitual almost to idiosyncrasy: a way of tilting any subject every which way in talk, with prolonged and exquisite elaboration and scruple. He was after the truth, the truth about specific events or things, and the truth about his own impressions and feelings. By truth I mean what he would chiefly mean: correspondence between what is said and what is the case — but what is the case at the utmost reach of consciousness. Now this intent has been delicately and justly distinguished from the intent of art, which is to make, not to state, things; and a self-dedication to truth on the part of Shakespeare or Mozart (Ageean examples) would indeed strike us as peculiar. On the other hand, with philosophy dethroned and the rise of great Realists, truth-telling has often seemed to devolve almost by default upon the responsible writer, enabling everyone else to have it both ways: his truth as truth if they want it, or as something else if they prefer, since after all he is merely an artist. Jim Agee, by nature an artist and responsive to all the arts, took up this challenge to perceive in full and to present immaculately what was the case.

Think of all that conspired to make him do so. The place of Truth in that awareness of the living God that he had known as a child and young man and could not forget. The place of truth at the university, *Veritas*, perennial object of the scholar's pains. New techniques for finding out what was the case: among them, in particular, sociological study, works like *Middletown* in the United States and *Mass Observation* in England, answering to the perplexity of that age, and the "documentary" by which the craft of the cameraman could show forth unsuspected lineaments of the actual. (An early and what would appear a commonplace example of this craft, *The River,* by Pare Lorentz, excited Agee and myself.) Then, to sicken and enrage him, there was the immense new mud-fall of falsehood over the world, not ordinary human lying and dissimulation but a calculated barrage, laid down by professional advertisers and propagandists, to corrupt people by the continent-load. Finally, day by day, he had the given occupation of journalism, ostensibly and usually in good faith concerned with what was the case. In the editing of *Fortune* all the other factors played a part: the somewhat missionary zeal of the Founder, a certain respect for standards of scholarship, a sociological interest in looking into the economic conditions and mode of life of classes and crafts in America, an acquiescence in advertising and in self-advertisement, and, of course, photography.

The difficulties of the period were, however, deepened by an intellectual dismay, not entirely well founded but insidious under many forms: *What was the case* in some degree proceeded from the observer. Theoretical in abstract thought for centuries, this cat seemed now to have come out of the bag to bewitch all knowledge in practice: knowledge of microcosmic entities, of personal experience, of human society. Literary art had to reckon with it. To take an elementary example, Richards would put three Xs on a blackboard disposed thus ∴ to represent poem, referent, and reader, suggesting that a complete account of the poem could no more exclude one X than another, nor the relationship between them. Nor were the Xs stable but variable. *Veritas* had become tragically complicated. The naive practices of journalism might continue, as they had to, but their motives and achievements, like all others, appeared now suspect to Freudian and Marxian and semanticist alike; and of what these men believed they understood, James Agee was (or proposed to make himself) also aware. Hence his self-examinations, his ambivalences ("split" feelings) on so many things. As he realized well enough, they could become tedious, but they were crucial to him and had the effect that what he knew, in the end, he knew with practiced definition. It must be added that the more irritated and all-embracing and scrupulous his aspiration to full truth, "objective" and "subjective" at once, the more sharply he would know his own sinful vainglory or Pride in that ambition, in those scruples; and he did. Few men were more sensitive to public and private events than he was, and he would now explore and discriminate among them with his great appetite, his energy, his sometimes paralyzing conscience, and the intellect that Richards had alerted. I am of course reducing a long and tentative and often interrupted effort into a few words.

I named three books arbitrarily as stars principal in our first years at Harvard; I will name three more, arbitrarily again, to recall the planetary influences after graduation. In the spring of 1934, after Judge Wolsey's decision, Random House published *Ulysses* for the first time legally in America, and even if we had read it before, as Jim and I had, in the big Shakespeare & Co. edition, we could and did now read it again, in a handier form suitable for carrying on the subway. Or for the Agee bathroom, where I remember it. Joyce engrossed him and got into his blood so thoroughly that in 1935 he felt obliged, as he told a friend of mine, to master and get over that influence if he were ever to do anything of his own.

Céline's *Voyage au Bout de la Nuit* was our first taste of the end-of-the-rope writing that became familiar later in Miller and later still in Beckett. Malraux's *Man's Fate* had another special position. This story, with Auden's early poems, counted as much as the Russian movies of Eisenstein and Dovzhenko in swaying Jim toward communism. The attraction in any case was strong. The peaceful Roosevelt revolution had only begun; there was a real clash of classes in America. I had myself, in a single day of reporting, seen the pomp of high capitalism to be faded and phoney at an NAM convention in the Waldorf and the energies of laboring men to be robust and open at a union meeting. On one side of his nature Jim was a frontiersman and a Populist to whom blind wealth and pretentious gentility were offensive. Besides this he had the Romantic artist's contempt, "considerable contempt," for the Philistine and for what were then known to us as bourgeois attitudes — though he distinguished between the human souls that inherited them. For poverty and misery in general he had a sharp-eyed pity. The idea of a dedicated brotherhood working underground in the ghastly world held his imagination for several years — spies amid the enemy, as Auden had imagined them; at the same time he had no great difficulty in seeing through most of the actual candidates for such a brotherhood, including himself. The Party fished in vain for Agee, who by liking only what was noble in the revolution liked too little of it.

9

Embedded in *Fortune* for those years are several of Jim's best efforts at telling how things really were. As in the description of the Tennessee River, these are most often concerned with American landscapes and American living. In September 1934, for example, there was this opening to an article on the Great American Roadside:

> This continent, an open palm frank before the sky against the bulk of the world. This curious people. The automobile you know as well as you know the slouch of the accustomed body at the wheel and the small stench of gas and hot metal. You know the sweat and the steady throes of the motor and the copious and thoughtless silence and the almost lack of hunger and the spreaded swell and swim of the hard highway toward and be-

neath and behind and gone and the parted roadside swarming past. This great road, too; you know that well. How it is scraggled and twisted along the coast of Maine, high crowned and weak-shouldered in honor of long winter. How in Florida the detours are bright with the sea-lime of rolled shells. How the stiff wide stream of hard unbroken roadstead spends the mileage between Mexicali and Vancouver. How the road degrades into a rigorous lattice of country dirt athwart Kansas through the smell of hot wheat and this summer a blindness and a strangulation of lifted dust. How like a blacksnake in the sun it takes the ridges, the green and dim ravines which are the Cumberlands, and lolls loose into the hot Alabama valleys. How in the spectral heat of the Southwest, and the wide sweeps of saga toward the North-west, it means spare fuel strapped to the running board. . . . Oh yes, you know this road; and you know this roadside. You know this roadside as well as you know the formulas of talk at the gas station, the welcome taste of a Bar-B-Q sandwich in midafter-noon, the oddly excellent feel of a weak-springed bed in a clap-board transient shack, and the early start in the cold bright lone-some air, the dustless and dewy road.

In October of the same year, on the Drought:

That this has been by all odds the most ruinous drought in U.S. history is old stuff to you by now. So are the details, as the press reported them, week by broiling week, through the sum-mer. But all the same, the chances are strong that you have no idea what the whole thing meant: what, simply and gruesomely, it was. Really to know, you should have stood with a Dakota farmer and watched a promissory rack of cloud take the height of the sky, weltering in its lightnings . . . and the piteous meager sweat on the air, and the earth baked stiff and steaming. You should have been a lot more people in a lot more places, really to know. Barring that impossibility, however, there is the clear dispassionate eye of the camera, which under honest guidance has beheld these bitter and these transient matters, and has re-corded this brutal season for the memory of easier time to come.

These quotations must suffice, and they are not carelessly chosen. In 1935 he did a thorough reexamination of the TVA, published in

May, and a study of Saratoga, New York, published in August. These and other examples of sheer ability won him a taste of the freedom he craved. Beginning in November, *Fortune* gave him a six months' leave of absence, most of which he and Via spent in Florida on a small coastal island, Anna Maria, south of St. Petersburg and Tampa.

In a notebook of his, half-filled with jottings of that winter, I find the first entry amusing at this distance: it was a name and an address — *The New Masses* — later canceled out by a scribble. He was now steadily devouring Freud and recording his dreams. "Read Freud until midnight" is an entry several times repeated. There are pages like Stephen's or Bloom's waking thoughts in *Ulysses*. There are notes and self-injunctions about writing. For instance:

> My need for tone, tension & effect in writing limits me very badly. Yet cd. be good. But in many ways needless effort. And in many ways false. Its attempt in long run: to give, at once, frame and fluescence to pic. of universe. Seem to feel I have no right to give the looseness till is established the tightness wherein it moves. . . . Must throw brain into detail. And into fearlessness, shamelessness & naturalness abt writing. . . . Poem or prose in line between The Barge She Sat In and a social report of a wedding. What was worn. Who was there, etc. / Bks not of one thing — stories, poetry, essays, etc. / but of all, down to most casual.

In December he wrote some ottava rima, a few stanzas mocking something Sir Samuel Hoare, then British foreign minister, had said in the course of diplomacy that winter over the Italian war against Ethiopia. It was the last spasm of *John Carter*. He read *Crime and Punishment*, Caroline Spurgeon on *Shakespeare's Imagery*, and *The Counterfeiters*. Gide, he wrote,

> makes me realize more clearly than I have for a long time what a damned soft and uncertain customer I am. Had again, still have, though now my head and purposes are woolly, feeling of necessity to go plain to the bone and stay there. The 40-day fasts and that kind of thing. Misnamed virtues: they clear you: which is a state of grace or virtue. / Virtual / feel in many words, suddenly like little puffs of light, nowadays, the shine and silver quality wh. is equivalent (EQUIVALENT is such a word) to a

whole certain tone in Bach. Does Bach and don't many com-
·posers reduce to 2 or 3 dominant tones? & I don't mean idioms
either. Same with writers. Mozart's very skillful chromatic de-
velopments & returns that an ear holds a lot less surely than
much trickier 20th Century stuff. Analyze (can you) quality of
excitement in minuet of Jupiter. Sense of a full orchestra in
a Beethovenish way of being full, even in 1st measure when
woodwinds have it. Mozart's queer "darker" music, something
like Hopkins' love of the dappled, the counter, original, spare,
strange. In some rather homely themes of scherzi — and, likelier
to turn up in them than in slo mvts & finales? 1st mvt of G-minor
has some of it, too. Also vide great values of the prosy & verbose
line in poetry, & of bromide almost. Note some of Mozart's
more strenuous & some of his more tossed off slow mvts; lyrics
in Songs of Innocence; many passages in Schubert; quite a few
in Beethoven.

Among many entries on music, there is one noting "the great beauty
of West End Blues" and another, written firmly with a fresh pencil as
if he wanted badly to get it down:

> Swing music is different from any contemporary Art Mouth-
> piece. Barring straight folk stuff and vaude & burlesk adlibbing,
> runs roughly this way. Writing last had this freedom in Eliza-
> beth's time, with something half like it but crippled in Byron.
> Sculpture of Africans has it. Music lost it (roughly) with Moz-
> art. Beethoven had but did not use and finally buried it. The
> 19th and 20th centuries are solidly self-conscious and inhibited.
> Only swing today is perfectly free and has in its kind a complete
> scope. Some directors have it. Eisenstein does or did. Disney
> does or did. Chaplin did. There may be bits of it in some surre-
> alist art. With words, does Perelman have some? and Groucho
> some? and Durante some? But all pretty much of a kind: not at
> all capable of wonderful lyric scope of swing. Can words spoken
> or written possibly break through it again, break through and
> get free.

He worked on some of the poems that were published over the next
three years or so, on some that were never published or worth publishing, on others that have not survived. He drafted autobiographical

material that would serve him years later in the novel published after his death, as the following entry indicated: "Have been working (c. 12–15,000 words) on the footloose in Knoxville idea. Don't know." One entry of great importance, because it stated an obsession that had its relevance to everything and especially to "Church" and Christianity, was this: "Truth goes much less far than falsehood: at every transition, more misunderstanding comes aboard: gradually becomes handleable by those too corrupted by falsehood to handle bare truth. Radium into lead." I have been quoting these notes generously in the hope that you will hear at least remotely a voice in them and get at least an inkling of what his talk was like. But one final entry I will quote as a thing in itself, comparable to one of Hopkins's beautifully delineated studies of nature in the *Notebooks*. This was during a walk on a misty night under an almost full moon down the beach on Anna Maria.

> Surf as rounded point, coming in at acute angle, running along its edges on shallow sand with tearing glistening sound, like drawn zipper opening. Then around pt., meet surf broadside. In darkness you see it, well out on the dark, explode like opening parachute, and come in. Another kind: where in 2-3 parts on single line it whitens and the white widens — again the glistening zipper action — till all white meets and in it comes. Also: smallish tendons of it, private to themselves, bearing up (no white) and smacking themselves straight down on hard sand beneath a few inches of water with great passion and impact, PFFUHHH. Also, lovely and violent, competent folding-under of seam, pursing as of lips, when wave crest falls so prematurely as to undermine its own back: so you get a competent, systematic turning under in long lines. Also sink and drying of water in sand as shallow wave draws down.

10

In May 1936, some time before the great day of the assignment in Alabama, Jim and I journeyed together to Bennington to read our verses to the college. In that budding grove he was almost inaudible, as usual when reading his own or other poems, but then as a kind of encore he did a parody of a southern preacher in a hellfire sermon, and this was more than audible: it brought down the house. You do not hear much of his parodies. You do not hear much, either, of his mimetic powers, great as they were, though years later he had a bit part as a "vagrant" in one of his movies. At the time I am thinking of, one of his best acts was a recital of "When the lamp is shattered" in the accent and pitch of rural Tennessee.

We saw a good deal of one another all that spring — by this time I was married and working for *Time* — but by midsummer he was gone into the Deep South with Walker Evans on the tenant farmer job. Walker has written very well about that in his short foreword to the 1960 reissue of *Let Us Now Praise Famous Men*.

Jim's passionate eye for the lighted world made him from boyhood a connoisseur of photography, and among all photographers I think the one who had moved him most was Mathew Brady. The portraits and Civil War photographs of Brady were a kind of absolute for him, calling him and sounding in him very deeply. Another near-absolute was the photography in von Stroheim's *Greed*; he especially loved the burning-white powdery kind of sunlight produced by the "orthochromatic" film of that period. These kinds of studied finality and fiery delicacy in images of contemporary existence he found above all in the photographs of Walker Evans. Their work together that summer made them collaborators and close friends for life. It is strange that Jim never wrote much about Evans's photographs. Perhaps this was because only a couple of years later the Museum of Modern Art held a big Evans exhibition for which Lincoln Kirstein wrote a full and handsome introduction. Jim did write, in 1942, an introduction for a proposed book of photographs by another artist he admired, Helen Levitt. For a full and pondered statement of what photography meant to him, you will do well to consult this book, A *Way of Seeing*, finally published in 1965 by the Viking Press. The heart of what he wrote is this:

> The artist's task [in photography] is not to alter the world as the eye sees it into a world of esthetic reality, but to perceive the esthetic reality within the actual world, and to make an undisturbed and faithful record of the instant in which this movement of creativeness achieves its most expressive crystallization. Through his eye and through his instrument the artist has, thus, a leverage upon the materials of existence which is unique.

After the summer in Alabama I should guess that he got his *Fortune* piece done in September or October, and I remember it hanging fire in the autumn, but I can't be sure of these dates. Why did the magazine in the end reject the article that the editor, knowing Agee and therefore presumably knowing more or less what to expect, had assigned him to write? Well, one reason was very simple: the editor was no longer the same man. He was no longer the same man because *Fortune's* repute in the Duquesne Club and the Sky Club and the Bohemian Club — in those places, in short, where subscribers met — had been damaged by what appeared to the subscribers as a leftward drift in the contents of the magazine. In 1935 Jim's piece might have been printed, but in 1936, by the excellent disposition of Providence, the new editor, not much liking his duty, did his duty and turned it down.

Now all hands at last had more than a glimmer of a fact I have alluded to earlier — that Agee's vocation, at least at that point and as up to that point meditated by himself and inflamed by his recent experience, was in competition with *Fortune*. It appeared that the magazine, committed of course to knowing what was the case, had had the offhand humanity and imagination and impertinence to send an ex-president of the *Harvard Advocate* into the helpless and hopeless lives of cotton tenant farmers, but that it did not have the courage to face in full the case he presented, since the case involved discomfort not only for the tenants but for *Fortune*. Anything but that. Well and good, this gave him his chance to show *Fortune* and everyone else how to treat the case: he would make the assignment his own and make a book of his own on the tenant farmers. His friend Edward Aswell at Harper & Bros. induced that firm to offer Agee and Evans a contract and an advance, but for the time being Jim did not accept it, fearing that it might affect the writing. He remained loosely attached to *Fortune*. I believe no high words passed.

In 1937 he was in and out of the office on three jobs. The most interesting took him to Havana on an excruciating Caribbean "vacation cruise," of which his narrative, appearing in September as "Six Days at Sea," was a masterpiece of ferocity, or would have been if it had been printed uncut. He had become grimmer about American middle-class ways and destinies, and would become grimmer still. His inclination to simple cleanliness, for example, turned to anger for awhile as he discerned meanness and status and sterility even in that.

In the good poems of this period, the one to his father in *Transition*, the one called "Sunday: Outskirts of Knoxville," and some of the lyrics in the *Partisan Review*, he did things unachieved in *Permit Me Voyage*. But most of the topical poems in quatrains, published or unpublished, are not so good. He never did as well in this vein as in the epigrammatic "Songs on the Economy of Abundance" that he had sent to Louis Untermeyer for the 1936 edition of *Modern American Poetry*. His skill with traditional meters declined; it remained, now, mistrusted and for long periods unused or used only casually and briefly. The Auden-MacNeice *Letters from Iceland* came out that year with a section of brilliant Byronics, and if Jim had had any intention of going on with *John Carter* — as I believe that by now he did not — those pages might have dissuaded him. Auden's unapproachable virtuosity may, in fact, have had something — not much, but inevitably something — to do with Jim's writing verse more seldom. "Seen this?" he came in saying one day, with a new book in his hand, and read aloud the Auden poem that opens with such beauty:

Out on the lawn I lie in bed,
Vega conspicuous overhead,
In the windless nights of June

In the Bickford's Cafeteria at Lexington and 43rd, over coffee at some small hour of the morning, we read together and recognized perfection in a set of new lyrics by Robert Frost in the *Atlantic*; one was the short one beginning: "I stole forth dimly in the dripping pause / Between two downpours to see what there was." Perfection of this order Jim now scarcely any longer tried for in verse.

Under one strain and another his marriage was now breaking up; I remember the summer day in 1937 when at his suggestion we met in Central Park for lunch and the new young woman in her summer dress appeared. It seems to me that there were months of indecisions and revisions and colloquies over the parting with Via, which was yet not to be a parting, etc., which at length would be accomplished as cruelly required by the laws of New York. Laceration could not have been more prolonged. In the torments of liberty all Jim's friends took part. At Old Field Point on the north shore of Long Island, where the

Wilder Hobsons had somehow rented a bishop's boathouse that summer, a number of us attained liberation from the *pudor* of mixed bathing without bathing suits: a mixed pleasure, to tell the truth.

One occasion in this period that I remember well was a public meeting held in June 1937 in Carnegie Hall by a "Congress of American Writers," a Popular Front organization, for the Spanish Loyalist cause. Jim and I went to this together, and as we took our seats he turned to me and said, "Know one writer you can be sure isn't here? Cummings." MacLeish spoke, very grave. His speech was a prophetic one in which he might very well have quoted "Ask not for whom the bell tolls: it tolls for thee." Then he introduced Hemingway. It must have been the only time in his life that Hemingway consented to couple with a lectern, and as a matter of fact he only stood beside it and leaned on it with one elbow. Bearish in a dark blue suit, one foot cocked over the other, he gave a running commentary to a movie documentary by Joris Ivens on a Spanish town under the Republic. Jim Agee hoped for the Republic, but I don't think he ever saluted anyone with a raised fist or took up Spanish (my own gesture — belated at that). He had joined battle on another ground.

In October he put in his second vain application for a Guggenheim Fellowship. His "Plans for Work" (of which he kept a carbon) are printed in *The Collected Short Prose of James Agee* and will give you an idea of his mood at the time, maverick and omnivorous as a prairie fire, ranging in every direction for What Was the Case and techniques for telling it. As in 1932 he did not fail to indulge in those gratuitous honesties (now about communism, for instance) that would make it tough for the Guggenheim committee. I do not know how he lived that winter, or lived through it.

Not, however, till the spring of 1938 did he take the Harper contract and settle down with Alma Mailman, in a small frame house at 27 Second Street, Frenchtown, New Jersey, to write or rewrite and construct his book. Jim wrote for the ear, wanted criticism from auditors, and read to me, either in Frenchtown or in New York, most of the drafts as he got them written. There isn't a word in *Let Us Now Praise Famous Men* that he — and I and others — did not ponder many times. Frenchtown was then quiet and deep in the dense countryside, traversable whenever and as far as necessary in an ancient open flivver; they had a goat, God knows how acquired, in the back-

yard; there was a tennis court in the town. Jim played an obstinate
and mighty game, but wild, against my obstinate and smoother one.

He labored all summer and fall, through the Sudeten crisis and
the international conferences and the Nazi mass meetings at Nurem-
berg and elsewhere that sent the strangled shouting of *Der Führer* and
Sieg Heil, Sieg Heil in an ominous rhythmic roar over the radios of
the country. He labored into the winter. I have found among his
things a journal in which he noted on December 1 that when the rent
was paid he would have $12.52 in the world and in the same breath
went on with plans for his wedding to Alma later that month. In January or February *Fortune* came to the rescue with an assignment: the
section on Brooklyn in an issue to be devoted to New York City. For
the rest of the winter and spring they moved to a flat in St. James

Place, taking the goat with them. When Wilder Hobson went to see them once he found that the neighborhood kids had chalked on the front steps: "The Man Who Lives Here is a Loony."

11

In the living room or backyard of that place I heard several drafts of his prose on Brooklyn and by some accident kept two drafts in a file. Twenty-four years later these turned out to be the only vestiges of this work in existence. In this case, too, *Fortune* found Jim's article too strong to print, and it did not appear in the New York issue (June 1939). *Fortune*'s editor, however, appreciated this labor. As epigraph to the tamer article (by someone else) that finally got into print, the editor lifted one lyric sentence from Jim's piece and quoted it, with attribution. Jim's preliminary draft was titled *Southeast of the Island: Travel Notes*. The later version prepared for *Fortune* editing on May 15, 1939 (by the "ditto" process, which produced a number of legible

copies), was shorter by nearly half and lacked the particularity of the earlier piece. Compression and generality served him well in one passage only, funny and biting if you remember that *Fortune* was rather given to Ripley-like statistical play:

> Courtship and marriage are difficult matters to speak of, and it will be the better part of valor not to speak of them, beyond remarking that no park has ever been more eloquently designed beneath the moon for its civic purpose than Prospect; that more homes are owned in Brooklyn than elsewhere in New York City; that there are more children per capita; that the divorce rate is only . . . per cent per head that of Manhattan; that there are 48,000 electric refrigerators in Flatbush alone; and that if all the perambulators in Brooklyn were pushed end to end, at the pace of a walking mother, they would soon reach three times around the origin of species, the history of religion, the cause of imperialistic war, sexual ethics and social fear, and the basis of private property and universal prenatal spiritual suffocation.

After the Brooklyn interlude, the Agees returned to Frenchtown for the summer. Some weeks before we heard Mr. Chamberlain's weary voice declaring that a state of war existed between His Majesty's Government and Nazi Germany, Jim Agee's manuscript of a book entitled *Three Tenant Families* was in the hands of the publishers. The war began, and the German armored divisions shot up Poland. In the Harper offices Jim's manuscript must have appeared a doubtful prospect as a rousing topical publishing event. The publishers wanted him to make a few domesticating changes. He would not make the changes. Harper then deferred publication; they could live without it. He was broke and in debt, and in the early fall he learned that fatherhood impended for him in the spring. I had just fallen heir to the job of "Books" editor at *Time*, so we arranged that he should join me and the other reviewer, Calvin Fixx, at writing the weekly book section, and he and Alma found a flat far over on the west side somewhere below 14th Street.

Now for eight or nine months we worked in the same office several days and/or nights a week. Early that year or maybe late the year before, I can't remember precisely when, the Luce magazines had moved to a new building called the Time & Life Building in Rockefeller Center between 48th and 49th Streets (now superseded by a later and of course bigger and better T & L Building farther west). We had a three-desk office on the twenty-eighth floor with a secretary's cubbyhole. Our secretary, or "checker," was a girl I had known in 1934 when she was Lewis Gannett's secretary on the *Herald Tribune* — a crapshooting hoydenish girl who used to get weekly twenty-page letters from a lonely and whimsical young man in a San Francisco YMCA, by the name, then unknown, of William Saroyan. In the years between 1934 and 1939 Mary had been in South Africa and had come back statelier but still *au fond* not giving a damn; her father was an Episcopal canon. She kept track of the review books and publication dates and spotted errors in what we wrote. The other reviewer, Fixx, was a Mormon, a decent, luminously inarticulate man engaged in living down some obscure involvement in the Far Left. He knew a great deal about that particular politics and history, now a great subject for "reevaluation" after the Ribbentrop-Molotov embrace.

Each of us read half-a-dozen books a week and wrote reviews or notes — or nothing — according to our estimates of each. Jim Agee of course added immeasurably to the pleasure of this way of life. If for any reason a book interested him (intentionally or unintentionally on the author's part) he might write for many hours about it, turning in many thousands of words. Some of these long and fascinating reviews would rebound from the managing editor in the form of a paragraph. We managed nevertheless to hack through that barrier a fairly wide vista on literature in general, including even verse, the despised quarterlies, and scholarship. With light hearts and advice of counsel we reviewed a new edition of the classic *Wigmore on Evidence*. One week we jammed through a joint review of Henry Miller, for which Jim did *Tropic of Cancer* and I *Tropic of Capricorn*, both unpublishable in the United States until twenty years later. Our argument that time was that if *Time* ought to be written for the Man-in-the-Street (a favorite thought of the Founder), here were books that would hit him where he lived, if he could get them. In all our efforts we were helped by T. S. Matthews, then a senior editor and later for six years managing editor and a friend to Jim Agee.

Not because I idolize Jim or admire every word he ever wrote but again to show his mind at work, this time in that place under those conditions, I will quote the first paragraph of his review of Herbert

Gorman's *James Joyce* and the final paragraphs from his review of *The Hamlet* by William Faulkner.

The utmost type of heroism, which alone is worthy of the name, must be described, merely, as complete self-faithfulness: as integrity. On this level the life of James Joyce has its place, along with Blake's and Beethoven's among the supreme examples. It is almost a Bible of what a great artist, an ultimately honest man, is up against.

Whatever their disparities, William Faulkner and William Shakespeare share these characteristics: 1) Their abundance of invention and their courage for rhetoric are bottomless. 2) Enough goes on in their heads to furnish a whole shoal of more temperate writers. 3) By fair means or foul, both manage to play not for a specialized but for a broad audience.

In passages incandescent with undeniable genius, there is [in *The Hamlet*] nevertheless not one sentence without its share of amateurishness, its stain of inexcusable cheapness.

12

Of the physical make and being of James Agee and his aspect at that time, you must imagine: a tall frame, long-boned but not massive; lean flesh, muscular with some awkwardness; pelt on his chest; a long stride with loose knee-joints, head up, with toes angled a bit outward. A complexion rather dark or sallow in pigment, easily tanned. The head rough-hewn, with a rugged brow and cheekbones, a strong nose irregular in profile, a large mouth firmly closing in folds, working a little around the gaps of lost teeth. The shape of the face tapered to a sensitive chin, cleft. Hair thick and very dark, a shock uncared for, and best uncared for. Eyes deep-set and rather closely set, a dull gray-blue or feral blue-gray or radiantly lit with amusement. Strong stained teeth. On the right middle finger a callous as big as a boil: one of his stigmata as a writer. The hands and fingers long and light and blunt and expressive, shaping his thought in the air, conveying stresses direct or splay, drawing razor-edged lines with thumb and forefinger: termini, perspective, tones.

His capacity for whiskey, as for everything else, was very great. I saw him once or twice violent with drink, but I never saw him disabled by it and don't know anyone else who ever did. As a rule, with every drink he only became more interested in any subject or line of action — any except going home and going to bed. A little conviviality was enough to get his comic genius off the ground and into such flights as his one-man rendition of the Bach Toccata and Fugue as arranged by Stokowski — a magistral act in which varieties of fruity instrumentation were somehow conveyed by voice and gesture, e.g., the string section by a flapping left hand and "fiddle-faddle, fiddle-faddle, fiddle-faddle." At the invention of American place names, or personal names, Jim had no peer; one of his best compositions, brought off while wandering late at night with Wilder Hobson, was the man's name, "George F. Macgentsroom." Very rarely, he might follow through with an inspiration from one of those evenings. In his war against middle-class folkways he struck a happily premeditated blow at the Christmas card custom by sending out, one Christmas, a card bearing as its olde winter scene a photograph of a pair of polar bears in innocent copulation, with season's greetings.

At the piano he sat well back and more than erect, head withdrawn and watchful, eyes downcast over the length of arms and fingers in hard exertion at the keyboard. It was the old upright that his grandmother had given him; I think he had it for twenty years. When he played he would have the whole form of the sonata or whatever it was before him in his mind. Battered conclamant notes, quite a few near misses, very little sweet shading or pianissimo. At his writing he looked the same: his left hand pinning down at arm's length a stack of yellow second sheets, leaning far back from it frowning (by this time he was getting farsighted; he tried, but discarded, some steel-rimmed glasses), power flowing through the sharp pencil into the tiny closely organized script. Wholly focused on it, as I remember him in warm weather once, oblivious to the closed office window behind him, stifling in a fog of cigarette smoke, with a small pure space cleared before him amid mountains of litter.

He wore blue or khaki work shirts and under the armpits there would be stains, salt-edged, from sweat; likewise under the arms of his suit jacket, double-breasted dark blue, wrinkled and shiny. He was too poor to afford a lot of laundering, and he didn't believe in it, anyway. After the baby arrived in March 1940, I remember one big scene in which Jim was engaged in spooning Pablum into Joel. The

father sat, all elbows and knees, in an armchair upholstered in some ragged and ancient fabric that had grown black absorbing through the years the grime of New York. The infant in his lap mouthed with a will at the Pablum but inevitably gobs of it splattered down even on the richly unsanitary arms of the chair, whence Jim would scoop it in long dives lest it drip — irretrievably, you could hope — on the floor.

The time was about over for all fragile arrangements and lightness of heart. In those days the German airborne troops were taking Norway. There was nothing we could do about it. One fine day in late spring, playing tennis with Jim on some courts south of Washington Square, I broke a bone in my instep. *Life* with a wealth of illustration

Agee at *Fortune* and *Time*   75

assured us that General Gamelin was the flower of military science and the French army the finest in Europe. Within a week or so it looked as though *Life* had exaggerated. While I was still getting around on a plaster clubfoot, the British were evacuating Dunkirk and the panzers were going through the Ardennes. The dress parade of the German army down the Champs-Élysées was reported by the *World-Telegram* with a photograph of the Arc de Triomphe and the headline ICI REPOSE UN SOLDAT FRANCAIS MORT POUR LA PATRIE. I looked at this and realized that so far as I was concerned a decade had come to an end, and so had a mode of life, to flatter it by that term, that included working for *Time*. To see what could be done about my *modus vivendi* in general, I turned over "Books" to Agee, Fixx, and Whittaker Chambers and departed, taking my first wife away to the west and eventually to Santa Fe for the winter. There I settled down on my savings to do unnecessary and unpaid work for the first time in five years. I had resigned. Taking no offense, and with great accuracy of foresight, the people at *Time* made it a leave of absence until a year from that October. I intrude these details because I am about to quote a few passages from Jim's letters to me during the year. At some point in the spring or summer Houghton Mifflin, to their eternal credit, accepted the manuscript that Harper had released to him. Well, from a letter in December:

> Excepting Wilder, whose getting-a-job has done him a favor as leaving-it has you, everyone I see, myself included, is at a low grinding ebb of quiet desperation: nothing, in most cases, out of the ordinary, just the general average Thoreau was telling about, plus the dead-ends of one of the most evil years in history, plus each individual's little specialty act. I don't think I'll go into much if any detail — for though I could detail it blandly and painlessly and some of it is of "clinical" interest, it could possibly have an intrusive and entangling effect. So I can most easily and honestly say that it isn't as bad as I've perhaps suggested, except by contrast with health and free action — is, in fact, just the average experience of people living as people shouldn't, where people shouldn't, doing what people shouldn't and little or nothing of what people should. Journalists, hacks, husbands, wives, sisters, neurotics, self-harmed artists, and such. Average New York Fall.

The book is supposed to be published January or February—
no proofs yet, though. I now thoroughly regret using the subtitle
(*Let Us Now Praise Famous Men*) as I should never have forgotten I would. I am rather anxious to look at it, finished and in
print—possibly, also, to read it in that form—but I have an
idea I'll be unable to stand to. If so, it might be a healthy self-
scorching to force myself to: but that's probably my New England chapel-crank blood. Mainly, though, I want to be through
with it, as I used to feel about absolution, and to get to work
again as soon as I can. I am thirty-one now, and I can conceiv-
ably forgive myself my last ten years only by a devotion to work
in the next ten which I suspect I'll be incapable of. I am much
too vulnerable to human relationships, particularly sexual or in
any case heterosexual, and much too deeply wrought-upon by
them, and in turn much too dependent in my work on "feeling"
as against "intellect." In short I'm easily upset and, when upset,
incapable of decent work; incapable of it also when I'm not upset enough. I must learn my ways in an exceedingly quiet marriage (which can be wonderful I've found but is basically not at
all my style or apparent "nature") or break from marriage and
all close liaisons altogether and learn how to live alone & keep
love at a bearable distance. Those are oddly juvenile things to
be beginning to learn at my age: what really baffles me is that,
knowing them quite well since I was 15, I've done such thorough
jobs in the opposite direction. Well, nothing would be solved or
even begun tonight by any thing I wrote or thought, or at any
time soon: my business now and evidently for quite a while to
come is merely to sit as tight and careful as I can, taking care
above all to do no further harm to others or myself or my now
virtually destroyed needs or hopes, and doing a timorous or dras-
tic piece of mending when or wherever there seems any moment's chance to. I haven't been very intelligent—to say nothing
of "good"—and now it's scarcely a chance for intelligence or
goodness—only for the most dumb and scrupulous tenacity. On
the whole, though, it's time I had a good hard dose of bad going,
and if I find I'm capable of it the winter will be less wasted than
it otherwise might be. Meanwhile, though, I find I'm so dull I
bore myself sick. A broken spirit and a contrite heart have their
drawbacks: worst of all if at the same time the spirit is unbroken

and ferocious and the heart contrite only in the sense of deep grief over pain and loss, not at all in true contrition. . . .

I thought *The Long Voyage Home* quite awful. . . .

I feel very glad you like the reviews. I wish I did. As a matter of fact I have hardly judgment or feeling, for or against, and on the whole, not a bad time with the job, except a general, rather shamed feeling, week by week, that with real intelligence & effort I could do much better, whatever the limitations of space and place. Then a book as important as Kafka's *America* can't even get reviewed, and I shrug it off again. . . .

The magazine you write of [an imaginary one — R.F.] makes my mouth water. I spend a lot of time thinking of such things and of equivalent publishers. They really existed in France and Germany and even in England. The fact that they don't here and I suppose won't ever, by any chance, makes me know just a little better what a fat-assed, frumpish hell-on-earth this country is. Last stronghold of just what. . . . But I do love to think about magazines like that. And the writing *can* be done — the only really important thing — whenever and wherever qualified people can cheat their inferiors out of the time it takes. Thank God you're getting it.

That is the longest excerpt. A shorter one, from a letter of February or March (he never dated his letters):

I'm in a bad period: incertitude and disintegration on almost every count. Somehow fed up and paralytic with the job; horribly bad sleeping rhythm; desperate need to live regularly & still more to do new work of my own; desperate knowledge that with all the time on earth I could as I spiritually feel now be capable of neither. . . . Alma is in Mexico — so is Joel — nominally, presumably, perhaps very probably, that is broken forever. And so far, I am not doing the one thing left me to do if it is ever possibly to reintegrate: entirely leave knowing Mia. It is constantly in the bottom of my gut — petrifying everything else — that I must, and will; and I still do nothing. A kind of bottomless sadness, impotence and misery in which one can neither move a hand nor keep it still without some further infliction on one or another. . . . For some doubtless discreditable reason it is of some good to speak of it, but I hope I don't do so at your expense,

in sympathy or concern (I've known such things to derail me) —
There is truly no need; as I say, I'm only too detached and
anesthetized.

I delayed 2 months in all this trouble, in correcting proofs, but
all is done now so I presume the machinery is turning. Don't yet
know the publication date though.

Another one from about June 1941:

Your last letters have sounded so thoroughly well in the head
and health and so exciting in potentiality, that the thought of its
shutting-off in a few more months, with your return to work, has
made me probably almost as sick as it makes you.

I think this could be rather easily solved as follows:

What with one expense and another I shall nowhere near
have paid off my debts by October and so will nowhere near be
free to quit work and get to my own. So why don't I continue at
this work and you continue at yours, for 6 months or 8 or a year
(we can arrange that) during which I could send you and
Eleanor $100 a month.

That would be very scrawny to live on most parts of this country; but apparently in Mexico would be: in Mexico City an adequate poverty; elsewhere an amplitude. This would, then, involve living where perhaps you might rather not; but a living,
and free time, would be assured. And when I am able to quit
work, if you are ready or need to come back, you could do likewise for me on some general equalization —

I think that by this or some such arrangement we & others
might really get clear time when we are ripe for it, and it seems
a better chance than any other — What do you think?

Another a bit later:

Nothing on earth could make me feel worse than that you
should for any reason whatever have to come back now that you
are ripe for so much.

As for the money, I feel as you do, that it belongs to him who
most needs it at a given time — your need for it for the next year
or so is far out of proportion to any I could have short of a year
or so of freedom first, and greater too than you would be likely
to have again, without a long stretch of preparatory freedom. I

think neither of us should think twice about your later paying me back — that is a wrong conception of the whole thing. I'll be able to take care of myself, one way or another, when my time comes for it — meanwhile I'll be best taking care for things I care for most, if I can make freedom and work possible for you when you can make best use of it.

I'm talking badly out of turn in all this walking-in and urging — I hope you can forgive it. It seems terribly crucial to me that you stay free at this particular time, and criminal if you don't. . . .

Chambers is still moving Books at *Time* — Stockley does Letters, and an occasional review. If you should come back — which God forbid — I imagine I could get switched to movies & you could replace me here.

13

I hope an occasional reader will understand that the foregoing private things are quoted after long hesitation and at the expense of my heart's blood. I think I am aware of every way in which they — and he, and I — can be taken advantage of. Jim Agee's agonies and his nobleness are equally the affair of no one who cannot keep still, or as good as still, about them, and there is no chance that all of you can. But some of you can, and some of you are thirty or thirty-one and hard beset and bound to someone in brotherhood, perhaps in art, and you may see that the brotherhood you know is of a kind really wider than you may have thought, binding others among the living and the dead. It is best, at any rate, that you should have the living movement of his own mind about his New York life and the dissolution of his second marriage, and it is essential that you should see proof of selflessness in a man who often appeared self-centered, and often was.

Before the publication of *Let Us Now Praise Famous Men*, just before I returned to New York, I received the book in September 1941 for review in *Time*. When Jim got word of this he wrote at once, airmail special, to make sure whether I had been consulted, whether I had time to spare for it, and whether if, consulted or not, I did have time and would write the review, we shouldn't agree that he would not read it. I wrote a review, but the editor who had invited it thought it was too stiff and reverent (he was right) and sent it back. He reviewed the book himself, recognized great writing in it, but classified it as "a distinguished failure." By this he, as an old *Fortune* editor, did not really mean that if *Fortune* had done it, it would have been a success, but that was true: it would have been objective and clearly organized and readable and virtuously restrained, and would have sounded well and been of small importance beyond the month it appeared. A failure, on the contrary, it consciously was, a "young man's book," and a sinful book to boot (as Jim called it in a letter to Father Flye) and was thereby true to the magnitude and difficulty of the case including the observer. It is a classic, and perhaps the only classic, of the whole period, of the whole attempted *genre*. Photographs and text alike are bitten out by the very juices of the men who made them, and at the same time they have the piteous monumentality of the things and souls represented. Between them Agee and Evans made sure that George and Annie Mae Gudger are as immortal as Priam and Hecuba, and a lot closer to home.

I refused to take about a quarter of Jim's already mortgaged income, as he proposed, and returned to work for *Time* from October 1941 to May 1943, when to my relief I joined the navy. That October of my return he got "switched to movies," all right, and the last and perhaps the best phase of his life began. He and Mia Fritsch, who was to be his third wife, moved into the top-floor flat on Bleeker Street where they lived for the next ten years. Before I went to Fort Schuyler I managed to revise my manuscript of poems and put them together in a book, but not until Jim had commented on each in the most minute and delicate written criticism I ever had.

How more than appropriate, how momentous, it was, that after 1941 James Agee had "Cinema" for all occupation, could scarcely have been realized to the full by anyone, but a few of us at least felt uncommonly at peace about Jim's employment. He loved movies more than anyone I ever knew; he also lived them and thought them. To see and hear him describe a movie that he liked — shot by shot, almost frame by frame — was unquestionably better in many cases than to see the movie itself. Once when I was driving him across the Brooklyn Bridge in an open Model A, he put on beside me such a rendering of Jimmy Cagney in a gangster film that I had to take my eyes off the road and give him my close attention. There must have been moments on that ride when we were both absolutely uninsurable.

He had wanted for years to do a scenario for Chaplin; whether he ever did more than imagine it, I have been unable to find out. By the late thirties he had, however, not only written but published two scenarios, both stunning exercises in what must be called screenwriting as literature. The first, entitled "Notes for a Moving Picture: The House," was printed by Horace Gregory in a collection called *New Letters in America* in 1937. Detailing every shot and every sound, second by counted second, with his huge sensuous precision and scope, he constructed a screen fantasy for the camera, his angelic brain, before whose magnifying gaze or swimming movement a tall old house disclosed its ghastly, opulent moribundity until blown and flooded apart in an apocalyptic storm. Compare this with the efforts of more recently "rebellious" young men if you want to see how close to artistic nonexistence most of these are. His second scenario was published in the first number of a review, *Films*, edited by Jay Leyda in 1939. In this one he merely (if you could use that word of anything Jim did) transposed into screen terms the famous scene in *Man's Fate* in which the hero, Kyo, waits with other Chinese Communists to be thrown by the Nationalists into the boiler of a locomotive. I am told that Malraux, who thought he had got everything out of this scene, thought again when he read the Agee script.

Concerning his movie reviewing for *Time*, T. S. Matthews has told me of one incident. Matthews as managing editor late one Sunday evening received and read a cover story Jim had written, on Laurence Olivier's *Hamlet*, and in Jim's presence indicated that he found it good enough, a little disappointing but good enough and in any case too late to revise; he initialed it for transmission to the printer (*Time* went to press on Monday) and in due course left for home presuming that Jim had also done so. At nine the next morning Jim presented him with a complete new handwritten version. Fully to appreciate this you would perhaps have to have felt the peculiar exhaustion of Sunday night at *Time*.

Jim Agee, however, had now found a kind of journalism answering to his passion. Beginning in December 1942, he began the signed movie column for the *Nation*, every other week, that Margaret Marshall, the literary editor, invited and backed, and that in the next several years made him famous. He began to be called on at *Time* for general news stories to which no one else could do justice. Whatever he wrote for the magazine was so conspicuous that it might as well have been signed. In the Western Pacific I recognized at once his hand in *Time*'s page-one piece on the meaning of Hiroshima and Nagasaki:

In what they said and did, men were still, as in the aftershock of a great wound, bemused and only semi-articulate, whether they were soldiers or scientists, or great statesmen, or the simplest of men. But in the dark depths of their minds and hearts, huge forms moved and silently arrayed themselves: Titans, arranging out of the chaos an age in which victory was already only the shout of a child in the street.

. . . All thoughts and things were split. The sudden achievement of victory was a mercy, to the Japanese no less than to the United Nations; but mercy born of a ruthlessness beyond anything in human chronicle. The race had been won, the weapon had been used by those on whom civilization could best hope to depend; but the demonstration of power against living creatures instead of dead matter created a bottomless wound in the living conscience of the race. The rational mind had won the most Promethean of its conquests over nature, and had put into the hands of common man the fire and force of the sun itself. . . .

. . . The promise of good and of evil bordered alike on the infinite — with this further, terrible split in the fact: that upon a people already so nearly drowned in materialism even in peacetime, the good uses of this power might easily bring disaster as prodigious as the evil. The bomb rendered all decisions so far, at Yalta and at Potsdam, mere trivial dams across tributary rivulets. When the bomb split open the universe and revealed the prospect of the infinitely extraordinary, it also revealed the oldest, simplest, commonest, most neglected and most important of facts: that each man is eternally and above all else responsible for his own soul, and, in the terrible words of the Psalmist, that no man may deliver his brother, nor make agreement unto God for him.

Man's fate has forever been shaped between the hands of reason and spirit, now in collaboration, again in conflict. Now reason and spirit meet on final ground. If either or anything is to survive, they must find a way to create an indissoluble partnership.

Enough, and perhaps more than enough, has been said by various people about the waste of Jim's talents in journalism. It is a consolation and a credit to his employers that on this occasion, as on some others, he was invited and was able to dignify the reporting of events.

14

When I got back to New York in 1946 I found Jim in a corduroy jacket, a subtle novelty, and in a mood far more independent than before of Left or "Liberal" attitudes. He had become a trace more worldly and better off (I'm sure Matthews saw to it that he was decently paid) and more sure of himself; and high time, too. His years of hard living and testing and questioning had given him in his *Nation* articles a great charge of perceptions to express. His lifetime pleasure in cinema had made him a master of film craft and repertory. He had had some of the public recognition that he deserved. Most important of all, I think, this critical job had turned his mind a few compass points from the bearing Truth to the bearing Art. He was ready to take a hand, as he was soon to do, in the actual and practical making of films.

We were never estranged, but we were never so close again, either, as we had been before the war. The course of things for me (here I must intrude a little again) had not only broken up my own previous marriage and way of life but had brought me back in astonishment, with a terrific bump, into Catholic faith and practice; and though Jim intensely sympathized with me in the breakup, he regarded my conversion with careful reserve. He saw an old friend ravaged and transported by the hair into precisely the same system of coordinates that he had wrestled out of in the thirties. Or rather, not precisely the same. For in my turn I had reservations, now, about the quality of his old vision. It struck me that for him it must have been a matter of imagination and empathy, a profound and sacramental sense of the natural world, but only a notion of the incommensurable overhead, the change of light and being that leaves a man no fulcrum by which to dislodge himself from his new place. With my all-too-negative capability and other flaws, I could easily have been self-deceived, as he must have imagined. I was not, however. At any rate, I now wanted to lead a kind of life that Jim had rejected and, in his own and general opinion, outgrown; and there was (at most) one art that I might practice, the art of verse that he had likewise left behind.

All the same, the memory of what he had aspired literally to be, in college and for the first years thereafter, could return now and again to trouble him. One day in 1947 when he and Mia brought their first baby, Teresa, to spend an afternoon with my wife and myself, he handed me the two very sad and strange sonnets on the buried steed, published three years later in *Botteghe Oscure* and now included in the collection of Agee's poems recently edited by myself. His hand at verse had barely retained but not refined its skill, and there is a coarseness along with the complexity of these and other late sonnets. Two or three of the final poems are very beautiful, though. "Sleep, Child" certainly is, and so is the peerless Christmas ballad in Tennessee dialect (but I am not sure how late that one is, and have no clue as to when it was written).

The last verses that he wrote were some rather casually attempted drafts, by invitation, for a musical that in the late winter and spring of 1955 Lillian Hellman and Leonard Bernstein were trying to make of *Candide*. Both playwright and composer felt that these drafts wouldn't do, but Miss Hellman is not sure that Jim, who was more desperately ill than he knew, understood this before his fatal heart attack on May 16. "He was not a lyric writer," Miss Hellman says. "Good poets often aren't." At my distance I find the episode fairly astringent. In their most nearly completed state, the drafts appear in Agee's *Collected Poems* at the end of Part IV. They may be compared with the lighter lyrics by various hands, mainly Richard Wilbur's, for the show as produced in December 1956.

Helen Levitt has told me that only a year or so before his death in 1955 Jim seriously said to her that poetry had been his true vocation, the thing he was born to do, but that it was too difficult; on the other hand, work in films was pure pleasure for him. I think he had in mind the difficulty for everyone — not only for himself — of making true poetry in that time; I think, too, that what he was born to do, he did.

Jim's leaning to self-accusation does not seem to me very deplorable, however. It was, rather, part of what gave him his largeness among his contemporaries, most of whom were engaged in pretending that they were wonderful and their mishaps or shortcomings all ascribable to Society or History or Mother or other powers in the mythology of the period. I gather that he got cooler and tougher about everything in his last years, in particular about love. Before he went to the Coast, in the late forties, he wrote a draft scenario, never worked up for production or publication, in which with disabused and cruel objectivity he turned a camera eye on himself in his relations with women.

After my wife and I moved away from New York in the summer of 1949, we saw him only once again, for an evening, in the following spring. His last letter to me was from Malibu Beach in 1952: I had written to say how much I liked *The African Queen*. Of his final years I can have little to say. (I had been in Italy for two years when the shocking cable came to tell me of his death.) I am told that young men in New York began heroizing him and hanging on his words, but late one night at a *Partisan Review* sort of party a younger writer in impatience saw him as "a whisky-listless and excessive saint." I myself felt my heart sink when I began to read *The Morning Watch*; the writing seemed to me a little showy, though certainly with much to show; and I wondered if he were losing his irony and edge. It is pretty clear to me now that he had to go to those lengths of artifice and musical elaboration simply to make the break with journalism decisive. He never lost his edge, as *A Death in the Family* was to demonstrate — that narrative held so steadily and clearly in the middle distance and at the same time was so full of Jim's power of realization, a contained power, fully comparable to that in the early work of Joyce. Let the easy remark die on your lips. Jim arrived at his austere style fifty years and a torn world away from Edwardian Dublin and Trieste; if it took him twenty years longer than it took Joyce, who else arrived at all?

The comparison with Joyce is worth pausing over a moment more. Each with his versatile and musical gift, each proud and a world-plunderer, each choosing the savage beauty of things as they are over the impossible pieties of adolescence, each concerned with the "conscience of his race." Agee had less ice-cold intellect; he could not have derived what Joyce did from Aquinas. He had, of course, nothing like Joyce's linguistic range. His affections were more widely distributed and perhaps dissipated. He inherited the violence that Americans inherit: a violence, too (it will not have escaped you), no more directed against office buildings, employers, and bourgeois hor-

rors than against himself. The cinema that interested Joyce in its in-
fancy had by Agee's time become a splendid art form, a successor
perhaps to the art of fiction, and who else understood it better than
he? The record is there in two volumes. Joyce had more irony, but
Joyce, too, sentimentalized or angelized the role of the artist. In all
Agee's work the worst example of this is in the scenario of *Noa Noa*,
and anyone can see that script becoming at times a maudlin caricature of the artist-as-saint.

Jim's weakness and strength were not so easy to tell apart. Consider,
if you will, his early story "They That Sow in Sorrow Shall Reap."
Through weakness, through not being able to do otherwise, the boy
narrator brings the laborer to the boardinghouse and so precipitates
the catastrophe that leaves the scene and people in ruins. Or is it
entirely through weakness? Is it not also through a dispassionate willingness to see his microcosm convulsed for the pure revelation of it,
for an epiphany that he may record? Was it weakness later that kept
James Agee at *Fortune*, or was it strategy and will, for the sake of the
great use he would make of it? Ruins were left behind then, too, but
in New York journalism of the thirties no one created anything like
the Alabama book. Likewise, no weekly reviewer of the forties created
anything like the body of new insights contained in his *Nation* film
pieces. Again, no writer of film pieces prepared himself to write for
cinema with such clean and lovely inventiveness (barring the instance I have noted). Finally, no scriptwriter except possibly Faulkner
exercised, or learned, in film writing the control over fiction that
went into *A Death in the Family*. When you reflect on his life in this
way, weakness and strategy, instinct and destiny seem all one thing.

In one of the best novels of the sixties, a charmer by a southerner,
I find a sentence running like this, of cemeteries that at first look like
cities from a train passing at a slight elevation: "tiny streets and cor-
ners and curbs and even plots of lawn, all of such a proportion that
in the very instant of being mistaken and from the eye's own necessity, they set themselves off into the distance like a city seen from far
away."[2] It is an Agee sentence, so I conclude that his writing has
entered into the mainstream of English. But I share with him a dis-
inclination for Literary History and its idiom. Jim may be a Figure
for somebody else; he cannot be one for me. "This breathing joy,
heavy on us all" — it is his no longer; nevertheless, I have written this
in his presence and therefore as truly as I could. Quite contrary to

what has been said about him, he amply fulfilled his promise. In one of his first sonnets he said this of his kin, his people:

'Tis mine to touch with deathlessness their clay,
And I shall fail, and join those I betray.

In respect to that commission, who thinks that there was any failure or betrayal?

Notes

1. *Collected Short Prose of James Agee* (Boston: Houghton Mifflin, 1969).
2. From *The Moviegoer* by Walker Percy (New York: Knopf, 1961).

David McDowell

The Turning Point

When I first met Agee in mid-April of 1936, I was eighteen and on the verge of graduating from St. Andrew's School in Tennessee. I felt I already knew him, for he was the "Rufus" I had heard so much about since I was thirteen — from members of the faculty and staff of St. Andrew's, but most of all from Father and Mrs. Flye, his dearest friends and mentors. I could not get used to calling him "Jim" until 1948 when I had returned to this country after the war. By that time, even Father Flye had given up on anything but "Jim" (though Agee's mother spoke of him as Rufus until her death in 1966).

I knew that lovely spring was a turning point for me, but it was many years before I realized what changes were in the offing for Jim. He was twenty-six years old, trim, tanned, and vigorously handsome. He and his wife Via had just driven up from Anna Maria, an island off the west coast of Florida, where they had spent a six months' leave of absence. It had been his first real break from New York City since he had joined *Fortune* right after his graduation from Harvard in 1932. It had been a relaxed time of writing, reading, tennis, and swimming. He was never again to have so long a respite from work and pressure.

It was also Jim's first visit back to Sewanee Mountain since he had left St. Andrew's in 1924 at the age of fourteen. He and Via stayed with the Flyes in their cottage on the school grounds for a little over a month. Later in June he wrote Father Flye: "I agree with Mrs. Flye: no time or visit ever, anywhere, has been so good and meant so much to me. Much love to you both."

2

That time of year on the mountain offers beauty beyond compare. This is no place to dwell upon it, but I wish I could quote the whole chapter on Sewanee in William Alexander Percy's *Lanterns on the Levee* — a book perhaps then already in the writing, though it wasn't published until 1941. (Jim wrote a review of it for *Time* — if memory serves — and I remember his reading to me, in the summer of 1942, the sections on mountain woods and flowers.)

So it was a time and season that he remembered and reveled in, and as Father Flye had classes and papers to grade, Jim and I often walked the woods or the winding paths. He especially wanted to re-trace his steps to Sand Cut, an abandoned sand quarry now, as then, deep and filled with water. He made no mention of it in any literary way, but I am sure he was touching base with some of the memories and perceptions that would later be used so well in *The Morning Watch.*

We also walked out to the cliff at Piney Point, passing the cottage his mother and his sister, Emma, had lived in while he was a student at St. Andrew's. He made no comment and, as I remember, spoke little on these outings, except to respond to my talk about poetry or to marvel at how little things had changed. Many friends have written about what a brilliant talker Agee was, but only rarely has anyone pointed out what an incredibly sensitive and perceptive listener he was. Perhaps Louis Kronenberger came closest in his brief but beautiful memorial tribute to Agee in *FYI*, Time, Inc.'s house organ: "No one else I can think of absorbed so much from all he encountered — or related so much in encountering it. No one else I ever knew so quickly got the point or sensed the purport of what you were saying: with Jim, you almost literally never needed to finish a sentence."

Jim and I also talked a lot about the beautiful and intelligent girl I was in love with — the first great love of my life. Agee wanted to hear all about her and to meet her, which was easy, since she lived only two miles away in Sewanee and had her own car. So one Saturday afternoon, she came out and picked us up, and we drove all over the mountain top. Somehow Via did not come along, but she and Jim later became almost as taken as I was with that lovely creature.

During those weeks Jim was relaxed and in constant good spirits. He was completely at ease with himself and quite obviously happy to be back on his beloved mountain, which was still almost as isolated as it had been in his childhood. As Will Percy wrote in *Lanterns on the Levee:* "It's a long way away, even from Chattanooga, in the middle of woods, on top of a bastion of mountains crenelated with blue coves. It is so beautiful that people who have once been there always, one way or another, come back. For such as can detect apple green in an evening sky, it is Arcadia — not the one that never used to be, but the one that many people always live in; only this one can be shared." Jim once said to me — perhaps at Piney Point — that this was his favorite part of the world (it *still* is mine), and in the years we were both living in New York City, we often spoke of our mutual longing for it.

He was also probably in as good shape as he had ever been. The school's tennis court was about twenty yards behind Father Flye's house, and as tennis was not then a particularly popular sport at the school, it was usually empty. So we played fiercely almost every day. I usually won, but it wasn't easy, for Jim was both tireless and highly competitive. I was never again to see him so merry and serene or so healthy.

3

But I want to get back to poetry, for at that time it was the main concern of us both. On Anna Maria he had been working mostly on poetry, although he mentioned some autobiographical material about his childhood in Knoxville to Father Flye, and Fitzgerald quotes from a journal, "Have been working (c. 12–15,000 words) on the footloose in Knoxville idea. Don't know." We don't know either exactly what prose he wrote during those months in Florida, but his father's death haunted him. His mother told me that as early as his final years at Exeter he had told her that he wanted to write about that early death and its effects on those closest to him. So the genesis of *A Death in the Family,* whose central theme is the death of a young father of two small children, actually came some years before Agee started writing it.

We know much more about the poetry he was writing and which poems were later published, but we don't know how much of the "Knoxville idea" material was included in *A Death in the Family.* It seems likely that some of it was, because we do know that "Knoxville: Summer, 1915" was written on Anna Maria, for Jim read it to Father and Mrs. Flye shortly after his arrival at St. Andrew's. As I wrote in the editorial note to *A Death in the Family* in 1957: "The short section 'Knoxville: Summer 1915,' which serves as a sort of prologue, has been added. It was not a part of the manuscript which Agee left, but the editors would certainly have urged him to include it in the final draft." To be sure, it is not "poetry," but it contains more than most of the published poetry of the decade. At the 1972 St. Andrew's dedicatory symposium on Agee's work, Walker Percy remarked that Agee "brought back poetry into modern prose." The other panelists agreed.

During our talks, Jim made no mention of any prose at all. He read me some poems, and he showed me three or four he had written, but he showed more interest in the poetry I had been writing. For a couple of years, Father Flye had sent him from time to time some of my work, and I want to quote from one of Jim's replies. It contains good advice to young writers and kind encouragement. Agee's generosity was legendary.

David's poem is likable and moving as the first poems of Keats are to me — whether there's any such parallel in talent I don't know but only reasonably doubt. Which is vulgar, ridiculous & uncalled for but I do care not only that he should want to and enjoy continuing to write but for the writing as such. On that, excuse a few half-ideas. Most of the language and a good deal of the thought and feeling of the poetry is very naturally "literary" — which is the way & about the proportion it comes to nine out of ten writers bad or good or for that matter great, to start with — and from which Lord knows there is a lot to be learned. But also a great deal of harm to be absorbed which can be hard & even impossible to clear the head of. I was going to say I hope he can be talked with & shown the various & more important (in fact indispensable) other contents of poetry & of writing. But that is really stupid: except for certain & small pieces of help, those are either learned by yourself or not learned. But it has all caused me plenty of trouble, and is still doing that. My wish would be to save anyone else from it: but each person can only save himself: I shouldn't have mentioned it. I'm glad of this possibility of his coming to Yale: God knows he deserves it. No. Excuse my opinion which is both callow & only personal: he deserves everything which can open clear & sharpen his appetite and feed it, and I don't know at all that that is best to be had at Yale or Harvard though at such places it does exist in concentrated as well as disguised forms. I'm not such a dope as to think I or anyone can find his own way unassisted but the more of that and the less guidance & elaboration of the means, the better. College elaborated a lot of things out of recognition for me and that was partly my limitations, immaturity, etc. Thinking of it now I would give anything to have had access to a good library and perhaps also to lectures, and to friends & acquaintances of all sorts & to have let it go at that. But that's wishful and probably romanticized feeling. Probably I'd have thought no more clearly and used time no better than I did. And do. Phooey. I really deserve to have no opinions. But I wish only best luck to David, whatever that may mean or be, and will you give him my best.

As Robert Fitzgerald and others have lamented, Agee's poems were too little known, then and now. After 1936, he wrote less and less poetry, for he was at the great turning point of his life. He was to be tied up almost entirely with prose. At St. Andrew's he was unaware that on his return to New York he would be handed his most important assignment. He got back to *Fortune* in late May, and he wrote Father Flye on June 18:

I must cut this short and do a week's work in next twenty hours or so: have been assigned to do a story on: a sharecropper family (daily & yearly life): and also a study of Farm Economics in the South (impossible for me): and also on the several efforts to help the situation: i.e. Govt. and state work; theories & wishes of Southern liberals; whole story of the 2 Southern Unions. Best break I ever had on *Fortune*. Feel terrific personal responsibility toward story; considerable doubts of my ability to bring it off; considerable more of *Fortune's* ultimate willingness to use it as it seems (in theory) to me. Will be starting South Saturday. For a month's work.

Agee and Walker Evans spent July and August in Alabama living with three tenant families. Agee was preoccupied for the next four years with what became *Let Us Now Praise Famous Men*, then with film criticism and scripts, *The Morning Watch*, and *A Death in the Family*.

4

The school year was running out. Like all such times it was hectic, and the last week or so I saw less and less of Jim. However, he and Via did go to the commencement dance with my girl and me, and we all had a great time. It was the only time I ever saw Jim dance. He had gone south without a suit or tie, and as we were about the same size, I lent him one of mine. He put it to good use, wearing it to a faculty literary club in Sewanee and to the commencement ceremonies which were held a week after the dance.

My clearest memory of him and of that important time in my life has to do with a speech. I had to give a valedictory address. I had written what I wanted to say on that somewhat sad occasion, but I could not seem to find a satisfactory way to begin. After lunch on the day before commencement, in desperation, I went down to Father Flye's house to seek his help. He and Jim were talking in the living room. I explained my predicament, and as my speech was not long, I asked Father Flye to read it. When he finished, he said he would have to think about it some but that it would have to wait until after a faculty meeting he had to attend in a few minutes. As he got ready to leave, Jim asked if he could read it. Of course, Father Flye and I were delighted.

Father Flye had left before Jim finished reading it. He leafed

through it again quickly. Then he said, "I think I have an idea. I'll be back in a minute or so," and he disappeared into Father Flye's study, which adjoined the room we were in.

A half hour passed, then an hour; and I grew more and more nervous, thinking that Jim was finding the whole thing impossible or that it had put him to sleep. I was on the brink of fleeing to escape disgrace, after over an hour and a half had gone by, when Jim came out and handed me a couple of sentences in his minuscule script. "How do you think this will work as a lead?" he asked. Lead was a new word to me, but in that context I knew what it meant. Here is what he wrote: "Before another hour has passed, we of the senior class will no longer be students at St. Andrew's. We shall have been advanced into a world new to us and not yet clearly known to us."

I felt then — and still do — how clear, how simple, how appropriate to that occasion. But I thought, even more, of his generosity and his total *engagement* in everything he did.

I do not expect to see his like again.

WALKER EVANS

James Agee in 1936

At the time, Agee was a youthful-looking twenty-seven. I think he felt he was elaborately masked, but what you saw right away — alas for conspiracy — was a faint rubbing of Harvard and Exeter, a hint of family gentility, and a trace of romantic idealism. He could be taken for a likable American young man, an above-average product of the Great Democracy from any part of the country. He didn't look much like a poet, an intellectual, an artist, or a Christian, each of which he was. Nor was there an outward sign of his paralyzing, self-lacerating anger. His voice was pronouncedly quiet and low pitched, though not of "cultivated" tone. It gave the impression of diffidence but never of weakness. His accent was more or less unplaceable and it was somewhat variable. For instance, in Alabama it veered toward country-southern, and I may say he got away with this to the farm families and to himself.

His clothes were deliberately cheap, not only because he was poor but because he wanted to be able to forget them. He would work a suit into fitting him perfectly by the simple method of not taking it off much. In due time the cloth would mold itself to his frame. Cleaning and pressing would have undone this beautiful process. I exaggerate, but it did seem sometimes that wind, rain, work, and mockery were his tailors. On another score, he felt that wearing good, expensive clothes involved him in some sort of claim to superiority of the social kind. Here he occasionally confused his purpose and fell over into a knowingly comical inverted dandyism. He got more delight out of factory-seconds sneakers and a sleazy cap than a straight dandy does from waxed calf Peal shoes and a brushed Lock & Co. bowler.

Physically Agee was quite powerful, in the deceptive way of uninsistent large men. In movement he was rather graceless. His hands were large, long, bony, light, and uncared for. His gestures were one of the memorable things about him. He seemed to model, fight, and stroke his phrases as he talked. The talk, in the end, was his great distinguishing feature. He talked his prose, Agee prose. It was hardly a twentieth-century style; it had Elizabethan colors. Yet it had extraordinarily knowledgeable contemporary content. It rolled just as it reads, but he made it sound natural—something just there in the air like any other part of the world. How he did this no one knows. You would have blinked, gaped, and very likely run from this same talk delivered without his mysterious ability. It wasn't a matter of show, and it wasn't necessarily bottle-inspired. Sheer energy of imagination was what lay behind it. This he matched with physical energy. Many a man or woman has fallen exhausted to sleep at four in the morning bang in the middle of a remarkable Agee performance, and later learned that the man had continued it somewhere else until six. Like many born writers who are floating in the illusory amplitude of their youth, Agee did a great deal of writing in the air. Often you had the impulse to gag him and tie a pen to his hand. That wasn't necessary; he was an exception among talking writers. He wrote—devotedly and incessantly.

Night was his time. In Alabama he worked I don't know how late. Some parts of *Let Us Now Praise Famous Men* read as though they were written on the spot at night. Later, in a small house in Frenchtown, New Jersey, the work, I think, was largely night-written. Literally the result shows this; some of the sections read best at night, far in the night. The first passage of "A Country Letter" is particularly night-permeated.

Agee worked in what looked like a rush and a rage. In Alabama he was possessed with the business, jamming it all into the days and the nights. He must not have slept. He was driven to see all he could of the families' day, starting, of course, at dawn. In one way, conditions there were ideal. He could live inside the subject, with no distractions. Backcountry poor life wasn't really far from him, actually. He had some of it in his blood, through relatives in Tennessee. Anyway, he was in flight from New York magazine editorial offices, from Greenwich Village social-intellectual evenings, and especially from the whole world of high-minded, well-bred, money-hued culture, whether authoritarian or libertarian. In Alabama he sweated and scratched with submerged glee. The families understood what he was down there to do. He'd explained it, in such a way that they were interested in *his* work. He wasn't playing. That is why in the end he left out certain completed passages that were entertaining, in an acid way. One of these was a long, gradually hilarious aside on the subject of hens. It was a virtuoso piece heightened with allegory and bemused with the pathetic fallacy.

He won over almost everybody in those families — perhaps too much — even though some of the individuals were hard-bitten, sore, and shrewd. Probably it was his diffidence that took him into them. That nonassurance was, I think, a hostage to his very Anglican childhood training. His Christianity — if an outsider may try to speak of it — was a punctured and residual remnant, but it was still a naked, root emotion. It was an ex-Church or non-Church matter, and it was hardly in evidence. All you saw of it was an ingrained courtesy, an uncourtly courtesy that emanated from him toward everyone, perhaps excepting the smugly rich, the pretentiously genteel, and the police. After a while, in a roundabout way, you discovered that, to him, human beings were at least possibly immortal and literally sacred souls.

The days with the families came abruptly to an end. Their real content and meaning has all been shown. The writing they induced is, among other things, the reflection of one resolute, private rebellion. Agee's rebellion was unquenchable, self-damaging, deeply principled, infinitely costly, and ultimately priceless.

Participants:

EDWARD CARLOS

WARREN EYSTER

JAMES WARD LEE

DAVID MADDEN

FREDERICK MANFRED

FATHER MARTIN

WILLIAM STOTT

Let Us Now Praise Famous Men Panel

FATHER MARTIN: Our panel is going to discuss *Let Us Now Praise Famous Men*. The chair of the panel is Dr. William Stott, who is a member of the faculty of the University of Texas at Austin, a member of the Department of American Studies and of the Department of English. His doctoral dissertation dealt with documentary literature of the thirties and, of course, focused strongly on *Let Us Now Praise Famous Men*. I believe he feels this is the outstanding documentary of that time. Is that correct, Dr. Stott?

STOTT: I certainly do.

FATHER MARTIN: Also on the panel is Dr. Edward Carlos. He is head of the Art Department at the University of the South and is, I feel, especially qualified to speak to us with regard to the photography in *Let Us Now Praise Famous Men* and its relationship to the whole work. To his right is Dr. James Ward Lee, a member of the Department of English of North Texas State University in Denton, Texas, a

St. Andrew's graduate, and editor of the journal *Studies in the Novel*. We're very happy to have with us, also, from the preceding panel, the three writers who have come to be with us for this part of the week: Mr. Manfred, Mr. Eyster, and Mr. Madden. So, with that introduction, I will turn the panel to our chair, Dr. Stott.

STOTT: This morning, in the first panel, I think a great and proper stress was put on Agee's emphasis on trying to communicate something that he felt was essential, that he felt was crucial, about human experience, human experience in very broad and general terms. I think that everybody who comes to *Let Us Now Praise Famous Men* and succeeds in getting through the book is rewarded. I must say, in all honesty, that there are many people who come to it and who shipwreck on the first thirty pages and never get any further. I think Agee, in the first thirty pages, did all that he possibly could to alienate a reader. Each person will have different, essential experiences in the book, and what I am going to do is ask each panel member to talk about his essential experience in the book — what he considered we must know, what we must see, what we must take away from it. Since I am making this demand, I think it only fair that I begin, so let me very briefly say what I think is so remarkable about the book.

Let Us Now Praise Famous Men appeared in 1941 and was at the end of a long series of books about the problem of the sharecropper. The sharecropper was at the center of the thirties thought, rather in the way that the blacks have been at the center of thought in the time that you have been growing up, rather as the black revolution has been at the center of the sixties. The sharecropper figured in dramas, particularly the longest running drama ever to appear on the Broadway stage, *Tobacco Road*, which was, when it first appeared — difficult as it is to believe — considered primarily a work of social consciousness, although it was quickly understood and seen for what it actually was: really, a lurid piece of exploitation. But the sharecropper also figured in documentary films, including one made for *The March of Time* called *Trouble in the Cotton Country*. The sharecropper figured in a host of books with photographs published in the thirties.

Agee and Walker Evans — Evans then a photographer for the Farm Security Administration — began to prepare *Let Us Now Praise Famous Men* as a *Fortune* article in 1936. Agee was sent out by *Fortune* magazine to look at the indecency of the sharecropper problem, to look at the pitiably "deformed" people. I think that when we begin the book, we look at that picture and we say, "Yes, that's what it's going to be about. It's going to be hard to take." What we have on the front cover is a sort of atrocity picture of a little boy: his eyes wide with malnutrition; his face passive, fearful, haunted, hungry. Yet, what I think is so essential in the book, and what raises it so much above the documentary genre in which it was created, is exactly the energy with which James Agee and Walker Evans worked against the simplicities of the propaganda of which they were, in many ways, writing.

Let me read to you a little passage from this book. Agee and Evans are living with the Gudger family, and Agee gets involved with Emma, Annie Mae Gudger's sister, who is leaving the house. This is Annie Mae, one of Walker Evans's most famous photographs. These are, of course, not the people's actual names. Agee said that these people were "real"; that's why he didn't use their actual names. Annie Mae didn't want her sister to go.

> Annie Mae is strong against her going, all that distance, to a man who leaves her behind and then just sends for her, saying, Come on along, now; and George too is as committal over it as he feels will appear any right or business of his to be, he a man, and married, to the wife of another man, who is no kin to him, but only the sister of his wife, and to whom he is himself un-concealably attracted: but she is going all the same, without at all understanding why. Annie Mae is sure she won't stay out there long, not all alone in the country away from her kinfolks with that man; that is what she keeps saying, to Emma, and to George, and even to me; but actually she is surer than not that she may never see her young sister again, and she grieves for her, and for the loss of her to her own loneliness, for she loves her, both for herself and her dependence and for that softness of youth which already is drawn so deep into the trap, and in which Annie Mae can perceive herself as she was ten years past; and she gives no appearance of noticing the clumsy and shamefaced would-be-subtle demeanors of flirtation which George is stupid enough to believe she does not understand for what they are: for George would only be shocked should she give him open per-mission, and Emma could not be too well trusted either.

So this sad comedy has been going on. And the awareness of this passage seems to me quite extraordinary, the sort of awareness that one would get in a novel—a fine novel—where one character is aware of his relation to another and is aware of what the other character is thinking of him and what the other character isn't, perhaps, thinking of him, doesn't realize. I would suggest that this passage, far from coming from a piece of propaganda, would come from a piece of fiction of the highest order, Henry James's sort of fiction. This is a passage out of something as abstruse as perhaps *The Golden Bowl*. Then later on, when Agee, having rented a car, drives Emma to the truck that is to carry her off to her husband, with everyone else in the Gudger family in the car, we have another passage. Emma is a beautiful young, healthy, robust, blonde girl of about eighteen:

> Emma rode between me and her father, her round sleeveless arms cramped a little in front of her. My own sleeves were rolled high, so that in the crowding our flesh touched. . . . Our bodies were very hot, and the car was packed with hot and sweating bodies, and with a fine salt and rank odor like that of crushed grass: and thus in a short while, though I knew speed was not in the mood of anyone and was going as slowly as I felt I could with propriety, we covered the short seven mileage of clay, then slag, to Cookstown.

I would suggest that there was not another passage like this in all of the documentary literature of the thirties, as a matter of fact, in any kind of propaganda literature. That the awareness of a physical fact, the human presence of these victims of a social condition that he is speaking about, entirely lifts these people, redeems them, from this social condition makes us understand that what is essential in them, what is essentially human in them, is not their suffering brought on by the callousness of society but rather what is perennial in them, the human reality about which Agee was always speaking in his literature, certainly in the vocal work *Knoxville: Summer of 1915* very memorably: this awareness of the unacknowledged sexuality of all relations, all social relations—even those that we don't want to admit as such—sitting next to someone on a bus, sitting next to a pretty woman, between a teacher and a student of opposite sexes, or perhaps of the same sex as well. Agee would insist later in this book that the fact of the human relation, the unacknowledged sexuality of the vagrant liaisons of common experience, emphasizes the human reality of these people, which in many ways makes the social fact of their suffering sharper. I would think this would be one essential thing I would want to point to in this book—this emphasis on the human fact of these people.

Having broached that, may I ask each of you to suggest what you think students might want to look at in the book? What would you consider essential in the book?

CARLOS: I feel that the book, in terms of the photographs . . . sometimes it is very difficult to express things that are visual in words. I feel very much in tune with my experience of the book, not as a thing to read at this point. I'm almost too close to it. I want you to know where I am with this in order that you will understand my approach.

My experience with the book is both photographic and verbal. I think I am here to represent Walker Evans more than Agee, and I would like to get to the essence of what I found. I found the idea of the perennial fact of human existence and the sexuality of all relations to be keen and perceptible and I appreciate that. But when I approach some works, I find that I cannot discuss them. They are, in some instances, too holy. I have to approach them in certain kinds of silence. This is the role of the photographer . . . a tendency to non-verbalize, to approach them with a certain amount of silence. I feel this way about Renoir's *Boating Party*.

In the last panel on poetry, a couple of references were made to things that I think are particularly visual and photographic in that sense, and it's this that I'd like to begin on. Two of the gentlemen made reference to two things—the leaf falling from the tree and the light catching the leaf as it falls to the ground. That was a visual reference, a photographic reference. Then he made the reference that beyond the leaf is the sun. Yes, the sun, the light. That is the essence of photography, I really think. That was one condition. I would like to come back to it. It is a primal utterance in that sense—of obtaining the light, of being one with that experience of the sun. It is energy. It is sound. It is a visual utterance, but the sound in this case, being visual, is silent. It's very much there with the entire experience of what visuality means and what photography means. Its essence is light, the apprehension of light and all that comes with it, including the shade, the shadow, and the darkness.

The other instance that I can draw reference from is when the panel moderator turned to Father Flye and asked him a direct question. Father Flye paused. There was silence for a few seconds. Not awkward seconds, but beautiful, quiet, gradual, gentle, contemplative seconds. And it was in that pause . . . that's what photography is about. Between the rhythms, something stops, something is there. In that reality of that quietness between the rhythms — full of energy, marvelous imagery, beautiful expression — was that other kind of thing that is visual. Then he said, "Let me think." And he thought again, and then he expressed himself. That was one of the highest moments of the panel to me. It was in what was not said, as well as in what was being said, because it was, from my experience, visual. Nothing negative about the things that were said. I thought they were wonderful, and I have taken copious notes all through it to carry back with me and think about again. But my experience here is with the photograph.

I think the book is in its attempt to be without words and I think it is that. I see it as something akin to the writing of Joyce in which there's a certain moving on and going. There are ritual habits obvious in the book. The references to "on the porch," returning to the porch at night to think, to listen, and, if I can draw my reference first to Agee and then come back to Agee and to Evans, I would like to read a passage, too, because, in discussing the essence of the verbal end of it, I have to use Agee himself.

In the very closing parts of the book, there's a reference where he's sitting on the porch again. In his meditation, in that pause each evening, which I think is essentially visual, the photograph pauses; it catches an experience right there in the reality, whatever the reality is. Agee himself made reference to Margaret Bourke-White, in which she said a photograph, maybe one photograph, can lie a little, maybe. That may be the idea of artifice we talked about in the last panel, but not really "lying." You have a series of photographs such as Evans has taken. It does not quite tell the truth, because so many aspects of the experience come out of the work, one-to-one, in the relationship. And it is sensual — in the sense of touching and feeling and experiencing — or, if you wish, sexual. The quote I would like to offer is when Agee is listening:

There was the frightening joy of hearing the world talk to itself, and the grief of incommunicability. In that grief I am now as then, with the small yet absolute comfort of knowing that communication of such a thing is not only beyond possibility but irrelevant to it; whereas in love, where we find ourselves so completely involved, so completely responsible and so apparently capable, and where all our soul so runs out to the loveliness, strength, and defenseless mortality, plain, common, salt and muscled toughness of human existence of a girl that the desire to die for her seems the puniest and stingiest expression of your regard which you can, like a proud tomcat with a slain fledgling, lay at her feet; in love the restraint in focus and the arrest and perpetuation of joy seems entirely possible and simple, and its failure inexcusable. . . . [A]nd though, even, I know that a more gifted human being, and even I myself, could come nearer giving it, I do not relinquish the ultimately hopeless effort with entire grief: simply because that effort would be, above most efforts, so useless.

In terms of technical references to the book, I mentioned the formlessness which I think is part of this work, an attempt to be more than the forms we know, to move into something greater, more significant. I think that's transubstantiation. It is recognizing the spiritual in the physical, the spiritual in the material.

The photographs have something akin to the primal utterance in their technique. They are almost snapshots, not photographs, yet they're almost photographs, too. I've drawn a distinction in that, a distinction I always make with my beginning students. They come in, having taken snapshots which are pictures of things that they're interested in, with little understanding of the relationships of the parts to the whole. Everything is centered on the object, so to speak. It hasn't yet become subjective, only hinting at it. And these photographs have this sense to them.

But they are not beginning photographs. They have comprehended classic form; they are extremely classic in their approach. They are centrally oriented in their composition almost throughout. They are objects captured out there, and yet through the mastery of techniques and understanding of the darkroom and the taking of the pictures, Walker Evans has returned to some of his primal things, some of the beginning attempts at photography, and done it with marvelous insight in terms of these beings there to whom he is tuned and whom he is trying to comprehend through the lens and to be one with.

I think he accomplishes it. I could have looked at them, I think, carelessly and shallowly and not seen that they are more than just snapshots. That there's something more. The one of the young man sitting on the porch . . . as you look closely at the composition, you see there is distribution of light and dark. Okay. That's design. That's easy. But then we see there's a hand dropping out of the top, and there's part of a body back here, and it cuts in through the face and makes an awkward dark shape around the hand, and the feet are cut off at the bottom. Yet it helps you get into the photograph because it's severed and cut here and there.

But there are distracting elements in it — these little details around the side. Why is that hand postulated up there? Is it to represent something symbolic? No, I think this book denies symbolism. To me, one of its greatest joys is that it rejects literary symbolism. It's there because it's a return to formlessness after having conceived, recognized, and comprehended the form that is given to us classically, simply, by our very existence. We have an entire historical heritage; we are all classical; we are all symmetrical in this sense. But the real sense of understanding is to try to break from it, to break forms, to grow out of it, and then to come back to it and see it again. And I think Walker Evans has done this consistently through his photographs.

I could talk about them individually. I won't do that. I do make reference to that one because he repeats that pattern time and time again: centrally located object, the clutter that is almost there, yet not. It becomes a framing device, returning to the shape of the structure, the rectangle or the square. Yet there is inside it a content and meaning. There is a continuance of the subject matter — of the tenant, his home, his farm, his children — centrally located, the expressions in their faces, which is part of that subject matter, part of that literalness of them. And there is the capture of the light, which goes back to its form again. There's a marvelous comprehension of these, that darkroom process: these were taken not before one has learned to print but after one has been in the darkroom and seen, with a touch of light, the emergence of an image and the emergence of a form. This is the essence for me in the book, and I see a parallel between the photography and text which I would rather pass on to those people who comprehend Agee's part in it.

STOTT: Thank you. Mr. Madden, may I ask you for your response to the book?

MADDEN: I'd really rather hear Mr. Lee's views, since I was talking the hour before. Would that be all right?

STOTT: Mr. Lee?

LEE: I was thinking of some way to get even. I am ill at participating in panels. It's one of the things I do worst. That may be especially the case today because on this panel I fear that I find a great deal to object to in Agee's classic work, *Let Us Now Praise Famous Men*. And finding objections to James Agee's works is not a popular position to take at this time and in this place.

But I lived in Alabama in the thirties, at the exact time covered by Agee's text and pictured in Walker Evans's photographs. Looking back on those days, I can't help but remember a line from A. E. Housman — "Some can gaze and not be sick / But I could never learn the trick." It is hard for me to gaze back on those days and on those people and not be sick at heart for the poverty they suffered and the awful conditions of life forced on them by outside circumstances. Life along the Tennessee River in Alabama was bad in those dark years of the Depression. To romanticize it, to wax lyrical over it, as is sometimes the case with Agee, simply won't do. Sentimentality will hardly ever do, and I find a great deal of sentimentality in this book. I don't know any better definition of sentimentality than one I read in a book somewhere. It is probably a famous definition, and everybody in the room but me probably knows where it came from, and I probably can't state it exactly right. But here is how I remember it: "Sentimentality is being more concerned with God's creatures than God is." And I find Agee's treatment of the Alabama poor sentimental. He cares for them more than God did, but he also finds them somehow romantic and noble for having been born into poverty.

What we have heard here in this symposium dedicating the Agee Library has been uncritical panegyric — and I really do praise this famous man, James Agee — but I think more praise is to be found in honest criticism. Nobody ever need make excuses for Agee's *A Death in the Family*. You can't do much better than that when writing a novel. I am a great admirer of *The Morning Watch*, *Agee on Film*, and *The African Queen*, but *Let Us Now Praise Famous Men* I find wanting in many ways. Let me read you some of the notes I made when reading the book.

I said to myself, Agee can't decide what he is doing. He can't decide whether he is writing a novel or whether he is writing journalism; whether he is writing philosophy or sociology or history or some sort of aesthetic treatise. There is a good deal of talk about aesthetics in the book. Talk that I find laden with sentimentality all too often. He might have found plain and simple beauty in a Number 3 washtub that the woman of the house used to scrub the family clothes. But my Aunt Rene, a farm woman who lived in an Alabama four-room, unpainted house belonging to someone else, never did. I prefer her view of the Number 3 tub, for my aunt saw it as an implement, not as a grail of some sort.

I find much to criticize in the style of the book. I recognize all the echoes of Hopkins, Blake, e. e. cummings, Archibald MacLeish, Faulkner, and Joyce — all the Modernist gods. I think anybody will admit that the punctuation and capitalization are strange. I can excuse it — nay, admire it — in e. e. cummings. I know what cummings is doing. When he writes "poor But-ter-fly" in a poem, he is echoing the popular song of the thirties and showing us how to intone his poem. But I see no excuse for it in *Let Us Now Praise Famous Men*. Here is a book about plain people that should have been written plain. The style of a book like this should not call attention to itself; the material of the book calls for its own attention.

There is much in the book to admire. When he tells the sad and pitiful story of Alabama tenant farmers, I am moved. But when he offers up all his sentimentalized reactions to that life, I am not moved. Agee says, "[I]n God's name, don't think of it as Art." He then proceeds to be arty for four hundred pages. I don't, for instance, know what "wounded honey" means, but I know it is arty. Of the book, Agee says "The whole job may well seem messy to you." It does. "[F]orget that this is a book," he says. I can't. How could I, for the artiness overwhelms me and makes losing myself in the narrative impossible.

The section on overalls takes flight. I stand second to nobody in my admiration of that utilitarian and supremely comfortable garment, but my admiration is different from Agee's. It may be the limitation of my background. There may be something to be said for being an old country boy from Alabama, but it may spoil the glories of *Let Us Now Praise Famous Men's* glamorizing of Carharts and 401s and Dickeys and White Mules. I may know too much. I may have seen too many poor men in overalls, men despised by the townsfolk for their ignorance and poverty. It may even be that having worn overalls for much of my life, I resent the arty presentation of them in this book.

My southern background never kept me from appreciating *The Sound and the Fury* because it didn't seem to me that Faulkner patronized his characters. And I think that may be my quarrel with Agee. Here is a guy who went from St. Andrew's to Exeter to Harvard and who has now gone into Alabama to do a job. Agee's heart shows in many places, and I think he had a good heart, but in many ways he could never put aside his superiority when he was with these half-starved, ignorant — we would now call them "disadvantaged" — people. I hate to say "white trash," but that is what it comes down to, and I don't think Agee could ever forget that.

I wish I had been asked to comment on *A Death in the Family.* I think it is a first-rate novel. It gets down to the crux of things when it tells how it felt to be six years old and have your father suddenly killed. It tells the story with economy, and I appreciate that. *Let Us Now Praise Famous Men* lacks economy of telling most of the time. But there are times in the book when Agee at his best comes out. In those passages the prose is tight and the story is economical. Parts of the book are well done. The quality of life in Alabama in the thirties is well rendered. But, all in all, I have to say — and I hate to in this gathering — that the book is mixed, that it is all too often posturing and overblown and arty. I guess, finally, I have to say that it will not do.

STOTT: Mr. Lee, thank you for a very therapeutic qualification, and I hope that some of the writers to my left will want to respond to this or perhaps amplify.

MADDEN: I think we should pause for some applause. The applause is suppressed here, I think. [Applause from audience] I think that what Mr. Lee has done is very important. For a whole week of Agee, it's important that, in the middle, those of you who aren't as swept away as some of the rest of us are have a chance to have your say and your spokesman and to applaud what he had to say. There needs to be this kind of moment and this kind of viewpoint, although it needs to be stressed that it is mainly about this one piece that he feels this way. He's a great admirer of *A Death in the Family*, but I think an interesting reader problem arises that I, as a writer, am very conscious of when I write and that I have tried to deal with in some material that is rather similar to *Let Us Now Praise Famous Men*. I want to touch on Agee's influence on me in this book, about which, I must say, I had some of the same feelings when I first read it.

I am from Knoxville, Tennessee, James Agee's hometown, and I reacted sometimes a little bit toward *A Death in the Family*, set in Knoxville, the way Mr. Lee reacts to *Let Us Now Praise Famous Men* set in his home state. But not as violently and not as strongly. I think that there's a problem here. He says that *Let Us Now Praise Famous Men* is full of sentimentality and romanticizes, and I think that there are similar passages in *A Death in the Family*. It's interesting that he doesn't see them there. It's only when Agee gets on his home ground that he gets upset.

And the same thing is true of me when I was about twenty-three years old and this book first came out. I was writing a novel set in Knoxville, Tennessee, based partly on some of my own experiences. And I reacted in much the same way: "You're talking about *my* territory. Who the hell do you think *you* are? Just because you were born two blocks down the street from where I am living doesn't mean that you can write about my territory." And I think it's a natural reaction.

People have reacted to my writing about eastern Kentucky where I was an alien and a stranger. I was fascinated, imaginatively, by the coal-mining country in eastern Kentucky, which, when I wrote about it, was being written about in a journalistic fashion, pretty much the way the South was being written about or Alabama and the share-croppers were being written about in the thirties. This was during the time that John Kennedy was going down to eastern Kentucky and saying: "Look at all these poor impoverished people: their horizons are limited; their experiences are stunted; their lives are stunted; their emotional, cultural growth is stunted; this is pretty pitiful compared to what we rich people or we middle-class people have, and we should bring them up to the level of middle-class experience."

I personally was finding the middle-class experience very much open to criticism myself. Knowing people of eastern Kentucky, knowing the people of Tennessee, the country people and writing about them, I felt their inner lives, their relationships among themselves are just as rich and interesting and as fascinating and as worthwhile as what you're holding up as being better, which is the middle-class way of life. So I felt pretty much the way Agee did when he went into Alabama.

Agee said the facts really don't express the life being lived here: the fact that they are starving, the fact that they have to wash in this wash-tub, which Mr. Lee was referring to, and that they should have a nice bathtub instead; the fact that they have only one fork per person in the family, and only two or three plates, not enough to go around, not enough plates to eat off of, not enough food to eat, not enough shelter in the winter, ragged clothes. That doesn't tell the whole story. He had this desire to show their fundamental humanity.

Now I faced, as a young writer, the same problem with eastern Kentucky. In "The Singer" I wanted to tell a story about a girl who walks into the faith-healing tent one night, gets caught up in the emotional experience, has a kind of visitation from God, and feels she has a mission to sing for Jesus. She starts singing right there in the tent and beautifully, "Power in the Blood." It's a marvelous song. Everybody is carried away, and they want to follow her when she leaves the tent. She just keeps walking.

The idea is that she can't speak. She's mute, struck dumb by this visitation from God, except that she sings when the spirit moves her. Wherever she might be when the spirit moves her, she sings. And they say that before she came to the tent, there wasn't anything wrong with her. She was just an ordinary girl.

Well, I felt that to simply tell this story straight I would lapse into romanticizing, and I would sentimentalize this girl with long hair and big blue eyes. I could just see myself describing her with all kinds of phony lyrical styles, describing the Kentucky landscape — which I love, which I was fascinated by — including the horrible old shacks that people are so appalled by. I thought they were beautiful. I feel the way James Agee does, that these old overalls, these old shacks, have a kind of beauty that transcends the misery that people are experiencing. And that beauty is part of the whole scene. You cannot let the misery completely swamp it. I disagree with Mr. Lee that the writer shouldn't try to describe and deal with those elements in the scene that don't simply have to do with the stark facts of survival.

From reading *Let Us Now Praise Famous Men*, I knew that I had to find a way to avoid some of the problems that Agee got himself into. Although it was an object lesson in what not to do, it was simultaneously an object lesson in what to do. The solution I found was to present on the page something very different from what I personally felt so that the reader, because of these juxtapositions, would experience something like what I wanted him to experience but couldn't describe, because I think that no writer could describe the things I really wanted to describe. This is something that young writers find out, to their dismay, somewhere along the line: that you can never really describe the very things that make you want to be a writer. Agee, especially, was fascinated by these things. The way the light looks on the side of a building, the way a man looks standing on the corner — you can't really describe those things in words, so you have to find a technique that will enable you to spark an emotion or an insight in the reader without stating it on the page.

Now what Mr. Lee is objecting to is that, too often, Agee tried to state it on the page and sometimes he really soared and the language really succeeded, but a lot of the time the language failed. But what he's not realizing is that Agee was very conscious of what he was doing with these different techniques.

Mr. Lee says Agee didn't know whether he was writing a documentary, poetry, or a novel. He *did* know that he couldn't write any of those things, that he could not do the whole job using any of those techniques. So then he tried, instead, to juxtapose different techniques, to go from a documentary listing of facts to a personal, lyrical expression of his own emotion, hoping that when these two different things were juxtaposed, along with Walker Evans's photographs, that the very thing he knew he was failing to express would somehow happen. One place where you can really study this, where it comes most dramatically, is on page 111 (*Let Us Now Praise Famous Men*, Boston: Houghton Mifflin, 1988). Look at the last paragraph, where Agee writes of the landscape he is about to enter: "That steep withdrawal and silence and meditation of whose need I spoke; we are now drawn back at the peak of in quite silence: whence let me hope the whole of that landscape we shall essay to travel in is visible and may be known as there all at once: let this be borne in mind, in order that, when we descend among its windings and blockades, into examination of slender particulars, this its wholeness and simultaneous living map may not be neglected, however lost the breadth of the country may be in the winding walk of each sentence."

There's a very painful consciousness of his limitations, no matter what technique he will use, as he proceeds with this novel, documentary, whatever. Then he goes in bluntly on the next page, "Part II: Some Findings and Comments." He is deliberately saying, "I'm going to give you the kind of things that I was sent here to get and that I think are inadequate. I am going to shove it violently, yoke it violently, with my own lyrical outpouring." Then the next page is entitled "Money." Almost as stark as, and as simple as, one of Walker Evans's photographs. "MONEY!" And then a quotation to give it authority. This is almost like some of the old-fashioned English courses where they tell you how to do an essay. Well, quote some authority. "'You are a farmer. I am a farmer myself,' said Franklin D. Roosevelt." And, of course, Agee is using that ironically because he's saying you're a millionaire and you're saying that you're a farmer. He's saying that this is ridiculous. He's also saying I am ridiculous, as a Harvard graduate, graduate of Exeter — even if he did go to St. Andrew's — it's kind of ridiculous to pretend to be a farmer. He knew that he was out of place.

That is what Agee was trying to do. I did the same thing in "The Singer." I have a guy get up who wants to make a documentary movie. He's got the raw footage up on the screen, he's got the audience, and he says: "We went into eastern Kentucky and we took all these pictures here to expose the bad conditions and I just want to show you all the horrible things there." And he reels them off, one after the other. And he's got a partner standing over here who's from Ohio. He's not a southerner. And the other partner is an advance man who goes in and prepares the people for the cameras, and he sits there, listening skeptically, and the audience wonders, "Well, now what's his attitude?"

Well, Pete the PR Man draws him in and says, "Wayne, I want you to say a few words." And Wayne comes in and begins to talk about the sheer humanity of the people, what really interested him about the people — not their suffering but their way of talking, their way of acting, and so on. And in the back is Fred, who is a mute who took the pictures. What happens is that gradually Fred begins to intercut with the expensive beautiful color, documentary shots, shots of the singer, which are lovingly done. I just want to show you this girl. She walks around and suddenly she starts singing for Jesus. I don't have the sound, but there's the picture of her. I just want you to look at this and look at that, and enjoy this and enjoy that, you see, and the hell with all these details and this documentary footage.

I was influenced as a novelist, as a Knoxville author, by the technique that I am demonstrating here in *Let Us Now Praise Famous Men*. Agee goes on for a few pages and he says, "Shelter." Another title somewhat similar to "Money." And then he says, "Shelter in Outline." This is an English course. So we've got to give you an outline of the things we are going to talk about, and so he lists all these things — the furniture, the altar, the tabernacle — the things that he's going to take up in the piece. Now this is another technique, a use of forms of communication, a reaching out for another medium through which to express what he wanted to say. He's not satisfied with any of these forms.

So I have to say out of the side of my mouth, and out of one side of my sensibility, I agree with Mr. Lee, but I think Mr. Lee is sentimentalizing, in an inverted way, the importance of that experience which he has now transcended. He's living a very different kind of life, and it's as if he's saying, "Well, I want that life to remain important in a different way." He's laying his claim on the experience he's had. He is making the claim that this has happened to me. It's my experience. Agee doesn't have a right to do some of the things he did with the experience. There's truth in it, and there's a lie in what Mr. Lee is saying, just as there is truth and there are lies in what Agee was doing. Unconscious in both instances.

But I have learned as a writer from this experience. I've looked for a way not to fall into some of the excesses, the personal objective excesses that Agee did, which means that I am slightly cowardly in a way. At the same time, I want to use some of the techniques to achieve what I want to achieve and to let the experience happen in the reader, not in me.

One final observation I think Mr. Lee is getting at. In some of those passages, but not all, what we are doing is watching a man experience something, rather than his making us experience it, and I think that sometimes readers really object to this. I think this is what happens in Jack Kerouac or Thomas Wolfe. We are watching the spectacle of a man devouring an experience, rather than his enabling us to experience it ourselves.

STOTT: Thank you very much. Mr. Eyster, may we pass the torch to you?

EYSTER: The first thing that comes to mind is how important the perspective of the reader is when he goes to the work, as to how he comes away from the piece of work. In my case, this is one of the ten most influential pieces that I have ever read, far more than *A Death in the Family* was. I am not saying better or worse for the moment. Simply, it had a strong influence on me. I'd like to try to describe why.

I had a feeling here, when Mr. Lee was talking, that we were both looking at the same thing, but it was like one man was up high looking into a dark well, and I was down in the well looking up at the light. I grew up on a background of people like Willard Markley, James Farrell, Upton Sinclair, and down south Erskine Caldwell. At first, I was kind of impressed: it sounds kind of hard, it's like life was. I was living in the Depression myself in a steel mill town, and gradually it began to rub on me that this wasn't getting to life. All this rubbing and what they call "naturalism" and the physical reality was somehow exaggerated and was missing the point, and I was tired of it. It was overdoing it, and when I came to Agee, the idea of reading something about a guy who went down to report on tenant farmers, I thought, "Oh, Lord, here we go again." To me, with all the flaws and all the exceptions and all the imperfections, I pretty much agree with the question as to the importance of them. But, for me, what really came through was almost like what Wordsworth had done earlier—a reaffirmation for the value of the human being in any living condition. He is just as vital, just as alive, just as important, whether he's down there grubbing for a living or whether he's a New York executive.

Now I would say, in thinking over what has been said, that a mistake that Agee made was his feeling that the audience didn't want to "buy" the common man and that he needed to magnify and insist upon the message to get that part through. I really feel that was the voice of the narrator. I don't really mind when the Harvard grad goes down, by the way. I was born in Pennsylvania, a steel mill town, and, of course to me, anything that told me about the South was new to me. I didn't know the South. I only got down to Winchester, Virginia. It's just barely over into southern territory. I felt like I was in the Deep South. With this kind of background, anything I learned about the South was new to me.

But I had smelled something wrong in the South of Caldwell and the South of writers down in New Orleans, Frank Yerby and that type — the kind that magnified the old pre–Civil War South. Either of these views, they rubbed wrong. When Agee came down, he really represented me, as the alien, going into the place and trying to say, "I am not going to try to kid you; I'm not going to try to pretend I'm the Alabama voice in this. I am going down there as what I am, a reporter from *Fortune*, a man who's been educated at Harvard, and I am going to give you me and those people as honestly as I can."

I almost feel that he recognized some of the imperfections that he was putting into it and that is some kind of honesty. I have always felt that the one thing I liked about Agee more than anything else was his honesty, the desire that he would have to sit with any human being and not pretend he was interested but *be* interested. I think that's it, and that's what this book was an effort at. There are many, many failures in it, and maybe the total thing is a failure, but for me, if it is a failure, it's a grand try. I could elaborate on particular passages that I liked, but I really think that would be beside the point. I think I'll just let it ride.

STOTT: Thank you. Mr. Manfred, may we turn to you?

MANFRED: I'd like to talk about Louise. I won't read it, but he tells how he noticed her, a ten-year-old girl. He remarked about her movements and the way she was looking at him with her pure clear eyes. There's another passage a little later. "She sits squarely and upright in her chair, as I have told, silent, and careful of the child . . . and I come soon to realize that she has not once taken her eyes off me since we entered the room." At that point the book lit up for me. The whole thing — all joy, life. Ever since I can remember, before I went to school, I, somewhere as a male child, had to have a girl. If I went to church, one of the meanings of the church for me was, besides what I heard from the pulpit and the advice from my father and mother to sit still and not make wiggly movements, to find some girl in church with whom I could catch eyes. I'd catch her eye for one second, and then she'd look at me in a certain way and look away, and right away the whole church service was great! I don't know how many of you boys have experienced that or how many have experienced a Fourth of July picnic. The day became special when there was a girl around somewhere who caught my eye, with whom I could exchange glances. The most beautiful part of it was exchanging glances with her before I got acquainted with her. After that, after we became acquainted, the whole thing disappeared. I don't know what's wrong with me, but I don't mind it. I like it still. Coming to this town, I've been alert, waiting for some girl with whom I can exchange glances. I hope I have this until I'm dead.

I think this is going on in James Agee's eyes, because he has this girl, and from that point on, he lit up. There was some *ideal*. I use that arty word because all good things come from the top down, never from the bottom up, at least creatively speaking. There's some power in me that asks for a certain kind of image and keeps looking until it finds it. That girl over there is my exact whole opposite. And I think this happens to me.

Now on the next page he says that he hopes that he will continue to watch her. "[A]nd after a little, not long at all, she raises her eyes again, and an almost imperceptibly softened face, shy, as if knowledgeable, but the eyes the same as before; and this time it is I who change, to warmth."

And this is what makes that whole passage lift up and become something whole and wonderful; it suddenly makes a book like Nabokov's look cheap. They're only simple by comparison. There's smirking and smiling and nowhere is *Lolita* very serious to me or believable. I read the book. I had a little trouble reading it because it's salacious and full of lust and all that stuff. That's not in my nature. By the time I was through with it, I was rather sick of it. Somehow I, too, in my own mind have had the need for something ideal. I think that's what causes this . . . sister, mother, and so on Agee caught for me. Since then, the book has been fine, and I am willing to accept all these things that they say are wrong with it.

STOTT: Well, as you can see, there is not one *Let Us Now Praise Famous Men* but at least four or five, maybe six of them here on the stage, and I am sure many of you who have had any acquaintance with the book at all have other *Let Us Now Praise Famous Men*. But let me suggest that perhaps you have questions you'd like to ask or observations you would like to make about this book or how it came to be.

EYSTER: Are there any of you here who can read fiction and get into it and say, well, this isn't really real? I remember when I was little and someone would tell me a story. I would ask, "Did it really happen? Is that guy real?" I always wanted to know about real people. That's one thing that bothered me. What are you doing writing novels if you don't trust fictional people? I always felt that I would like to write about real people, about people that really existed. I always thought of people like Napoleon or the presidents, or somebody big, wheeling and dealing. When I read, even in fiction by authors like Dos Passos, biographical passages about Henry Ford and so on, I always felt so down. I hated most biographies, and I couldn't understand this. This book came closest to cutting the boundaries between fact and fiction to get the values of both. Agee makes you see how important the real person is but also how important the vision of the author is. Fiction is two entities.

MADDEN: I'm really eager to hear some reactions from out there to what's been said up here or your own reflections on this piece.

AUDIENCE: What really got to me was the description of the house.

EYSTER: What I think Agee was trying to say in the interminable middle section of the book where he describes the house right down to the dust in the corner of the drawers . . . I think he's trying to say that it's all valid. It all needs attention. It all needs to be attended to. He wanted to make you see it.

CARLOS: I'd like to make a comment, if I could, about sentimentalizing. It doesn't bother me when something is sentimental. I'm a romantic sentimentalist. I was thinking about your washtub. That really hit me because my mother used a washtub, too, and I grew up with it. I don't like it in painting, sometimes, which is my field; I get violent, too, about the washtub. My mother was tickled pink when she could buy a washer and dryer and put the old tub away. But she's never thrown it away. It's still in the basement, I think, because, for her, there's some sort of necessity in retaining that. She doesn't go down and look at it. She doesn't go down and pray over it, and she doesn't use it unless the washing machine breaks down and she's forced to. But she's never let it go. I come along as her child. She was born the same year that Walker Evans was. So I have my stories of the Depression. I was born at the end of it. I don't remember it, unfortunately, but I'd like to take that tub and that washboard and bring them down here and hang them in my living room. I've done it with other things that I can get away with. I do it with the family photographs — she won't let those go either — and I think basically there's something poetic about those things. I know we go back and we sentimentalize. It's not much fun living in a dirty coal town. That's my province, too, but I didn't come from middle-class western Pennsylvania. It's middle class now, but it wasn't then. The Depression was still too new to it.

LEE: Let me just say one thing. I'm a sentimentalist. I still have my grandmother's iron and her doghouse trunk, but that's my sentimentality. I don't approve of it in other people or in my students. I'm rather harsh on them. Don't talk nonsense to me. If there's any nonsense talked to you, I'm going to talk it. It's all right for me to be a sentimentalist. I just don't want him to be one.

MADDEN: Yes, let's put it this way. I want to take a bath when I go back to the Holiday Inn. It would be nice if my old washtub were there for me instead of that impersonal modern thing they've got set up there. But I want to wash in *my* old bathtub, not *his* old bathtub.

That's where sentimentality in art does not work. Sentimentality . . . we should retain it in our own lives, though an excess of it there can be very dangerous, too. I think that readers who respond to sentimentality in another person's poem or story are having a relatively shallow experience or are simply using that poem as an occasion to reminisce about one's own life, not experiencing a work of art. I really would strongly urge you to reject sentimentality in works of art and cultivate it in your own life in the deepest way. Nostalgia, too. Albert Camus once said that he had a nostalgia for poverty, and I think that's what's behind my own responses to things like old washtubs.

I would like to have again the smell of Knoxville with coal smoke coming out of all the chimneys. Now almost nobody burns coal. I grew up with the smell of the polluted air of Knoxville, the little tiny balls of soot rolling around on the "winder sill" where we put the butter out during the night because we didn't have an electric refrigerator. We brought it in in the morning, and it always had these tiny flecks of soot that I inhaled all day long and that I now have painfully beautiful memories of. I, too, grew up in extreme poverty in Knoxville, far more than Agee ever experienced. I look back on it as something absolutely beautiful and wonderful. Like some of the guys from eastern Kentucky said, "We just didn't know we were miserable, didn't know we were unhappy, didn't know our horizons were limited till some journalist came along and told us."

AUDIENCE: I read that Agee went down to Alabama as a reporter for *Fortune* magazine. What about Agee's feelings for the sharecroppers? Did they get in the way of his role as the reporter?

MADDEN: Yes. That's a wonderful question. The interesting thing about Agee was that he was always getting these jobs like *Fortune* and other jobs that were, in a way, against his nature. In fact, Warren Eyster, driving up from Louisiana, told me, "When I first met him, I was a little leery of him because he kept talking about all these money-making projects that he was into—which probably he was into so that he could finance the time to write." But Warren's sensitivity was such that he was really appalled. He felt, "You're supposed to be an artist. What are you doing with all these Hollywood things and so on?"

But the thing to keep in mind about Agee was that he had such integrity that no matter what job he did, he brought everything he had to it. The thing about this *Fortune* assignment was that the experience was so overwhelming that he couldn't stay within the limits. Now I think it's interesting when you study Agee to keep in mind the limitations of each form that he worked in, and it's interesting that when he had to work for *Time* magazine, reviewing movies, that he did have a space problem. It's interesting to see how he worked within this very narrow space and how much perception and feeling he packed into it, although I imagine the reviews were probably four times longer than they ended up being in print. They probably cut them—I don't know the history of that—but it's interesting to see what happens when he just can't go on and on, as he could in this piece.

AUDIENCE: What about that passage, when he was lying there with the girl, and he was thinking about death? What is the connection of the scene with death?

MADDEN: I don't remember the scene that clearly. But, just intuitively, the way I respond to that is that any time you experience something that intensely, that's beautiful. You experience simultaneously a sense of its transience, that every beautiful thing has inherently the seed of decay in it, and it probably made him think of death because it was so full of life. It's sort of like Keats's poems being full of his awareness that his own body was disintegrating with disease. Even if you don't have that in you physically, you have it spiritually. This constant awareness that there is a death in you. Wright Morris is one of my favorite writers. If you really want to study the use of pictures in texts, look at some of his books where he, as a novelist, took his own photographs and wrote the prose beside it. Part of his book *The Inhabitants* came out in *New Directions* at exactly the same time as *Let Us Now Praise Famous Men*. Morris has a line in one of his novels where Uncle Dudley sees this beautiful girl on the corner in Hollywood, and she was so beautiful that he had to look away. You can't take it, in a way, and one reason why you can't is that you just know it won't last. I think that's one of the perceptions he was working at.

While I'm on Wright Morris, I want to say that James Agee should have taken his own photographs for this book. It would have been a more coherent piece if he had, and if he had interspersed the photographs in the text, not "illustrating" something on the opposite page. There's something about having them all as a bunch at the front, even though they're by a different man, that always bothered me. Think about what it would have been like if Agee had taken his own pictures, which later on, of course, he did by participating in the movies.

III

Film Reviews and Cinema

Louis Kronenberger

A Real Bohemian

Relatively few people are altogether easy to share an office with; Jim was an ideal one. Partly from having been brought up in the South, but preeminently from having the most delicate sensibilities, he was the most courteous of men. He had equally sensibilities of thought as of feeling; you had only to start a sentence to find him anticipating the rest of it. In the office, as I remember, we seldom stopped working to talk at length; but we traded comic items and literary tidbits back and forth, and every so often, late in the afternoon, we would go out for a drink. These proved to be extremely pleasant sessions but dangerously protracted ones which I would eventually have to call time on, even so arriving home more tardy, if possible, than tipsy. Jim's losing all sense of time was, in my experience, his only failure of "thoughtfulness" and of course not that at all; it came about through his love of talk, often involving the pursuit of ideas, and it constituted a facet of his essential bohemianism. He was a real bohemian, beginning with how he wanted to live, which was in no particular way; but far from any element of conformity, there was no apparent element of rebelliousness. He seemed adaptable to almost any situation, this not so much because nothing human was alien to him as that almost everything human was interesting. He was a steady and heroic drinker, though on "social" lines; never really unsteady so long as he was seated and went on talking away with great verve or intensity, gesturing in great wide arcs of space, and drinking, it sometimes seemed as unawarely as breathing, in great easy draughts. The only trouble — and it became a subject of humorous despair for the friends whose houses he went to — was that 2 A.M. or 3 A.M. or 4 A.M. might come, and Jim would show not the slightest inclination to go home. This, should you have a seven months' pregnant wife, or have to be up by seven o'clock, or, as the host, just not be able to keep awake, might have its inconvenient side. Then, suddenly penetrating the haze that never muddled his eloquence, Jim would become aware that it might be awfully late, and he would stand himself up, lunge contritely forward and somehow, ceremoniously apologetic, take his leave.

Dinner at the Agees' — which was on the fifth and top floor of an old building in the Village — had about it a kind of charming unpunctual punctilio, an engaging, unthought-out yet thoughtful, hospitality. Mia, Jim's Austrian-born wife, was a calm-mannered likable woman and a very good cook; and dinner, equally for how good it tasted and how festively it was consumed, was a very pleasant meal. It might be preceded, during an hour or more of drinking, by a need for milk or bread or bottled goods, with Jim possibly dashing twice down four flights of steep stairs and then up them — a routine matter it would seem, and no doubt straining the heart condition which he knew about and seemed to dismiss and from which he died. At dinner, drinking wine with the rest of us, might be an Agee four-year-old in a high chair; and toward the end of dinner, there was perhaps another dash downstairs for cigarettes. It was all of a piece, all a pleasure, and somehow rather memorable.

Having achieved by his movie criticism in *Time*, and even more in the *Nation*, a great recognition and prestige that reverberated in Hollywood, Jim somewhere around 1950 resigned from *Time* to go there, but he continued to write periodically for *Life*. The last time that I saw him he stuck his head through my office door, suggesting a drink,

and we had a longish session in which he talked of movies he had been asked to write and of others he wanted to. Hollywood, I gather, used him rather badly, which was perhaps foreseeable, since Jim simply disregarded not only money but the protective clauses of modern business life. He had even ignored the insurance arrangement available to Time-Inc-ers. Of the people I have known he was one of the few who truly had something large, open, magnetic about them and a touch — but no Midas touch — of genius.

This doesn't mean that he lacked faults or weaknesses; they, indeed, are implicit in the legend that he hastily became. Something demonic, or priapic, or reckless, or mysterious, or doomed would seem to be a necessary ingredient of such legendry, from Marlowe to Shelley and Byron, from Rimbaud to Baron Corvo and Jack London and, contemporary with Jim, Dylan Thomas.

The legend of course is never really the man and indeed often misrepresents him. I never knew Jim well enough, and I am not psychologist enough, to feel I could even tentatively provide a portrait.

His "life," though unimportant beside his personality and his work, had its standard ingredients of legend-making: there were wine and women in it, and moments of rage, and others that suggested bravura; but the first two things fit the sense of physical size he imparted and the personal magnetism; and the last two are less significant in themselves than indicating, in a greatly gifted man of gentleness and courtesy, the "required" intensity. What perhaps, in the man one knew, provided a resonant inner voice and an added dimension was Jim's religious nature, which ran very deep in him. His rage seemed a kind of denial of rancor — something heated and impassioned, not petty. He had magnanimity but not, I think, strength. There was something — though there is perhaps a better word — weak about him, partly owing perhaps to his physical endowments, which must have seemed inexhaustible, as must also have seemed his talents. The something weak was not something flabby but just not sufficiently firm. In the man, and from a desire to seize on all experience, it perhaps derived from a kind of scorn of something so middle class as willpower. In the writer, with gifts evocative of genius, there was seldom the exacting judgment and long-range control to produce a great work; what emerged were great passages. Jim had considerable control and judgment, but nothing to cope with the swell of language, the onrush of imagination in his writing; as well try to filter a waterfall. The filter and the file are what his work most needed. There was a much less costly element of this in Jim's talk. Now and then toward the end of a session I found myself bored from a sense of excess, repetitiousness, undirected intensity in what he said. Much of this is, of course, part of many legends; legends, as a matter of fact, don't grow up around men of logical thought and disciplined action. Nor can one be both religious and rational by nature or in one's encounter with life both immensely responsive and restrained. Each way of life sets *faults* in opposition as well, and Jim's way had no touch of expediency, calculation, self-serving forethought.

For *FYI*, Time's in-house publication, Louis Kronenberger wrote the following memorial:

> You did not need to know Jim Agee personally to grasp how marvelously special he was. His signature was upon everything he wrote, whether critical or creative, books or movies, prose or

poetry. There was a richness and, in the words of Keats, a "fine excess" about it; an imagination furnished out with miraculously right words. In his movie criticism there are countless examples of Jim's ability to penetrate, encompass, and above all enlarge his subject. In his creative writing there are passages that — quite simply — it took genius to write, but that not even genius could have written without an accompanying largeness of heart and mind.

But those who did personally know Jim knew what was incalculably greater. I don't mean only the charm, the humor, the sweetness, the passionate aliveness. He was one of the very few — they are really painfully few — men of great gifts who are even more distinguished as human beings. Jim saved nothing of himself for his writing — all the sympathy, generosity, nobility of feeling that beat through his words shone equally in his actions. He lived his gifts, and if this was at a certain cost in concrete achievement, living them as he did was a far rarer achievement. No one else I can think of absorbed so much from all he encountered — or released so much in encountering it. No one else I ever knew so quickly got the point or sensed the purport of what you were saying: with Jim, you almost literally never needed to finish a sentence. As for his place here, he was *Time's* finest writer and will remain one of its most beautiful memories.

T. S. Matthews

Agee at *Time*

If you've played tennis all your life, you can get a pretty fair idea of a man's character after half a dozen sets of singles with him. By the same token, you can get to know a man by working alongside him. Perhaps you don't know him as well as if you had often sat up all night drinking together or as if you were both survivors in the same open boat after a disaster at sea; all the same, if you work with a man you will read him — not like a book, perhaps, but at least like its chapter headings.

It was by working with Agee on *Time* that I got to know him. We had a few friends in common; I remember seeing him at a Greenwich Village party; and once I paid him a visit when he was in the hospital after an operation — for appendicitis, I think. But most of our meetings took place at the office and were strictly business: he was a *Time* writer (mainly of cinema reviews) and I was his editor.

There was no one at all like Agee on the *Time* staff, although there were some others who were also out of the ordinary and who behaved as if they had a special license. Agee's office mate, Whittaker Chambers, was one of these. Physically and temperamentally they could not have been more unlike, and politically they were at right angles, but they shared a preference for working at night, and this habit led first to a mutually tolerant acquaintance and then to a warm friendship.

Many years later, recalling those days, and with Agee and Chambers (and one or two others) in mind, I tried to characterize these difficult individuals — difficult, that is to say, from a managing editor's point of view. I wrote:

> I learned to value the steady man, the slogger, the writer who got his copy in on time and did what he said he would. If it had not been for him and his kind, we should never have got to press. I often thanked God for him. But my real Te Deums were reserved for the uncertain performance of his unsteady brother. There were never more than three or four (out of fifty-odd) of this breed on the staff, and I suppose that was about as many as we could safely carry. In many cases, they were "hard to work with" — touchy, suspicious, arrogant, unpredictable. Their working habits were spectacularly individual. When they worked, they often worked all night, then disappeared for indeterminate periods. They were not only subject to temperamental tantrums but prey to fits of despair, and they had absolutely no feeling about going to press, one way or the other. They sometimes missed the target completely or failed to pull the trigger. But when they did make a hit, it was often a bull's-eye. They were regarded by the rest of the staff with mingled contempt and awe. I loved and cherished them. They were the seagreen incorruptibles who acknowledged no authority but some inner light of their own. These rarities were in journalism but never altogether of it. They gave their editors more trouble than anybody, but they made the whole undertaking worthwhile.

I had two episodes in mind as I wrote of Agee the journalist. Once, on his own hook, after a week of working late nights, he stayed up all night and completely rewrote a "cover story," a long review of

Olivier's film of *Hamlet*, because he thought I was a little disappointed in his original version. And I was, a little: it was well above *Time*'s standard but not quite up to Agee's. Nevertheless a respectable piece of work, and he was so late getting it in that there was no time to make more than minor changes. All I could do about his revised version was thank him and try to explain that there simply wasn't time now to get the story retyped, let alone set.

When people tell me about *"Time* style" or assert that *Time* has always written in some form of pidgin English, I remember Agee and the editorial he wrote on the atomic bomb just after we had dropped it on Nagasaki and Hiroshima. "When the bomb split open the universe and revealed the prospect of the infinitely extraordinary, it also revealed the oldest, simplest, commonest, most neglected and most important of facts: that each man is eternally and above all else responsible for his soul and, in the terrible words of the Psalmist, that no man may deliver his brother, nor make agreement unto God for him."

I have to say that though I admired and respected Agee, he does not play the hero's part in all the scenes I remember: not all are good and some are ambiguous. When he came to see me about a leave of absence I urged him to cut loose and resign, telling him that if he had to come back to *Time* he could always be sure of getting his job again. I hoped he would go off to some quiet spot and write whatever he felt he had to write. Instead he did a couple of pieces for *Life* and then went to Hollywood to work with John Huston, of all halfway people.

I knew or suspected that he had a violent temper; all the same, it was a shock when I picked up my office telephone one night and by some accident of crossed wires overheard Agee, his voice thick with drink and anger, cursing the telephone operator as if he hated and despised her. And I learned with an equal shock, this time of relief, that his knocking down a girl at a *Time* party was an accident: I was afraid that it had been an act of drunken rage.

And there were questions to which I never knew an adequate answer: why did he leave so much of his own work unfinished, partly finished, or not even begun? Why, after quitting *Time* — and none too soon — did he waste his substance on Hollywood movies? Why didn't he get his teeth fixed and smoke and drink less; did he *want* his life cut short?

But all such questions and doubts are of no account in the light of what he saw, what he was, and what he tried to do. He saw something sacred in the hopeless poor. He was "human": that is to say, contradictory and unworthy of himself. By the seriousness of his intention, a seriousness that pervades his writing as veins and arteries branch through a body, he makes us feel like the liars we are.

Perhaps he was torn apart by all the different things he was or might have been: an intellectual, a poet, a cineaste, a revolutionary, God's fool. A wild yearning violence beat in his blood, certainly, and just as certainly the steadier pulse of a saint. He wanted to destroy with his own hands everything in the world, including himself, that was shoddy, false, and despicable; and to worship God, who made all things.

SCOTT BATES

Agee on Film

This is a checklist, a rapid run-through, of Agee's preferences in regard to film. You are going to see *Open City* tonight, a watershed in film, one of the most important films to hit America, especially at the time it did, right after World War II. It hit Agee very hard, and he wrote a good deal about it in the *Nation*, the periodical that he wrote for as a film critic. To understand his reaction to the film and the importance that he attached to the film, I think that you really have to understand the main lines of Agee's criticism—what were his main interests and preferences, what kinds of things did he like in films, and what did he hope that films could do.

I made up a checklist of his preferences out of about five hundred films that he reviewed. I am going to talk a little about each one and see if we can work out some kind of pattern in his film criticism— his main lines, what he liked, his ideas, his aesthetics. This is a problem I set for myself and I set it for you. I hope you can work it out with me, because up to this point, the usual statement on Agee's film criticism is that it is more or less formless. It's impressionistic. He likes what he likes, and he doesn't like what he doesn't like, and it's variable.

I have written down here the films that he particularly liked before the thirties — that is, the twenties films for the most part and even before that: Chaplin two-reelers, that is to say, the shorts, and *City Lights*, the full-length film, which came out in 1928; some of the films you saw last night — Mack Sennett comedies, Griffith's *The Birth of a Nation*; Keaton two-reelers, too — the best things that Keaton did, like *The Haunted House* and the full-length feature *The Navigator*. Agee also liked *The General*, which some of you may have seen, about the Civil War train. Then he liked the great Russian films, the Communist directors, Eisenstein, particularly *Potemkin*, which is the marvelous film history of the failed 1905 Proletariat Revolution in Russia; Pudovkin's *Mother*, a picture of a strike that failed to be put down by the capitalists in Russia; Von Stroheim's *Greed*, which he mentioned many times and which particularly appealed to him. It's about grim naturalist greed in this country — little people fighting for money and turning into jealous, bitter people. And Murnau, the famous *Last Laugh*, about a hotel doorman — a little person who gets too old to handle the big trunk and gets demoted to an attendant in the washroom. It seems like a very small plot, and it is. But it is made into a very great picture, and Agee often referred to it as such.

In the thirties, the films he preferred above all else were Chaplin's *Modern Times*; Dovzhenko, another Communist director, and his *Frontier*, a film made in the mid-thirties; and then Jean Vigo's *Zero de Conduite*, about which I'll say something later.

We have now a few references to movies in the letters to Father Flye. The first one that I could find was this one. "Did you ever happen to see any of the Silly Symphonies by Walt Disney? On the whole, they are very beautiful, a sort of combination of Mozart, super-ballet, and La Fontaine." That was in 1934, about when three Silly Symphonies, in color, had been produced. You may know one of them. One was *The Grasshopper and the Ant* — all set to music with no dialogue, an animated cartoon. *Flowers and Trees* was probably the first one and the most musical. And the one about three little domestic animals and a wild savage animal who was hunting them down, *Three Little Pigs*. Agee praised these films at this time; he probably wasn't aware of the larger allegorical significance of, at least, the last film, *Three Little Pigs*, which soon became in the thirties a kind of escapist moral lesson for keeping the wolf away from the door by hard work and courage. "Who's Afraid of the Big Bad Wolf" became a theme song in the thirties, at the time of the Great Depression, for holding your head up and fighting it through.

Later on in the decade, he turned against Disney. He felt that the cartoons had become cruel, and this is important in Agee's regard for animals, in his regard for innocence — animal innocence as well as human innocence. The last film script that he wrote about in his last letter to Father Flye is about animals and about their corruption by mankind. The film is about animals and it is about music. Perhaps he got his love for both here at St. Andrew's, or partly, perhaps, but I'd like to check this out. He was here for four years and couldn't see any movies here, as the theater wasn't opened in Sewanee until 1929. I don't think there were movies shown here, but I may be mistaken.

A Death in the Family, for those of you who read it, begins with a description of a Chaplin movie which he saw with his father. It must have been when he was very young. His father died when he was six. Perhaps his separation from movies here and his enjoyment of movies with his father created a special interest in this.

He could see movies when he went to college at Harvard in Boston. Agee became a film buff after he left here, one of the greatest of our time. His next reference to Father Flye is the new Charlie Chaplin, *Modern Times*, in 1936. "If it comes and if it doesn't conflict with Lenten rule, it's a wonderful thing to see, a lot, to me, as if Beethoven were living now and had completed another symphony." Here's an analogy to music again, to Beethoven. I suspect he got, here too, a great love for music, also a need to communicate this interest and to get other people interested in the things that he was interested in, to sell his taste — which he became superbly good at. So he is trying to sell *Modern Times*, and he'll do that with Chaplin all his life. He'll push Chaplin as hard as he can, and we'll see at the end of his critical career that he's pushing *Monsieur Verdoux*, a late Chaplin, very highly still.

The next reference I have here is from Robert Fitzgerald, his college friend who describes himself as going with Jim to see many movies in the thirties: *The Informer, Man of Aran, The Blue Angel, Grand*

Illusion, and so forth. These were the most talked about films among the intellectuals of the thirties. These were the films that were labeled as "the ones to see." The ones that seemed to go farther than the usual Hollywood trash of the time. And the films that really got involved with simple people, as in *Man of Aran*, a documentary on Irish peasants living a very grim life on the coast; *The Informer*, a story of the Irish Revolution; either *Grand Illusion* or *Mayerling*, a story about little men caught in war, and here a sympathy not only with (this is World War I) the French about whom it was made but with a German captor — those who captured the French; *The Blue Angel*, a German film that introduced Marlene Dietrich; *Mädchen in Uniform*, significantly, a movie about an all-girls' school and the difficulties of the adjustments between the girls and some of the tyrannical teachers. He recommended, in his letters to Father Flye, films about that pupil-teacher relationship: *Good-bye, Mr. Chips*; *Mädchen in Uniform*; *On Borrowed Time*, which is about a little boy and an elderly man who is dying — perhaps his father shows up in this one; later on, *A Cage of Nightingales*, again a pupil-teacher film about a progressive teacher in a reform school; and *Farrebique*, a French equivalent, you might say, of *Let Us Now Praise Famous Men* — in other words, a film about tenant farmers and their year. It's a very naturalistic, very realistic account, a documentary of what it's like to be a farmer. You really have the smells, almost the taste of the farm: the manure, a birth, a death — everything that goes on in this very natural environment, a very primitive and a very poor environment. So you can see why he would like this film, certainly, after having written *Let Us Now Praise Famous Men*.

In the forties, he became an actual journalistic critic for the *Nation* and for *Time*, and he started turning out regular weekly reviews for these periodicals. Many critics have pointed out that this was a particularly unfortunate time for Agee to be a film critic. Never have American films slumped so low as in the first five years of the forties. There were really bad films at this time, and he had very little to choose from. Of course, the war was going on, there was no money, and there were a lot of propaganda films of all kinds. In 1941, the one film he really seemed to like was W. C. Fields's *Never Give a Sucker an Even Break*. He liked Fields all the way through the thirties. He felt the best Fields films were *The Bank Dick*, made in the late thirties, and *It's a Gift*, an earlier film. He especially liked Fields's more or less rebellious stand against everything that is held dear by classical American taste: mother, children, family, sobriety, and so on.

In 1942, he started at the *Nation* at the end of the year, so we don't have a chance to see what he thought of other films during the year, but in any case, he says, without question, Chaplin in *The Gold Rush* is the best film of 1942. It was made in 1925, and it goes along with the silent-comedy type.

In 1943, the best film he chose for that year was *Desert Victory*. It is still a very fine film. It is a documentary about the British Expeditionary Force in Africa, the hunting down of the Desert Fox, Rommel, Hitler's best general. It's a brilliant film describing this war. The runner-up was another documentary, *The Battle of Russia*, one of the "Why We Fight" films that was shown to men in the service to give them the idea of what they were doing overseas. This one is in favor of Russia, one of our major allies at the time, a very patriotic film in the Russian sense, as well as in the American sense, for the great battle that the Russians were putting up against the Germans on the Russian Front. This picture, incidentally, was suppressed after the war by Joe McCarthy because it was so pro-Russian. It was not released by the government until the mid-fifties.

Other films that he praised — and he always criticized at the same time — were *Mission to Moscow*, which he liked because of the Russian-American relations, and *The Ox-Bow Incident*, an intellectual film about a lynching, which he found a little bit too arty still — a very grim film in which the wrong man gets lynched. So negative a film in the sense of the usual Hollywood "happy ending" when something usually happens at the last minute. It was touted by intellectuals as a very different kind of film, a new kind of film that dared to say the truth. Agee found that they were artificially daring to tell the truth, that they were too self-conscious about it; therefore, it did not tell the truth as much as it pretended to. *Bataan* was a movie about fighting in the South Pacific; *Casablanca*, a very famous film about spying in the war — well, actually the nonwar, the outer war region of North Africa — with Humphrey Bogart and Ingrid Bergman; and *Watch on the Rhine*, a very militant, anti-Nazi film from the play by Lillian Hellman, which he liked with reservations. He thought it was a little stagy. He strongly criticized the anti-Nazi film *The Moon Is*

Down; the Steinbeck novel made into a film, *Shadow of a Doubt.* He's not always too kind with the Hitchcock films. He finds that they are often a little bit too shallow, pretentious, and uninteresting. Bogart in *Sahara* was another film about North Africa, fighting in the African Desert, and he also found it stagy and artificial and phony.

In 1944, the best film for him was a nineteen-minute documentary, *The Marines at Tarawa,* which he felt really gave you the feeling of the fighting. This is important. He wanted the audience to get involved with what they were a long way away from. This kind of "film truth," what they now call *cinema verité,* was very important to him — to get as much across as possible. Now, you can check back with certain things in *Let Us Now Praise Famous Men,* particularly his beginning of that work when he talks about the importance of the camera. I have a short quote: "[T]he camera seems to me, next to unassisted and weaponless consciousness, the central instrument of our time." This is a very strong statement when you think that he could have mentioned a pen, for example, as a central instrument, the one that he was using. Of course, *Let Us Now Praise Famous Men* works with a still camera, not a movie camera, but he says some interesting things about it, which I think I should quote at this point, because it shows what he expects out of film. He says: "For in the immediate world, everything is to be discerned, for him who can discern it, and centrally and simply, without either dissection into science, or digestion into art, but with the whole of consciousness, seeking to perceive it as it stands: so that the aspect of a street in sunlight can roar in the heart of itself as a symphony, perhaps as no symphony can: and all of consciousness is shifted from the imagined, the revisive, to the effort to perceive simply the cruel radiance of what is."

The camera is an absolute documentary recorder of what is! Get it in the full feeling, the full texture, a "You Are There" kind of feeling. That's what he wanted. "This is why the camera seems to me . . . the central instrument of our time," he goes on. You have a feeling that what he is wanting to do with these documentaries is hoping that they will do that — give you the feeling that you are there on the front and that you will experience the war as much as you can in your theater seat.

His runners-up that year were four other documentaries: *Memphis Belle, Underground Report, Attack: The Invasion of New Britain,* and

The Battle for the Marianas. At this point now, Agee has come to the point where it is not enough to put you there. You have to explain why you are there. He becomes interested in communication — the way in which the recording is done, rather than just sending the camera down, letting it take a picture, and getting the results; in other words, a kind of editing, still with the documentary, working with the camera, instead of letting it tell the whole story. That year he found the best fictional film to be the horror film by Val Lewton, whom he always admired, *The Curse of the Cat People*, an unpretentious B movie, rather well made, unlike some of the more pretentious films that he criticized, like *Lifeboat*; *Wilson*, an attempt by Hollywood to make a serious film biography (They really thought they were doing it; this was a film by Darryl Zanuck. They said, if this one fails, we'll never make another film. It really did fail intellectually, but it had a fairly good success commercially); *Winged Victory*; *Air Corps*; *Keys of the Kingdom*, a propaganda film taken from the novel of the same name about a missionary in China.

He praised, with reservations, Odets's *None but the Lonely Heart*, a film that Cary Grant insisted on making about a poor boy and his mother, who is played very well by Ethel Barrymore; *Miracle of Morgan Creek* and *Hail the Conquering Heroes*, two folk comedies by Preston Sturges, a very good creative director of American comedies; *Phantom Lady* by Hitchcock, which he didn't like too much; and *Cover Girl*, a musical with Rita Hayworth . . . he didn't like the American musicals. *To Have and Have Not*, another *Casablanca* brought up to date, with Lauren Bacall and Humphrey Bogart, not at all Hemingway, even though it was based on the Hemingway story or novel; *Meet Me in St. Louis*; and *National Velvet*, Elizabeth Taylor's first movie, made when she was about twelve with Mickey Rooney — a movie about a horse race and a very exciting movie. I saw it in the army, and it had the GI audience on its feet at the end. It's well done and still holds up.

So that year, again, the documentaries were the most important. These other films were good. They were certainly the best films of the year. If you go through all the films produced that year, you find that these are the only ones that stand out at all. The other hundreds of films turned out by Hollywood were JUNK!

In 1945, he picked as the best *GI Joe*. Here the war is ending, and you have the feeling he was looking all the way through the war for a film that was really good about the GI, one that was accurate and truthful, that really showed him not glamorized as all Americans tend to glamorize their war heroes but as he was, as in *Up Front with Mauldin*, for example, a cartoon. He felt that this succeeded. The runner-up, and it's surprising that he didn't pick this first, was John Huston's *San Pietro*, a half-hour documentary by a major director, taken in Italy of the action that he was engaged in and taken right up in the front. It's a very powerful documentary because, again, you have a feeling that you are there.

Now he began to worry about being there, about experiencing those things that you are not a part of physically. Is it right, he wonders, for you to belong to a scene where people are suffering and dying when you're sitting there comfortably chewing popcorn? How much right do you have to see that film? And I think he asked that about the film that you will see tonight, *Open City*, which is a film taken right after the Allied victory in Rome, about the suffering and dying of Italian resistance leaders against the Nazis and which is taken right from the resistance leader's notebook. When he made the film, Rossellini talked to the resistance leaders. They found one who told them what happened, and they filmed it there on the spot with people who had seen such action, in the atmosphere and feel of the situation. That's what you are going to see tonight. You're going to be there, right after the war. Is this really sacrilegious to enjoy watching them suffer? How much right do you have to be there? So this is the question of film truth that you can discuss after you have seen the film. For the same reason, he disliked the atrocity films that were shown after the Allies captured Dachau, the concentration camps — horrible films of the cadavers, inmates, half of them dead or dying, and used at this time to stir up hatred against the Germans and settle for a hard peace. He felt that they were used for propaganda, and he was against these "vengeful" films, as he called them.

That year appeared Renoir's *The Southerner*, which he was very interested in because it was about tenant farmers in the South, but he said that it was all wrong. It was a good try, but they didn't really get the feeling of the situation, the atmosphere, the emphasis on hard, miserable work, and so forth. But at least they tried. Graham Greene's *Confidential Agent* he liked, a story about the Spanish Civil War, about the Republican side of that war. *The Last Chance*, a European film about refugees from Nazism, and *Goupi Mains Rouges*, a film about French peasants. He disliked *The Picture of Dorian Gray*, which he thought was dead, phony. *Spellbound* was a phony intrusion into psychoanalysis with a Dali type of decor, which he said looked like a Bergman window in New York. And it's true. It does.

In 1946 — here we come to *Open City*. Now this is very shortly after the end of the war. It's the first major European film he's seen in a long time — *The Last Chance* was a good one, but not a major one — and he was overwhelmed, no doubt, by this film. You can read between the lines. He had to take a couple of weeks to think about it before he could write about it in the *Nation*. His review is very carefully thought out. Therefore, I hope that all of you will read that review after you see the film tonight. Get your own ideas about it; be sure you know what's going on and why you think what's going on should go on, and so forth, and what's wrong about it. Then compare it with what Agee said.

After having a general idea of the kind of films he does like, the kind of things he wants to see in film, you'll be able to appreciate his criticism better. He said, "By all odds, the best film of the year." He said this again at the end of the year when he'd seen everything else. "It goes far in the best general direction movies might take now and in the discernible future," and that's absolutely correct. The movies have taken this direction since *Open City*, a film that was made outside the studio, in the streets, with the people who were involved, with little people who were involved who became great actors. Actually, Anna Magnani, the greatest actress of the film, was a professional actress at this time, but she was not well known. He immediately picked her out and described how great she was in his review. It's a passionately felt and intimately understood picture. And although, as he admitted, it was Communist propaganda — it has a Communist point of view in it — that's great, he says. It lets us understand what the Communists are thinking and doing and how they participate.

The runners-up that year were *Henry V*, the Olivier production; *The Best Years of Our Lives*, a picture of Hollywood production, but rather well done, about returning GIs and their letdown after three or four years of risking their lives and coming back to the home front and their disorientation, their lack of a base to start off from; *Brief Encounter*, a romantic Noël Coward movie, but very carefully and realistically done; and *The Raider*, a British picture, a semi-documentary.

In 1947, running rather quickly past *Open City*, he praised highly Jean Vigo's *Zero de Conduite*, which had been put out by the son of an anarchist in 1932, whose father had been killed by the police. He was a young anarchist who was rather bitter about the police and about society. He was dying. He died very young, at twenty-eight — after having made two masterpieces, *Zero de Conduite* and *L'Ata-lante*, both of which Agee liked very much. Now, here we are again, with a teacher-pupil relationship. Here we have a small boarding school, not private, a public school, but a boarding school in France, with the old structure of the rather conservative rigorous system, and we have a revolution. The kids rise up and revolt against their teachers. It's about education with an anarchistic plot. In a film that some of you may have seen [*If*], it was imitated, and the imitation was not as good as the original. Yes, *If*, another picture about the boys with the machine guns and mowing down the teachers at the convocation service at the end. A very violent picture, but not as good, not as well done. I wish Agee were around to comment on it. And then the other film that he really liked this year was Chaplin's *Monsieur Verdoux*, the film that "did Chaplin in" in this country because it was suppressed with unofficial censorship by the film theater owners. They refused to show it. It was attacked by the Catholic League of Decency as immoral. It was attacked by critics as being a failure, as being not a very funny film, and certainly an immoral one.

Well, Agee picked up his lance and really went to war for this film. He wrote three long articles in the *Nation* defending it against the syndicate and the American public, fighting for Chaplin, his hero with whom he identified perhaps more than anyone else in film, and the man about whom he wrote to Father Flye who was equal to Beethoven. Well, he fought for *Monsieur Verdoux*, which is the story of a rather eloquent Frenchman who has a beautiful wife and child and who marries rich widows and kills them for their money to support his wife and child — an interesting plot. Agee finds this an allegory of the American human condition, the world human condition, the upright citizen, who does do unfortunate acts for good reasons: "The wrong things for the right reasons." Chaplin works this out magnificently. Agee goes into this at great length, and it's a fascinating review. Incidentally, Chaplin left the country in a huff around this time because of this and other things; he was not appreciated by Americans, and his coming back this year was a tremendous event in modern film history.

Runners-up that year were *Shoeshine; L'Atalante*, another realistic Italian film like *Open City; To Live in Peace*, an Italian film pushing for the peace of all mankind; *Man's Hope*, a film made during the Spanish Revolution of the thirties from the Republican side by André Malraux, who also wrote a book that very much influenced Agee in the thirties, *Man's Fate*, again, a pro-Communist work about the battle against Chiang Kai-shek and his troops by the Chinese revolutionaries; *The Fugitive*, a biography about a crusading priest; *Boomerang*, a crime film; and *Beauty and the Beast* by Cocteau.

In 1948, he's back with John Huston, whom he began to see as the great film producer/director in America. *The Treasure of the Sierra Madre* he found the best film of that year; *Day of Wrath*, another film he had to fight for, by the Danish producer Carl Dryer, an apocalyptic film about a witch-hunt in the seventeenth century; and *Farrebique*, a film about peasants, which he recommended to Father Flye.

This will give you, then, a quick survey of the kind of films he liked, what he wanted to see, films that he had most hoped for, and the fulfilling of the dream of the great American art form — the movie. He believed in the movie. He liked a lot of bad movies, probably because he saw what they could have been. He saw what they tried to be and did not succeed in being, and he had his own ideas of what he thought the movie should contain.

And what are these ideas? That is the question. What pattern do you find in this general run-through? These are the great films on anybody's list. You look through those ten years, and you can't find better films than these. Yet Agee's reasons for liking them may be a little bit different and odd. What does *Open City* have that these films have, too? Let's see if you find any patterns in films that Agee is really fighting for.

AUDIENCE: He liked films about the character outside society — Chaplin, the tenant farmers.

BATES: Yes, the outsider, the little kid kicked around by society.

AUDIENCE: He also couldn't stand the propaganda films.

BATES: Yes, the typical black-and-white type of film he couldn't buy — German planes come screeching over the horizon, and the

American planes mow them down. There's not one of those films on his list.

AUDIENCE: He didn't seem to like Bogart that much. So why did he write for Bogart in *The African Queen?*

BATES: Do you want to answer that question?

AUDIENCE: I don't think he said he didn't like Bogart, because he also praised *The Treasure of the Sierra Madre* and *Sahara.*

BATES: Yes, *Sahara* he didn't like much, but *Sierra Madre* he loved. Also, he liked *To Have and Have Not.* He said it was simple-minded of him to like it, but he liked the rough-tough, obviously hokey but poor guy and beautiful doll type. He saw what Bogart could do in *Sierra Madre* and presumably, if he had any favorites, he approved of Bogart acting in *The African Queen.* What other things? What about respectability? He showed in *Monsieur Verdoux* how the family situation fell apart because it was dependent on murder and dependent on a false ideal of innocence, keeping them separate from things that count, keeping his wife and child separate. It would have been better if they had been poor and going through things together. Perhaps Agee was thinking of his own life a little bit. How about his subjects? How about *Zero de Conduite,* innocents in that sense? Those who hadn't had a chance to be corrupted by society yet. The elephants in his last film script. Innocence always attracted him, in animals, children, tenant farmers — a kind of horrible innocence because they didn't have a chance.

AUDIENCE: Why did he like foreign films?

BATES: Good question. Because they didn't have the old Hollywood one-two, the studio's phony commercialism of the thirties. This film tonight is not studio-made. At that time it was really something to be out in the streets of Rome. We're used to films made on location now, but at that time it was a rarity. In Europe, they didn't have any money for studios, and they didn't have the facilities for producing a movie inside. So they had to go in the streets because they didn't have any sets. This was a realism forced on the foreign film.

AUDIENCE: Would you say Agee was one of the first in his reviews in the *Nation* and elsewhere to take film seriously as an art form?

BATES: He took them so seriously that he felt they were the major art form of our century. Seeing the potential in film, he had such a brilliant mind that he saw what film could be, and this is what destroyed him really — the thought that all his time, energy, and effort and all his brains were going into something that was garbage. And so he wanted it to be great, and he said, "This is . . . why in turn I feel such rage at its misuse: which has spread so nearly universal a corruption of sight that I know of less than a dozen alive whose eyes I can trust even so much as my own." He felt that the camera had not begun to be used with its full potential. He pushed a lot of bad films because he wanted to encourage people to keep on making films, even though they did not succeed that time.

EDWIN M. STIRLING

Open City Panel

I am going to address myself to Agee's film criticism this morning. James Agee, in his film criticism, has again and again called himself an "amateur." I am falling back on some of the things that Agee accused himself of doing, falling back on what is called subjective criticism or "I just know this is a good movie and let me tell you why." I also have no critical standard, no kind of criterion to present to you. He's been called a "descriptive" critic and by this, I suppose, his strength is in his capacity to point out the elements within the film that compose its form, its shape.

I think that's why he liked John Huston so much. You're going to see a John Huston film, *The African Queen*, and certainly one major strength in John Huston is content. His moral point of view has been objected to by many, some in this very community, but I think that Agee finds in Huston this strength of content. What I thought I'd do is lay out what I feel are the major critical standards operating in

Agee's criticism and then apply them to *Open City*, the film that you saw last night.

Dr. Bates, I believe, yesterday spoke of Agee's faith in the camera. We see him saying this directly in *Let Us Now Praise Famous Men*. For Agee, the camera could be as truthful as the most accurate scientific instrument. It could demonstrate truth in its most absolute form when properly used. In this sense, he's a unique critic for his time. Again and again, one sees James Agee referring to camera work in a film, praising it, suggesting the importance and centrality of the camera as being the major aesthetic aspect of the film.

I think Agee called himself a critic or became a critic for two major reasons: first, I would suggest that he is absolutely disgusted with what is coming out of Hollywood in the late thirties and particularly disgusted by his sense that there are so many critics in the public press praising what is little more than pure trash. And so he senses, at least on one level, his role as a critic to offset those who would blindly praise the films coming out of Hollywood in the late thirties and early forties.

But more important, I think Agee sensed that the film, more than any other art medium, had the capacity to be available to all men. Unlike the poem, and to a degree unlike the novel or the play, more people in contemporary society could come into contact with the film. Thus, he saw its importance as being a kind of democratic art medium, an art medium for the people. Therefore, he demanded that film be a proper record of the people, that it be truth to the people, that it be responsible, not just to an intellectual and artistic elite, a special group who are especially qualified to understand and enjoy the art object. It goes far beyond that for James Agee. I think that Agee demanded that the film demonstrate reality, be truthful to what it sees. He does praise films that have a kind of fantasy quality about them. But more commonly he praises the film that seems to be true to things as they really are. One finds him, again and again, praising the documentary, particularly the documentaries of John Huston. One finds him praising Walker Evans in *Let Us Now Praise Famous Men* for his camera work, because of its truth, because it demonstrates this reality. It is interesting that a man who was so much a part of the world of words — a poet, a novelist, and a critic — would place such faith in the film for its capacity to communicate this reality. The film, for Agee, I believe, was "the word made flesh," made real. He also had a strong, abiding faith in the film as an art medium capable of competing with the best of novels, with the best of poems, and with the best of plays. He says in one essay, "Hold up, in any given period, the best plays, the best novels, and the best poems with the best films, and you'll find that the films can compete and in many cases are superior to those other art forms."

Even so, he could be very demanding. He did not accept the Hollywood pronouncement that someday in the future a great film would be made. For James Agee, that was the "infinite number of monkeys on the infinite number of typewriters" argument. That simply would not work. The thing that Agee demanded again and again was, "Let's have great films now." Dr. Bates placed great store yesterday in Agee's belief that the film must involve the viewer in something that he is otherwise unlikely to participate in. Agee praised documentaries, and specifically those pertaining to the Second World War. He felt, at least in the first portion of his critical career, that men ought to be exposed to the suffering of war, the pain of war of the deprived Europeans who were in many ways the most poignant victims of war, and that Americans had to have the experience and knowledge firsthand, and that film provided that function. Yet he also said that the film must be true to the experience that it tries to communicate.

He hated "super patriotic" films. There was a very famous film and one that I am embarrassed to say that I liked myself, a film entitled *Purple Heart*, in which American air force pilots are shot down over Tokyo in a raid. They are captured by the Japanese and endure incredible suffering, but emerge from this as the absolute essence of American patriotism. Darryl Zanuck produced that film. Agee hated it. He hated it because it was not true to the experience. Men do break, you see, under torture. *Open City*, to a degree, demonstrates that.

Finally, it seems such a stock notion today, but Agee placed great faith in the director. It was not the actor, not the music, not the way that the film was edited. It was the director who was the most important figure in the making of the film. He's the God of the film. He's the deity. He's the creator, the shaper. If you've read any of Agee's letters to Father Flye, again and again he's coming back to the great directors in those letters, explaining why they are great directors. For Agee, I think, there were very great directors: the Russian film maker

Sergei Eisenstein, the great early American filmmaker D. W. Griffith, and John Huston. Obviously, his friendship with John Huston had something to do with his love of Huston's films. But I think Agee is right, that a very strong Huston is the early Huston.

Let me turn to Agee's essay on *Open City* for a moment and try to summarize it for you and suggest where I think Agee is right and where perhaps he's wrong, and try to give you some kind of alternative viewpoint on Agee's essay. If you have read the essay, you will recall that Agee finds both a strength and a weakness in *Open City* in terms of its usage of both the leftists, that is, the political resistance figures, and the Christians, particularly the priests. And he is slightly disturbed in that essay because he detects a kind of contradiction between the two, between the leftists and the Christians. Agee is clearly sympathetic to both points of view. He's not sure of the success of the fusion of the leftists and the Christians. But obvious to me is the fact that the priest is a figure that has real meaning for us today, is the Berrigan figure. He becomes, because of the circumstances he finds himself in, a political priest, and he finds himself forced to affirm the tenets of his belief in a real political situation, and Agee finds some success in the presentation of that priest. He feels, too, and I agree with him on this, that there is a real superficiality about the film, that there is not depth in character in any one of the major figures of that film, and I think that Agee is right.

Even so, he harkens back to what he says we must demand in film. *Open City* is immediate, and it involves us in a reality that we would not otherwise be able to be involved in. It involves us in a situation, a terribly desperate and despairing situation: the occupation of a city by forces who are not the inhabitants of that city—the brutal and cruel occupation of that city. And many people just accept it. Many people just give in to it. But some have the strength and the heroism to resist it, to fight against it. And here Agee, I think, suggests in the essay that we must be aware of that kind of strength in the human spirit. There are fine moments in that film. I think that Agee begins to suggest in his essay that the depravity and the corruption one finds particularly among the Germans and their allies suggest something within the human spirit that must be resisted and resisted heroically. These are not heroes from literature of the past. These are all common people. The pregnant mother and her son and a priest and men who would probably be tailors or cobblers if this situation were not upon them. They rise heroically against this horrible situation. Agee finds a real strength in the film director's capacity and ability to capture the normal qualities of these people, the common qualities of these people.

He later calls *Open City* the best film of 1946. I think, here too, there are reasons why. He found himself in such a wasteland in modern film that he was absolutely refreshed and overwhelmed, astonished by the strength, in contrast to the normal offerings of Hollywood. Also, I think he finds a strength in the truth of its presentation, of its creation. Sets weren't built for that film. The film was shot out in the city itself. And he speaks of the importance of turning to this way of making films. There is a truth there, too, as much as there is a truth in the characters involved in that city. If I may embellish a bit now on what I think he is saying, and I obviously put some interpretations on what he is saying, I would say that there is no hero or central character in *Open City*. The hero is the city itself—the city of Rome. We find it to be as brutal and terrifying as much as we find it to be tender and enduring. It can be perverted, but it can also be tremendously heroic.

The technique of the film interests me to some degree. I don't really know how to talk about technique. I've never had any formal training in filmmaking, and in a sense what I'm doing right now is probably the most pretentious thing you'll hear all week. But even so, I find a real beauty in the contrast between the adults and the children in that film, a real strength. If you'll remember, usually those instances pertaining to the adults are vividly presented. You think of the killing of the mother, a vivid close-up. You think of the coming of the Germans to the tenement house, very sharply photographed. You think of the torture of that resistance leader, done with daring close-ups again. All the gore is there for you to see — all the blood, all the cuts, all the pain in that man's face. And you think, finally, what a terribly disturbing moment, the execution of the priest at the end. You have a close-up of that priest's face — first when they don't shoot him and then when he's killed.

This is to be contrasted with the children. All their activity is usually very fuzzy. Do you really know what they did, for example, that night when they went out and blew up something—a train, I guess, or a warehouse? But we don't really get any idea of what occurs. All we get is the idea that these are terrified children—they come back and they huddle together, and there are anxious parents about—that they are ultimately children in the face of even such heroic action as the demolition of whatever it was that they blew up. So I see an interesting technique in the kind of hazy way that the children are treated and the clarity of image with which the adults are treated.

Something else that interests me in this film is the crippled boy. In a sense, he's an ironic figure; that is, on the surface he is crippled. Ultimately, we discover in the film that it is the Germans who are crippled because of their brutality. There are some Italians who accept what the Germans are doing, even to the extent of betraying their friends, their families. And so he becomes an ironic figure, very curious, and I think an important touch in the film.

Finally, there is a triumph of innocence. The children will clearly continue, but they are innocent, even in their continuation of their task. I would bring this back to James Agee. I think one of the very significant aspects of James Agee's art is his belief in, and affirmation of, innocence. Not just the films he praises, like *Open City*, but think about the film he made. You're going to see *The African Queen*.

One of my favorites is a film called *The Night of the Hunter*, an incredible film. I'd forgotten how wonderful that film is, how beautifully photographed. There again is a kind of adult world versus children: Robert Mitchum with the "love and hate" tattooed on his fingers, and probably the most memorable scene of that film is the children as they float down the river and the obvious crosscutting. By that I mean taking a section of film and applying it to another section of film, crosscutting the children with animals, back and forth, suggesting how closely identified children are with small creatures, how closely identified with rabbits and small creatures they are in this world. And, of course, they emerge victorious. Robert Mitchum doesn't get what he wants.

I would argue that, in *The African Queen*, the theme of innocence comes up in both the missionary figure and in old Humphrey Bogart and an innocence in a world not of their making. They didn't cause this war. They are caught up in it, and they emerge victorious over it largely because of their innocence and their strength and heroism. One sees that in *Open City*.

Participants:

Charles Angermeyer

Arthur Ben Chitty

Father Martin

The African Queen Panel

Father Martin: The purpose of this particular panel is to hear a couple of persons who have some special background on *The African Queen* and to get some of their ideas about it, to point out some of the good or even some of the weak points of the movie, and then to have questions from the floor. On my far left, we have Dr. Arthur Ben Chitty, who is the director of public relations and historiographer at the University of the South. And the gentleman on my left, I think, needs no introduction — our inimitable graduate of St. Andrew's School and director of our school movie, Charles Angermeyer, Class of 1961. So without further introduction, I will turn the panel discussion over to Dr. Chitty and let him begin with the analysis of *The African Queen.*

Chitty: Thank you very much, Father Martin. It is a pleasure to be here. He did not exaggerate when he said that *The African Queen* was a great favorite among movies for me. Of course, it was produced twenty-one years ago, and it was based on a novel written, oddly enough, the year I graduated from college at Sewanee, 1935. So this is not a brand-new thing on the American literary scene. As you know, the author of this novel is C. S. Forester, who died in 1966. He was born in 1899, so if he were living today, he would be seventy-three. He is an English novelist whose most famous works are the *Hornblower* series. He also wrote several other novels, most of them with a kind of military background: *The Gun* in 1933, *The General* in 1936, *A Ship of the Line* in 1939, and *The Commodore* in 1944. He wrote one play produced in 1934, *Nurse Cavell*, and he certainly deserves a considerable place in English literature.

I want to take a rather extreme position, perhaps, and say that I believe a movie script and a TV script deserve almost a separate category in literature. It may be that they are almost a new form of literature, although, of course, there is not a great deal of difference between the development of a movie script and a TV script and the development of a play, for instance. I believe that the poem is the most concentrated kind of literature, the most intensive, the most tightly focused. But certainly, in my opinion, next to the poem, the play (and I include the television script and the movie script) constitutes an extremely tight kind of literature. It might serve a purpose to say that play reading or script reading is a very efficient way of reading. Absorb an entire plot in a few pages in less time by reading the plot in the form of the play, rather than, for instance, in the form of a historical novel, which might run six hundred, eight hundred pages. I don't bring that home as a virtue for either the play or the historical novel. The matter of length or efficiency is merely a point.

Now, somewhere, after plays began to be produced, someone discovered that plays could be read profitably as well as be seen. And there are many people who read plays in preference to novels, and I think the same would be true of scripts. Reading this script, I'm impressed with the enormous technical knowledge that is required of the writer. Agee's description of *The African Queen* is highly technical. He has to know a lot about boats . . . this little river boat. He has to know a great deal about what the camera will do and what it won't do. His descriptions, his directions to the cameraman and to the director of the movie must be very detailed. Let's get the flavor of what this extremely skilled writer is able to do in considering a description of what the director has to interpret for the viewer. You see, he has to be aware of color. Then he has to be aware of what the camera will do. He has to describe for the director what he wants in the way of sound.

I am sorry to say that I didn't read the novel *The African Queen* to prepare for this. I would be interested to know how much humor, which was so obvious in the film, originally appeared in the novel, and how much of it was put in by James Agee.

ANGERMEYER: I'm going to take this strictly from the point of view of film. I don't know if any of you have seen the films of the French director François Truffaut, but he wrote an essay saying that film has nothing to do with literature. I am not trying to deny the importance of scripts or anything else, but I happen to think that films have a life of their own and that Agee is one of the most skilled writers in putting film into words that there ever has been. However, I think the experience of the film is different than reading the film.

CHITTY: I fully agree. I really do. These are two separate entities. This script is absolutely worth reading if you never thought you would ever see the film. And the film is absolutely worth seeing if you never thought you were going to read the script. I think that they are two separate forms, and both qualify wonderfully when they are this well done.

ANGERMEYER: Dr. Chitty is probably more familiar with the screenplay and the literary aspects; however, those distinctions become blurred as we talk about it. I haven't read the whole novel, but I read about the first fifty pages. It's very interesting to see the differences between the novel and the script and between the script and the actual shooting of the movie. The novel starts off with the brother being dead right away. We see Rose caught in this dilemma from the very beginning. In the film script, I believe, his death is delayed. In the film script, there is a description of the congregation singing, a rather detailed description. The actual film itself doesn't match the script.

What I'm trying to do is add the second element, saying not only does the film script not resemble the novel but the film itself doesn't follow the film script. And the reason for this is because the final decisions on making the film are made in the editing process, not in the scripting process. Even though Agee's scripts were very detailed, I personally think Huston's influence is tremendous. In the novel itself, there is no description of the scene with the cigar, which I think is an important point to see how he felt at the time he wrote it. Knowing where he was, how he felt, what anguish he had, what pain and what joy. I could appreciate what words he was choosing to tell me about it. It was at that point that the words began to mean something to me. I began to understand why they were arranged the way they were on the page. These were the only words he could find to catch that energy he had. Actually, this isn't the way that it works at all. The only reason that your eye is caught by anything in life is that you feel completely about something at the time. Your mind grasps and catches this energy that's been released in you. Actually, that's what poetry really is. It's energy captured in certain key words, which will express that original meaning. This energy may be free emotion, great feelings, great anguish, and so on.

AUDIENCE: Could you give an example of this energy in film?

ANGERMEYER: Something that happens to the brother — he gets hit in the mouth. Now that's something that film can do that you can't do in any other art form. You can almost feel that, can't you? Just wham! The only point that I'm trying to make is that the very nature of the medium of film makes it possible to do things that you cannot do in literature. And, going back to my original point, that is why a director like Truffaut will say that film has nothing to do with literature.

CHITTY: Most interesting. A very fine point. I'd like to take that up. You mentioned the delay of the death in the movie. Now, would someone like to hazard a guess as to why they changed that sequence from the novel to the movie, and why the death was delayed? We're talking about why the death of the brother hasn't already happened when the movie opens. The brother dies after the movie has gone on a bit. Now, would you like to say something on that?

ANGERMEYER: I think they show more than action when the brother dies. Do you remember the image in your mind when the brother dies in the film? Do you see him when he falls down? Then what? He comes in and she helps put him in the bed. Now, isn't that a shot? We get a close-up of her face there. And, traditionally, the contribution of the close-up shot in the film is made to communicate thought. Well, the difference is, in the film, it's not as explicit. It's left up to the audience to infer what she is thinking. For me the movie is much better than the novel because you can participate in the movie, whereas in the novel it is spelled out for you. That's just my idea.

CHITTY: Yes, it certainly introduced a strong motivation for her. Now, I want to ask a question. What in the movie was least believable? What in the movie was hardest for you to think really would work?

AUDIENCE: [Unintelligible]

CHITTY: The miracles by which they were floated out. You just didn't see how that boat could have survived that. That's asking a lot of credulity, alright.

But let's go back to what we were talking about a moment ago about the death scene. It seems to me that what happened before the death, in other words, showing this woman in that situation that she was in — out in the jungle alone with her brother — conveys an enormous amount of determination and capability and versatility. You remember the scene when she pays no attention to the horrible looking insect. She brushes the thing off. You know, this is a woman —

ANGERMEYER: That's an example of what is in the script but not in the film.

CHITTY: I beg your pardon. I thought it was in the film. But anyway, here is a woman who shows in the early part of the play what a very competent individual she is and how, when she finally does take command of the ship, you are not really surprised. I wasn't. I thought it prepared the way for her to take command.

ANGERMEYER: I would like to ask you what was most believable about the movie.

AUDIENCE: [Unintelligible]

ANGERMEYER: She is saying that people appeal to each other because they have the traits that the other person doesn't have. Can you give me an example, specifically, of where that takes place? I can think of one. She said that when he's drinking, what's he drinking? He's drinking gin. What's she drinking? Tea. She was shocked when he came in out of the rain. Okay. Now, what happened after she threw away all of his gin? How did he react to that?

AUDIENCE: [Unintelligible]

ANGERMEYER: What did he do ultimately, though? He shaved, didn't he? In other words, he took on some of her qualities. He even made a little speech about her, how it's nice to have a woman around to make him get cleaned up. On the other hand, what's the example of where she took on his characteristics? She was outspoken. What's the most obvious thing that she does that she'd never done before? She steers the boat. She helps push the boat with the poles. She goes under the water. She becomes another Alnot, in a way. The reason I bring this up is that my point of view on the film is . . . the boat itself is their relationship. And it's only through the adjustments that they make in the situation . . . it's like two people falling in love. Eventually, if they are going to stay in love, they have to take on respect for the other person's differences and at least tolerate them, if not participate in them. Because it's the boat that brings them together. And at the end of the film, you no longer need the boat. They are married.

CHITTY: What are the chances for happiness for that couple? Anybody like to make a statement on that? What are the chances that they really would make it now because everything that's happened has been under these highly specialized circumstances?

ANGERMEYER: I'd like to read a couple of statements about it, since it came up here. I took some notes during the film when they go through the rapids. I can make a little sexual analogy. What is it for her, or what is going through the first rapids like? She says it's the most stimulating physical experience she's ever had. Okay. I will say that there are many statements in the film where they use the boat to talk about their relationship. For example, he says, "Shall we drop the anchor, sweetheart? I'll let the anchor out. It will keep us out of trouble." There is a general usage of the boat, I believe, as a metaphor for their relationship: it goes through rapids, it goes through calms, it gets lodged in marshes, it's tested by nature, it's tested by man, and in the end it survives.

CHITTY: In other words, back on land, we think they might not get along very well. You're agreeing?

ANGERMEYER: Don't you think they were in love? You're not convinced? In all of the discussion, I didn't get my question answered. I wanted to know what you found most realistic in the film. This might help us out. I think we're getting around to this issue of what was believable. Very British. Just like the Union Jack. You're saying that the hatred for the Germans was most believable. The impact of the tropics. Right! I'd like to have a report for that myself. What are the implications you speak of? You're saying the willing suspension of disbelief? That's a nice phrase. You put that in your essays to Father Martin and you might get an A. Is that right? I think for me what makes the movie powerful and one of the greatest movies I have ever seen is the fact that the typical situation itself does require this willing suspension of disbelief.

FATHER MARTIN: Another thing along that line is what has come up again and again and that is, in Agee's mind, the triumph of innocence over all kinds of obstacles, including the most amazing kinds of difficulties and coincidences and everything else. And yet, in the end, in spite of all the evil and all the tragedy and all the frightening experiences, innocence does triumph.

IV

Fiction

DWIGHT MACDONALD

Jim Agee, A Memoir

In the twenties, James Agee and I both attended Phillips Exeter Academy, which then had an extraordinary English department:
Myron Williams, E. S. W. Kerr, Hank Couse, Dr. Cushwa, James
Plaisted "Cokey Joe" Webber, to set down the names of those who
taught us something about writing. Jim and I just missed each other
at Exeter, I graduating in the spring of 1924 and he arriving there
in the fall of 1925. I find I wrote an old Exeter friend, Dinsmore
Wheeler, in 1929, apropos of a project for starting an intellectual
community on his farm in Ohio: "Our generation is one of great
power, I think. There's talent running around like loose quicksilver.
A fellow named Jim Agee, onetime editor of the P.E.A. *Monthly*, has

The Stuff. I've never met him but I've corresponded with him. He is all there when it comes to creative writing, or rather *will be* all there."

Agee was then at Harvard and I on *Fortune*, and we kept on corresponding, mostly about movies, which interested us as a form of self-expression much more than writing did. "A fellow in my dormitory," he wrote me that year, "owns a movie camera (not the kind you set buzzing and jam into the diaphragm) and has done some interesting work with it. . . . It's possible we'll do two movies [a documentary on Boston and a film version of a short story he had written]. The idea is that I'll devise shots, angles, camera work, etc., and stories; he'll take care of the photography and lighting." (Like my own dream of an Ohio Brook Farm, neither of these projects seems to have come to anything.) We both admired the standard things — Griffith, Chaplin, Stroheim, the Russians, the Germans — despised the big American productions ("*Noah's Ark* is the worst and most pretentious movie ever made," he wrote), and looked desperately for signs of life in Hollywood: "Saw a movie today, *Hearts in Dixie* was its unfortunate title. The thing itself struck me as pretty swell [though] there was no camera work and very little else to recommend it from the real director's point of view." His enthusiasm seems to have been based mostly on the fact it was less melodramatic than *Porgy*. Similarly, his "Ever noticed Dorothy Mackaill? Along the general lines of Esther Ralston" was intended as a compliment. We really were hopeful then. "I'm going to spend the summer working in the wheat fields, starting in Oklahoma in June," he wrote May 10, 1929. "The thing looks good in every way. I like to get drunk and will; I like to sing and learn dirty songs and hobo ones — and will; I like to be on my own — the farther from home the better — and will; and I like the heterogeneous gang that moves north on the job. . . . Also I like bumming. . . . Finally, I like saving money, and this promises from $5 to $7 a day." That summer I got a pencil-scrawled note dated "Oshkosh, Neb., maybe August 1" (the postmark is August 5):

Dear Dwight —
    If pen and ink and white paper gave you trouble, this should rival the Rosetta stone. To add insult to injury, it's written in a wagon-bed — about my only chance to write is between loads.
    Am now working at hauling and scooping grain on a "combine" crew. . . . Kansas is the most utterly lousy state I've ever

seen. Hot as hell and trees ten miles apart. I worked near a town which proudly bore the name "Glade" because of a clump of scrawny, dusty little trees it had somehow managed to assemble.

The first town across the Nebraska line was so different I declared a holiday, sat on a bench in the courthouse park and wrote a story. I rather think I've stumbled onto the best possible surroundings and state of mind in which to write. I certainly was more at home with it than at Harvard, home or Exeter.

That night I saw a rather interesting movie, *The Leathernecks*. . . . It seems to me Richard Arlen is capable of pretty big stuff. I wish someone would give Von Sternberg a story for him. . . . Have to tackle a load now.

Jim

An extract from another letter, written in 1936, may be of interest:

It seems to me, comrades, that *New Masses* readers should treat Dostoevsky kindly yet strictly. There are inexcusable gaps and deviations in his ideology and they must not be condoned; on the other hand, we must not on their account make an enemy of a man who has come far and who may turn out to be inestimably useful to the Movement. (signed) Granville Hicks. I think *The Brothers Karamazov* deserves the co-operation of all the finest talents in Hollywood and wd. richly repay all research & expenditure. A fullsized replica, complete down to the last tpmizznmst, of the Mad Tsar Pierre (Charles Laughton). Papa Karamazov (Lionel Barrymore). His comic servant Grigory (Wallace Berry). Grigory's wife (Zasu Pitts). Smerdyakov (Charles Laughton). Smerdyakov's Familiar, a cat named Tabitha (Elsa Lanchester, the bride of Frankenstein). Zossima (Henry B. Walthall). . . . Miusov (Malcolm Cowley) . . . in Alyosha's Dream: Alyosha (Fred Astaire). Puck (Wallace Berry). Titania (Ginger Rogers or James Cagney). . . . Routines by Albertina Rasch. Artificial snow by Jean Cocteau. . . . Entire production supervised by Hugh Walpole. . . . To be played on the world's first Globular Screen, opening at the Hippodrome the night before *Jumbo* closes. Mr. Dostoevsky will be unable to appear at the opening but Charles A. Lindbergh has agreed to be on hand (you may recognize him by the smoked glasses & unassuming manner) and a troupe of selected ushers will throw epileptic fits during the intermission (courtesy Max Jacobs). Margaret Anglin will sell signed copies of Countee Cullen's *Medea* in the lobby. President Roosevelt will plant a tree. The Italian Expeditionary Force will observe two minutes silence in honor of the birth of the little Christ child. Artificial foreskins will be handed out at the north end of the Wilhelmstrasse to anyone who is fool enough to call for them. The film will be preceded by *Glimpses of the New Russia*, photographed by M. Bourkeovitz [Margaret Bourke-White who, after her marriage to Erskine Caldwell, no foe of the Soviets, did do some such book of photographs, as I recall]. . . . Suggested tie-ins for hinterland exhibitors: arrange to have your theatre picketed by your local chapters of the American Legion, the Catholic Church, the Parent-Teachers Association, the Sheetmetal Workers Union and the Youth for Peace Movement. Set up Jungle Shrubbery and a stuffed Gorilla in your lobby (your Police Station will be glad to furnish latter in return for a mention). If you are in the South, stage Negro Baptism (in white gowns) in front of your theatre. If in North, an Italian Saint's Day or a Jewish Funeral will do as well. Plug this feature hard. It will richly repay you.

Until I came to transcribe this, I had not realized how tasteless it is, calculated to offend the sensibilities of every right-thinking and wrong-thinking group in the country, minority or majority. It goes beyond buffoonery to express a nihilistic, destructive, irreverent, vulgar, alienated, un-American, and generally lousy attitude. And why drag in the Sheetmetal Workers Union? And if the union, why the cops? There is something very old-fashioned about the whole thing, more like 1926 than 1936 — and certainly not at all like 1962.

One of the unexpected things about Agee — and there were many, he was what used to be called "an original" — is that he was able to think in general terms without making a fool of himself, therein differing from most American creative writers of this century. This may have been because of his education or, more likely, because he had a gift that way. (He had so many gifts, including such odd ones, for intellectuals, as reverence and feeling.) Considering his hell-for-leather personality, Agee was a remarkably sophisticated, even circumspect, thinker. "Was just reading in *New Masses* Isidore Schneider welcoming Archie into the new pew," he wrote me in 1936.[1] "Still have my ways of believing in artforart and, more especially, of conviction. Marx — Marx plus Freud for that matter — isn't the answer to everything." Then he adds, with his typical balance, the last quality one would expect if one merely saw his picturesque side. "But just because Copernicus didn't settle all the problems of the universe is no reason at all to go on insisting that the sun moves around the earth and comes out a little southwest of purgatory." Jim was always moderate in an immoderate way, he was always out of step, and he had very little respect for the Zeitgeist. This was his tragedy and his triumph.

In his last letter to Father Flye, written a day or two before he died, Agee sketches out a fantasy about elephants — how they have been degraded by man from the most intelligent and the noblest of beasts to figures of fun. He felt he was dying and this was his last, most extraordinary insight. For wasn't this just what happened to him? Wasn't he also a large, powerful being who was put to base uses? The same note is struck in his fine parable, "A Mother's Tale" — also written toward the end of his life — in which a mother cow tells her children and nephews and nieces a strange tale that has come down through the generations about the ultimate fate of their kind. I venture that here too Agee was thinking of himself when he wrote about the slaughter of one species for the benefit of another. The cattle have their own life and purpose, as he did, and they are used by more powerful beings for a different purpose, as he was. This, at least, is how I imagine he may have thought, or rather felt (for it may not have been wholly conscious), about it in his last years. It was emotionally true for him and was also true in general. But looking at it more coldly, one must say something more. While Time, Inc., has in common with the Chicago packing houses one important thing — that its purpose is to convert something living, namely talent, into a salable commodity — it is not really an abattoir because those who, like Agee or myself, took its paychecks did so, unlike the cattle, of our own free will. The great question is, as Lenin once remarked of politics, who uses whom (I think he had a more pungent verb in the original Russian). It is possible to use instead of being used: Faulkner wrote Hollywood scripts for years. But Agee didn't have this kind of toughness and shrewdness. He was, in a way, too big and too variously talented.

There is something helpless about elephants precisely because of

their combination of size and intelligence; it is a fact they can be tamed and trained as few wild animals can. It's not the fault of the tamers. Henry Luce was a decent fellow when Jim and I worked for him on *Fortune*, and I'm sure Luce was, like me, charmed and impressed by Agee. But what a waste, what pathetic docility, what illusions![2] As late as 1945, after thirteen years with Time, Inc., Agee can still write to Father Flye that he has now been offered a job of "free-lance writing through all parts of the magazine," and this not in despair but hopefully. As if for a writer to be given the run of *Time* were not like a collector of sculpture being offered his pick of wax figures from Madame Tussaud's Museum. He was always looking for a way out — in 1932, his first year on *Fortune*, he is wondering whether he shouldn't try for a Guggenheim grant; two years later he is asking

Father Flye about the chances for a teaching job at St. Andrew's, etc. — but he also was always full of innocent, elephantine hope.

In his perceptive introduction to the letters, Robert Phelps states that Jim got his job on *Fortune* because they were impressed by "an ingenious parody of *Time*" he had put out when he was editing the *Harvard Advocate*. I wish this were the whole story, but I remember in 1932 recommending Jim, then looking for a postgraduation job, to Ralph Ingersoll, then managing editor of *Fortune*, where I'd been working since my graduation from Yale. And I've dug up a letter from Jim which is almost unbearable in dramatic irony, the audience knowing how it is going to turn out: "Noted contents of your letter with eyes rolling upward and stomach downward with joy, relief, gratitude and such things. I shall send a wire in the morning to beat this letter down. . . . I don't want to miss any chances of losing this chance (for which thank you, God, and Managing Editor Inger-soll). . . . Words fail me re. the job: besides the fairly fundamental fact that I don't want to starve, there are dozens of other reasons I want *uh* job and many more why I am delighted to get this one."

But I didn't do him a favor, really.

2

James Agee's *A Death in the Family* is an odd book to be written by a serious writer in this country and century, for it is about death (not violence) and love (not sex). Death is conceived of in a most un-American way, not so much a catastrophe for the victim as a mystery, and at the same time an illumination, for the survivors. As for love, it is not sexual, not even romantic; it is domestic — between husband, wife, children, aunts, uncles, grandparents. This love is described tenderly, not in the tough, now-it-can-be-told style dominant in our fiction since Dreiser. The negative aspects are not passed over — Agee is, after all, a serious writer — but what he dwells on, what he "celebrates," is the positive affection that Tolstoy presented in "Family Happiness" but that now is usually dealt with in the women's magazines. Very odd.

There are other original features. We are used to novels that de-scribe the professional and regional background more fully than the human beings, but here there is no "local color," and we are not even told what the father's occupation is. We are used to novels about "plain people" that are garnished with humanitarian rhetoric and a condescending little-man-what-now? pathos, as in *The Grapes of Wrath* and such exercises in liberal right-mindedness. But Agee felt himself so deeply and simply part of the world of his characters — the fact that they were his own family by no means explains this empathy — that he wrote about them as naturally as Mark Twain wrote about the people of Hannibal. The 1915 Tennessee vernacular sounds just right, not overdone yet pungent: "'Well,' he said, taking out his watch. 'Good Lord a mercy!' He showed her. Three-forty-one. 'I didn't think it was hardly three. . . . Well, no more dawdling. . . . All right, Mary. I hate to go, but — can't be avoided.'" The last sentence, in rhythm and word choice, seems to me perfect. We are used, finally, to novels of action, novels of analysis, and novels that combine the two, but not to a work that is static, sometimes lyrical and sometimes meditative but always drawn from sensibility rather than from intellection. It reminds me most of Sherwood Anderson, another sport in twentieth-century American letters — brooding, tenderminded, and a craftsman of words.

James Agee died in 1955 at the age of forty-five. He died of a heart attack in a taxicab, and the platitudes about "shock" and "loss" suddenly became real. A friend I had for thirty years respected intellectually and sympathized with emotionally and disapproved of temperamentally and been stimulated by conversationally had vanished, abruptly and for good. I had always thought of Agee as the most broadly gifted writer of my generation, the one who, if anyone, might someday do major work. He didn't do it, or not much of it, but I am not the only one who expected he would. He really shouldn't have died, I kept thinking, and now this posthumous book makes me think it all the harder.

The book jacket is, for once, accurate when it describes Agee as "essentially a poet." For this is really not a novel but a long poem on themes from childhood and family life. The focal point is the death, in an automobile accident, of Jay Follet, a young husband and father who lived in Knoxville around the time of the First World War. This is about all that "happens." There are other episodes grouped around the death, and they are often vividly rendered, in novelistic terms, but there is no plot, no suspense, no development, and thus no novel. The point of view is mostly that of Jay's six-year-old son, Rufus, who is in fact James Agee, who is writing about his actual childhood and about the actual death of his father. Even those parts that are not told directly in terms of Rufus Agee's experience are affected by this viewpoint. The father and mother, although they are major figures, are barely individualized, since to a small child his parents are too close to be distinctly seen. The more distant and lesser figures, like Aunt Hannah, are more definite. Parents are big, vague archetypes to a child (Strength, Love, or — alas — Coldness, Failure), but aunts are people. In this child-centered structure, at least, *A Death in the Family* is in the American grain. (Why are our writers so much more at home with children than with adults?) Many of the best things are connected with Rufus: his delight over his new cap, his comic and appalling relations with his little sister, his nightmares ("*and darkness, smiling, leaned ever more intimately inward upon him, laid open the huge, ragged mouth*"), his innocent trust in the older boys, who tease and humiliate him with subtle cruelty. These parts of it can be recommended as an antidote to *Penrod*.

Agee was a very good writer. He had the poet's eye for detail. "Ahead, Asylum Avenue lay bleak beneath its lamps. . . . In a closed drug store stood Venus de Milo, her golden body laced in elastic straps. The stained glass of the L&N Depot smoldered like an exhausted butterfly . . . an outcrop of limestone like a great bundle of dirty laundry. . . . Deep in the valley an engine coughed and browsed." He could get magic into his writing the hardest way, by precise description:

> *First an insane noise of violence in the nozzle, then the still irregular sound of adjustment, then the smoothing into steadiness and a pitch as accurately tuned to the size and style of stream as any violin . . . the short still arch of the separate big drops, silent as a held breath, and the only noise the flattering noise on leaves and the slapped grass at the fall of each big drop. That, and the intense hiss with the intense stream; that, and that same intensity not growing less but growing more quiet and delicate with the turn of the nozzle, up to that extreme tender whisper when the water was just a wide bell of film.*

I haven't watered a lawn in forty years, but I remember that was the way it was in Sea Girt, New Jersey. And this was the way trolley cars were:

*A street car raising its iron moan; stopping, belling and starting;
stertorous; rousing and raising again its iron increasing moan and
swimming its gold windows and straw seats on past and
past and past, the bleak spark crackling and cursing above it
like a small malignant spirit set to dog its tracks; the iron whine
rises on rising speed; still risen, faints; halts; the faint stinging
bell; rises again, still fainter, fainting, lifting, lifts, faints forgone:
forgotten.*

These passages are from "Knoxville: Summer 1915," which appeared in *Partisan Review* twenty years ago; the publishers have had
the good idea of reprinting it as a prelude to A *Death in the Family.*
*"We are talking now of summer evenings in Knoxville, Tennessee, in
the time that I lived there so successfully disguised to myself as a child,"*
he begins, and he concludes, *"After a little I am taken in and put to
bed. Sleep, soft smiling, draws me unto her: and those receive me, who
quietly treat me, as one familiar and well-beloved in that home: but
will not, oh, will not, not now, not ever; but will not ever tell me who I
am."* In between are five pages of reverie, lyrical and yet precise,
about the after-dinner time when families sit around on porches and
the fathers water the lawns. "Knoxville" is typical of Agee's prose: in
the weighty authority with which words are selected and placed; in
getting drama, as Dickens and Gogol did, out of description; in the
cadenced, repetitive, sometimes biblical rhythm; in the keyed-up
emotion that teeters on the verge of sentimentality ("soft smiling"
falls in, and "unto" comes too close for comfort); in the combination,
usual only in writers of the first rank, of acute sensuousness with
broad philosophical themes.

Although A *Death in the Family* is not a major work, Agee, I think,
had the technical, the intellectual, and the moral equipment to do
major writing. By *moral,* which has a terribly old-fashioned ring, I
mean that Agee believed in and — what is rarer — was interested in
good and evil. Lots of writers are fascinated by evil and write copiously about it, but they are bored by virtue; this not only limits their
scope but prevents a satisfactory account of evil, which can no more
be comprehended apart from good than light can be comprehended
apart from darkness. Jay Follet is a good husband and father, Mary is
a good wife and mother, and their goodness is expressed in concrete

action, as is the evil in the boys who humiliate their son or the lack of "character" Jay's brother, Ralph, shows in a family crisis. (Character is another old-fashioned quality that interested Agee.) The theme is the confrontation of love, which I take to be life carried to its highest possible reach, and death, as the negation of life and yet a necessary part of it.

Admittedly, the book has its longueurs, and very long longueurs they are sometimes, but for the most part it is wonderfully alive. For besides his technical skill, his originality and integrity of vision, Agee had a humorous eye for human behavior. The nuances of the husband-and-wife relationship come out in a series of everyday actions: Mary peppering the eggs to Jay's taste; Jay straightening up the covers of the bed ("She'll be glad of that, he thought, very well pleased with the looks of it"); Mary insisting on getting up at three in the morning to cook breakfast for her husband, and his mixed reaction: "He liked night lunchrooms, and had not been in one since Rufus was born. He was very faintly disappointed. But still more, he was warmed by the simplicity with which she got up for him, thoroughly awake." The bondage and the binding of marriage are both there. This is realism, but of a higher order than we have become accustomed to, since it includes those positive aspects of human relations which are so difficult to describe today without appearing sentimental. The uneasiness the Victorians felt in the presence of the base we feel in the presence of the noble. It is to Agee's credit that he didn't feel uneasy.

This livelier, more novelistic side of Agee appears in such episodes as the scene in which Aunt Hannah takes Rufus shopping for his first cap (up to then he had been allowed only babyish *hats*):

> He submitted so painfully a conservative a choice, the first time, that she smelled the fear and hypocrisy behind it, and said carefully, "That is very nice, but suppose we look at some more, first." She saw the genteel dark serge, with the all but invisible visor, which she was sure would please Mary most, but she doubted whether she would speak of it; and once Rufus felt that she really meant not to interfere, his tastes surprised her. He tried still to be careful, more out of courtesy, she felt, than meeching, but it was clear to her that his heart was set on a thunderous fleecy check in jade green, canary yellow, black and white, which stuck out inches to either side above his ears and had a great scoop of visor beneath which his face was all but lost. It was a cap, she reflected, which even a colored sport might think a little loud, and she was painfully tempted to interfere. Mary would have conniption fits. . . . But she was switched if she was going to boss him! "That's very nice," she said as little drily as she could manage. "But think about it, Rufus. You'll be wearing it a long time, you know, with all sorts of clothes." But it was impossible for him to think about anything except the cap; he could even imagine how tough it was going to look after it had been kicked around a little. "You're very sure you like it," Aunt Hannah said.
>
> "Oh, yes," said Rufus.

"Better than this one?" Hannah indicated the discreet serge.

"Oh, yes," said Rufus, scarcely hearing her.

"Or this one?" she said, holding up a sharp little checker-board.

"I think I like it best of all," Rufus said.

"Very well, you shall have it," said Aunt Hannah, turning to the cool clerk.

Agee was a very American writer, and this passage, in its humor, its sensitivity to boyhood, its directness of approach, and its use of the rhythms and idioms of everyday speech, seems to me to be in the peculiarly American tradition of Twain and Anderson.

A Death in the Family should be read slowly. It is easy to become impatient, for the movement is circular, ruminative, unhurried. He dwells on things, runs on and on and on. Perhaps one *should* be impatient. What Agee needed was a sympathetically severe editor who would prune him as Maxwell Perkins pruned Thomas Wolfe, whom Agee resembled in temperament, though I think he was superior artistically. A better comparison is with Whitman, who also runs on and on, hypnotizing himself with his material, losing all sense of proportion, losing all sense of anyone else reading him, and simply chanting, in bardic simplicity, to himself. Like Whitman and unlike Wolfe, Agee was able at last to come down hard on The Point and roll it up into a magically intense formulation; the weariest river of Ageean prose winds somewhere safely to sea. After pages of excessive, obsessive chewing-over of a funeral, including a morbid detailing of the corpse's appearance and several prayers in full, Agee comes down, hard and accurate, to earth and to art: "[Rufus] looked towards his father's face and, seeing the blue-dented chin thrust upward, and the way the flesh was sunken behind the bones of the jaw, first recognized in its specific weight the word, *dead*. He looked quickly away, and solemn wonder tolled in him like the shuddering of a prodigious bell." Should one be impatient? I suspect one should. Granted the preceding longueurs were necessary for the writer if he were to work up enough steam for this climax, it doesn't follow that they are necessary for the reader. Would not a more conscious, self-disciplined writer have written them and then, when he had reached the final effect, have gone back and removed the scaffolding? It would have been interesting to see if Agee would have done this had he lived to give final form to A *Death in the Family*.

Agee was seldom able to tell when he was hitting it and when he wasn't. That he should have hit it so often is a sign of his talent. There are many passages in A *Death in the Family* that can only be called great, much though the word is abused these days, great in the union of major emotion with good writing.

In some literary circles, James Agee now excites the kind of emotion James Dean does in some nonliterary circles. There is already an Agee cult. This is partly because of the power of his writing and his lack of recognition — everyone likes to think he is onto a good thing the general public has not caught up with — but mainly because it is felt that Agee's life and personality, like Dean's, were at once a symbolic expression of our time and a tragic protest against it. It is felt that not their weakness but their vitality betrayed them. In their maimed careers and their wasteful deaths, the writer and the actor appeal to a resentment that intellectuals and teenagers alike feel about life in America, so smoothly prosperous, so deeply frustrating.

James Agee was born in Knoxville in 1909. He went to St. Andrew's School, then to Exeter and Harvard. In 1932, the year he graduated from Harvard, Agee got a job on *Fortune*. For fourteen years, like an elephant learning to deploy a parasol, Agee devoted his prodigious gifts to Lucean journalism. In 1939, he moved over to *Time*, where he wrote book reviews and then was put in charge of Cinema. In 1943, he began writing movie reviews for the *Nation*, too. He resigned from *Time* and the *Nation* in 1948, specifically to finish A *Death in the Family* but also because he realized that otherwise he would never get down to his own proper work. There was reason for his concern. Although he wrote constantly, in a small, shapely script that contrasted oddly with his oceanic personality, he finished very little; I remember grocery cartons full of manuscripts he had put aside. In 1948 he was thirty-nine, and he had published, aside from his journalism, only a book of poems, *Permit Me Voyage* (1934), and a long prose work, *Let Us Now Praise Famous Men* (1941).

In the seven years that were left to him, he did manage to bring A *Death in the Family* close to final form and to publish a novelette, *The Morning Watch* (1951), and a short story, "A Mother's Tale"

(*Harper's Bazaar*). But again most of his energies were diverted. For before he settled down to work in his old farmhouse in Hillsdale, New York, with his third wife, Mia, he had to get out of the way two profitable articles for *Life*, which he planned to knock out in six weeks and which took him six months. One was on silent-movie comedians; the second was on the films of John Huston. Agee had already, in 1947, written the commentary for one movie, *The Quiet One*, a documentary about Harlem life that was a great *succès d'estime*, but he had never worked in Hollywood. Huston liked his article and commissioned him to do a script for a film version of Stephen Crane's story "The Blue Hotel." Huston never made the film, but he was impressed by Agee's script (and by Agee) and asked him to do one for *The African Queen*. This is mostly just another movie, but it does have several Agee touches — the Anglican service with only shining black faces in the congregation, Bogart's stomach rumblings at the tea party, the peculiar horror of the leeches and the gnats. It was ironical, and typical, that Agee's work with Huston was limited to a conventional adventure-romance film. Before they met, Huston made *The Red Badge of Courage*, and later he wanted Agee to work on *Moby-Dick*, but Agee had an interfering commitment. So two jobs that would have given scope for his powers were lost by luck, or was it destiny? Whichever it was, it was rarely on his side.

After *The African Queen*, Agee did a number of other scripts — for *The Night of the Hunter*, which is realistic and at times macabre in a most un-Hollywoodian way; for a delightful short comedy, *The Bride Comes to Yellow Sky*, taken from a story by Crane in which he played the town drunk; for a film on the life of Gauguin (this, said to be his most remarkable script, was never used); for *Genghis Khan*, a Spanish-language Filipino film; for an *Omnibus* television series on the life of Lincoln; for a documentary about Williamsburg. Then he died.

Although he achieved much, it was a wasted, and wasteful, life. Even for a modern writer, he was extraordinarily self-destructive. He was always ready to sit up all night with anyone who happened to be around or to go out at midnight looking for someone: talking passionately, brilliantly, but too much, drinking too much, smoking too much, reading aloud too much, making love too much, and in general cultivating the worst set of work habits in Greenwich Village.

This is a large statement, but Agee's was a large personality. "I wish I knew how to work," he said to a friend. He wrote copiously, spending himself recklessly there, too, but there was too much else going on. He seemed to have almost no sense of self-preservation, allowing his versatility and creative energy to be exploited in a way that shrewder, cooler men of talent don't permit. His getting stuck for so long in the Luce organization is an instance; like Jacob, he drudged fourteen years in another man's fields, but there was no Rachel in view.

"Jim seemed to want to punish himself," another friend says. "He complicated his creative life so much that he was rarely able to come to simple fulfillment. He would put off work until he got far enough behind to feel satisfactorily burdened with guilt. Somehow he managed to turn even his virtues into weaknesses. Jim was bigger than life, had enormous energy—my God, the man was inexhaustible!

He reacted excessively to *everything*. The trouble was he couldn't say no. He let people invade him, all kinds, anyone who wanted to. He thought he had time and energy enough for them all. But he didn't, quite. His heart trouble began on Huston's ranch out West, when he was working with him on the script of *The African Queen*. Huston was in the habit of playing two or three sets of singles before break-fast — *he* was a prodigal live-it-upper, too; that was one reason they got on so well together — and Agee, who hadn't played in years and was out of condition, went at it with him every morning, trying for every shot, until he collapsed on the court with his first heart attack. The doctors told Jim to take it easy, to drink, smoke, and live moderately. But that was the one talent he didn't have."

The waste one senses in Agee's career had other roots as well. He was spectacularly born in the wrong time and place. He was too ver-satile, for one thing. In art as in industry, this is an age of specializa-tion. There is a definite if restricted "place" for poetry; there is even a Pulitzer Prize for it, and poets of far less capacity than Agee have made neat, firm little reputations. But his best poetry is written in prose and is buried in his three books. Nor was he solely dedicated to literature. Music was also important to him, and the cinema, so closely related to music, was his first love, and his last. I think he never gave up the dream of becoming a director, of expressing him-self directly with images and rhythm instead of making do at one remove with words. His best writing has a cinematic flow and im-mediacy; his worst has a desperate, clotted quality, as though he felt that nobody would "get" him and was trying to break through, irri-tatedly, by brute exaggeration and repetition. But he was typed as a writer, and the nearest he could come to making movies was to write scripts — scripts that go far beyond what is usual in the way of precise indications as to sequence of shots, camera angles, visual details (the raindrops on a leaf are described in one), and other matters normally decided by the director. They are the scripts of a frustrated director.

The times might have done better by Agee. They could exploit one or two of his gifts, but they couldn't use him *in toto* — there was too much there to fit into any one compartment. In another sense, American culture was not structured *enough* for Agee's special needs; it was overspecialized as to function but amorphous as to values. He needed definition, limitation, discipline, but he found no firm tradi-tion, no community of artists and intellectuals that would canalize his energies. One thinks of D. H. Lawrence, similar to Agee in his rebellious irrationalism, who was forced to define his own values and his own special kind of writing precisely because of the hard, clear, well-developed cultural tradition he reacted so strongly against.

If his native land offered Agee no tradition to corset his sprawling talents, no cultural community to moderate his eccentricities, it did provide "movements," political and aesthetic. Unfortunately, he couldn't sympathize with any of them. He was always unfashionable, not at all the thing for the post-Eliot thirties. His verse was rather conventional and romantic. In the foreword to *Permit Me Voyage*, Archibald MacLeish, than whom few have been more sensitive to literary fashions, accurately predicted, "It will not excite the new-generationers, left wing or right. . . . Agee does not assume . . . a Position." Ideologically, it was even worse. In an age that was enthusiastic about social issues, Agee's whole style of being was individualistic and antiscientific. He was quite aware of this; oddly, considering the constellation of his traits, he had a strong bent toward ideas. Unlike, say, Thomas Wolfe, he was an intellectual; it was another aspect of his versatility. This awareness comes out clearly in a passage from that extraordinary grab bag *Let Us Now Praise Famous Men:*

> "Description" is a word to suspect.
>
> Words cannot embody; they can only describe. But a certain kind of artist, whom we will distinguish from others as a poet rather than a prose writer, despises this fact about words or his medium, and continually brings words as near as he can to an illusion of embodiment. [Here the frustrated moviemaker speaks, for if words cannot embody, pictures can, and without illusion—a picture is an artistic fact in itself, unlike a word.] In doing so he accepts a falsehood but makes, of a sort in any case, better art. It seems very possibly true that art's superiority over science and over all other forms of human activity, and its inferiority to them, reside in the identical fact that art accepts the most dangerous and impossible of bargains and makes the best of it, becoming, as a result, both nearer the truth and farther from it than those things which, like science and scientific art, merely describe, and those things which, like human beings and their creations and the entire state of nature, merely are, the truth.

As MacLeish observed, Agee appealed neither to the Left nor to the Right. "I am a Communist by sympathy and conviction," he wrote in the thirties, and at once went on to put a tactless finger right on the sore point:

> But it does not appear (just for one thing) that Communists have recognized or in any case made anything serious of the sure fact that the persistence of what once was insufficiently described as Pride, a mortal sin, can quite as coldly and inevitably damage and wreck the human race as the most total power of "Greed" ever could: and that socially anyhow, the most dangerous form of pride is neither arrogance nor humility, but its mild, common denominator form, complacency. . . . Artists, for instance, should be capable of figuring the situation out to the degree that they would refuse the social eminence and the high pay they are given in Soviet Russia. The setting up of an aristocracy of superior workers is no good sign, either.

The idiom ("the sure fact . . . figuring the situation out . . . no good sign, either") and the rhythm are in the American vernacular and thus hopelessly out of key with the style in which everybody else wrote about these matters then. Nor was Agee any more congruous with the Right. Although he was deeply religious, he had his own kind of religion, one that included irreverence, blasphemy, obscenity, and even communism (of his own kind). By the late forties, a religio-conservative revival was under way, but Agee felt as out of place as ever. "If my shapeless comments can be of any interest or use," he characteristically began his contribution to a *Partisan Review* symposium on Religion and the Intellectuals, "it will be because the amateur and the amphibian should be represented in such a discussion. By amphibian I mean that I have a religious background and am 'pro-religious' — though not on the whole delighted by this so-called revival — but doubt that I will return to religion." Amateurs don't flourish in an age of specialization, or amphibians in a time when educated armies clash by night.

The incompatibility of Agee and his times came to a head in the sensational failure of Agee's masterpiece, *Let Us Now Praise Famous Men*. It is a miscellaneous book, as hard to classify as that earlier failure *Moby-Dick*, which it resembles, being written in a "big" style, drawing poetry from journalistic description, and making the largest statements about the human condition. It is mostly a documentary account of three southern tenant-farming families, illustrated with thirty-one magisterial photographs by Walker Evans, Agee's close friend, who is listed on the title page as coauthor and whose influence was strong on the text. But it is many other things as well — philosophy, narrative, satire, cultural history, and autobiography. It is a young man's book — exuberant, angry, tender, willful to the point of perversity, with the most amazing variations in quality; most of it is extremely good, some of it is as great prose as we have had since Hawthorne, and some of it is turgid, mawkish, overwritten. But the author gives himself wholly to his theme and brings to bear all his powers; he will go to any lengths to get it just right. From this emerges a truth that includes and goes beyond the truth about poverty and ignorance in sociological studies (and "realistic" novels), the truth that such squalid lives, imaginatively observed, are also touched with the poetry, the comedy, the drama of what is unexpected and unpredictable because it is living. It is illuminating to compare Agee's book with one of those New Deal surveys of "the sharecropping problem." It is also interesting to read a professional work on grade-school education and then to read Agee's twenty-seven pages of notes on the subject:

> Adults writing to or teaching children: in nearly every word within these textbooks, for instance [he has three devastating pages on one of them, which every writer for children should read], there is a flagrant mistake of some kind. The commonest is this: that they simplify their own ear, without nearly enough skepticism as to the accuracy of the simplification, and with virtually no intuition for the child or children; then write or teach to satisfy that ear; discredit the child who is not satisfied, and value the child who, by docile or innocent distortions of his intelligence, is.
>
> The "esthetic" is made hateful and is hated beyond all other kinds of "knowledge." It is false-beauty to begin with; it is taught by sick women or sicker men; it becomes identified with the worst kinds of femininity and effeminacy; it is made incomprehensible and suffocating to anyone of much natural honesty and vitality.

The book grew out of an assignment to Agee and Evans from *Fortune* in 1936 to do a story on southern sharecroppers. For two months they lived in the Alabama backcountry. *Fortune,* unsurprisingly, couldn't "use" the article. Harper then staked Agee to a year off the Luce payroll to write the book. When it was done, they couldn't use it either; they wanted deletions in the interests of good taste, and Agee refused; since the higher-ups weren't enthusiastic anyway about this strange, difficult work, Harper stood firm. Finally, Houghton Mifflin brought it out in 1941. The critics disliked it — Selden Rodman, Lionel Trilling, and George Marion O'Donnell were honorable exceptions — and it sold less than six hundred copies the first year. *Moby-Dick* sold five hundred, which was six times as good a showing, taking into account the increase of population.

The mischance that dogged Agee's career is evident in the timing of his death. Those who knew him best say that in the last few years of his life Agee changed greatly, became more mature, more aware of himself and of others, shrewder about his particular talents and problems. In the very last year, he had even begun to pay some attention to doctors' orders. He was by then getting such good fees for scripts that he was looking forward to doing only one a year and spending the rest of the time on his own writing. He might even have found out who he was. *A Death in the Family* contrasts significantly with *Let Us Now Praise Famous Men.* It rarely achieves the heights of the earlier book — I think Agee's literary reputation will be mostly based on about half of *Let Us Now Praise Famous Men* — but it is written in a more controlled and uniform style; it has more humor and none of the self-consciousness that often embarrasses one in the earlier work; its structure is classical, without Gothic excrescences; and, most significant of all, human beings are seen objectively, with the novelist's rather than the poet's eye. There is also the remarkable short story, "A Mother's Tale," he wrote three years before his death: a Kafka-like allegory, perfectly ordered and harmonious all through, of the human situation in this age of total war. I think only a thoroughly developed writer could have done it. Like Keats, Agee died just when he was beginning to mature as an artist. That Keats was twenty-five and Agee forty-five doesn't alter the point. Agee was an American, of a race that matures slowly, if ever.

"He was at his best just short of his excesses, and he tended in general to work out toward the dangerous edge. He was capable of realism . . . but essentially he was a poet. . . . He had an exorbitant appetite for violence, for cruelty, and for the Siamese twin of cruelty, a kind of obsessive tenderness which at its worst was all but nauseating. . . . In his no longer fashionable way, he remained capable, and inspired. He was merely unadaptable and unemployable, like an old, sore, ardent individualist among contemporary progressives. . . . He didn't have it in him to be amenable, even if he tried." So Agee wrote after D. W. Griffith died. He may have been describing the film director. He was certainly describing himself.

Notes

1. The reference is to Archibald MacLeish, who had, under pressure from the Zeitgeist, temporarily edged over toward the Communists. Four years later the war had begun — no one ever had to ask Archie, "Don't you know there's a war on?" — and MacLeish was attacking Dos Passos, Farrell, Hemingway, and such as "The Irresponsibles" who had betrayed the American Dream. Shortly thereafter he was running Roosevelt's Office of Facts and Figures, as our wartime propaganda agency was at first quaintly called.

2. On both sides. In *Fortune*'s case, they never really knew just where to have this strange creature. When he first arrived on *Fortune*, Agee speedily became, largely because nobody could figure out any other way to use him, the staff specialist in rich, beautiful prose on such topics as Rare Wines, Famous Orchid Collections, and The World's Ten Most Precious Jewels. When this finally reached the attention of Henry Luce, he was indignant, for he had a theory that a good writer could write on anything — also, *Fortune* was supposed to be about business. He thought it somehow immoral that a writer should do only what he was best at — there was a lot of the Puritan in Luce. So he assigned to Agee as occupational therapy an article on The Price of Steel Rails, and furthermore announced that he, Luce, would personally edit it (as he often did in those days). It was a fascinating topic for anyone with the slightest interest in economics, since the price of steel rails, which had been exactly the same for some forty years, was the classic example of monopolistic price-fixing. But Agee, of course, had not even a slight interest in economics. He did his best and Luce did his best — "Now, Jim, don't you see . . . ?" — but finally Luce had to admit defeat and the article was assigned to someone else (me, I think) who did a workmanlike job. The trouble with Agee as a journalist was that he couldn't be just workmanlike. He had to give it everything he had, which was not good for him.

Participants:

ANDREW LYTLE

DAVID McDOWELL

FATHER MARTIN

JOHN REISHMAN

The Morning Watch Panel

McDOWELL: I conceive my function here is to introduce questions to Dr. Lytle and Dr. Reishman and to comment a little about the history of *The Morning Watch*. It was published initially in a magazine in Italy, *Botteghe Oscure*, in 1950. The very distinguished editor was an American woman, married to an Italian prince. She had tried very hard to get material out of American writers. Agee had worked for quite a while on *The Morning Watch*, and finally he decided to give it to her. It was published in book form in 1951. Its setting is here at St. Andrew's, and it deals with various types of ambiguities and religious experience. It has a very interesting structure and some important use of symbolism. Dr. Lytle, I think, would like to address himself to that.

LYTLE: I have read parts of this book three times. I read it when it first came out when I was almost as young as you. I was very moved by it, and I read it again, and I felt it was too long. I read it again last night, and I find that it's not too long, that it makes a perfect whole. You approach a piece of literature — you can approach it in many ways — but you can approach it through its structure. All of you are men and women; you have a certain structure as a man and a certain structure as a woman, but each of you is distinct and individual. That is part of the mystery of life, and this is what you have to look for in the character.

Now you know what time this is, the morning watch, where Christ is betrayed by the flesh. People couldn't stay awake an hour to see him out. His traitorous friend, Judas, gave him away for thirty pieces of silver, and this is one of the constant themes in life — betrayal by friends and fellows.

The young boy in *The Morning Watch* is an adolescent, and like all adolescents he feels that he is a little peculiar — a little set apart from the rest of the people here. He is basically and distinctively a believer, without which you cannot have faith in yourself or anything else. He goes through this morning watch, and what he suffers at the beginning of it is the frailty of the flesh and the frailty of attention. He goes through this in a worldly way. The worldly action that we all encompass is an imitation of Christ, and that's what he does here. He shows you the frailty of that imitation. While engaged in the watch, the young lad feels strange and looks around to see if he's done anything whereby people will notice him. All of this diverts him from the central vision of prayer, which he should be engaged in. He's so involved in these thoughts that he doesn't pray. Finally he goes out toward the sand pit. Remember that this is an imitation of the resurrection of Christ, which is a promise of rebirth. Indeed, at the last trumpet, you are going to confront four last things: death, judgment, heaven, or hell. Then what? I think everyone has to remember this: until Christ's mission, what the world knew was that everybody died except the king and the high priests. The word *hell* in Hebrew was nothing but a hole in the ground. It was with Christ's advent that everybody, no matter his status or his state, had a chance at those four last things: death, judgment, heaven, or hell. And so Christ — the creative act of God through whom all things are made — was crucified, suffered, and died. This was the great moment of death. The dark hour before Easter and the great resurrection.

The boy felt that he failed in the chapel, so he and several others broke the rule and left the chapel. In the end, everybody must break the rules to come to himself. Everyone has to commit a criminal act, that is, a *mild* criminal act. That's when you are the most saved. They go out to the sand pit and enter this murky water. Water, of course, is a symbol for life; it's also a feminine symbol. On the way, he finds the husk of an insect on the tree. Well, the insect is gone, but what does this represent? It represents resurrection. The locust, which is a biblical reference — the seven-year locust in Egypt — sheds his husk and the locust is reborn. In a sense, he's saying he sees that, yet he doesn't quite understand it. He himself goes down and risks death in the murky water of the sand pit, trying to be like Christ, but, of course, being mortal, he can only imitate Christ. He rises up from the dead, that is, from the water, and what does he see? The old serpent. But the serpent is shining and beautiful; he shed his skin, too, and so he is resurrected.

There is a constant threat of something evil: the things we live by in our lives, by which we learn our nature, are the opposites, good and evil. He is being reborn at the same time that the promise of Christ's rebirth is repeated each year. He comes back and feels himself strange at that moment. Then to keep the snake from suffering, that is, to show charity, even to the lowest of animals . . . he feels charity and a warmth or love toward the animal and takes the risk of killing it, which raises him in the eyes of his fellows, whom he felt had not thought much of him before. The wonderful thing there is what you get: the communion between himself and his own kind, which he's not had before. This is a kind of understanding of what life is, and that's what he's come to. After having failed in the chapel, he learns it in the sand pit.

McDowell: John, would you like to say a few things about *The Morning Watch*?

Reishman: I would like to begin with the history of preparing myself to read *The Morning Watch* and my first reading of it. I think it has some bearing on the way I estimate the work and the way I had estimated it in the past.

When I was thirteen years old, I went to a school on the Notre Dame campus in South Bend, Indiana, that was run by the Holy Cross Fathers of the Roman Catholic Church — not the Holy Cross monks of the Anglo-Catholic persuasion. We kept a morning watch, and we prayed the prayers, or at least some of the prayers, that form a part of the structure of that novel. We wrestled with the world in the terms that the hero of this novel wrestles with the world. I think that's one of the problems with the novel. The kind of piety that Richard practices, the terms of his religious experience are foreign to many people growing up today. I suspect that those of you who have read the novel find that your own sympathies are very different or very far from the hero of the novel. He's not like Huck Finn or Holden Caulfield or the hero of *A Separate Peace*, who talks in terms more of us can appreciate. What I would like to emphasize is that my experience was more like Richard's and less like Holden Caulfield's and Huck Finn's.

When I first read *The Morning Watch*, I was astounded. I read it as a freshman in college, and I couldn't believe that anyone had been through so much that I felt that I myself had been through. I had come to regard my own experience as unique and something of an anachronism, something that just didn't happen anymore, and here it had happened to someone else, in Tennessee. I was overcome, and I judged it to be an absolutely fantastic novel that perhaps only I and the author could understand.

I think the novel concerns a basic question that we are always asking ourselves, but more seriously at that time of adolescence, and that is the question of whether or not life is possible. Can we bear to live in the world that we are discovering? I don't want to suggest anything to you, but I think that it's not accidental that there is in this country right now a very high suicide rate among adolescents. I gather from what I can read that this is not a new phenomenon. I think that it's because a lot of people are asking this question. Richard, the hero of the novel, is asking this, I think, in all that he does. Finally, I agree with Mr. Lytle that Richard sees at the end that resurrection is possible, that life can be redeemed, and that all he senses that is peculiar and sinful and wicked in himself can be overcome. In the end he embraces life.

He begins waking up in a dormitory room to go ask himself this question. He confronts a God whom he sees as a God who is dying, a God with whom he tries to identify. In that process of death, Christ is attempting a reconciliation with his Father, and the hero in this novel experiences that same problem in his own life. You'll recall that his own father is dead. He recalls vivid memories of this dead father, and this is one of the problems that James Agee is facing. It's part of the problem of anyone growing up — reconciling himself with his father and reconciling himself with his parents. He confronts this personally and at the level of myth, or the religious level, through his particular response to the Christian mystery. That is what intrigues him about Christ. It is in dying that he attempts, in several ways that might strike us as ludicrous, to identify with the dying Christ. We hear so much in current religious expression about identifying with the resurrected Christ. The prayer that he says at the beginning seems remote and even bizarre when he asks to be taken into the womb of Christ. That's just something that we can't say anymore. The point is that it's something he moves beyond and overcomes. He wrestles with the problem throughout *The Morning Watch*. He tries to bring his attention around to the dying Christ, but life keeps getting in his way. The flesh, as Mr. Lytle says, keeps getting in his way.

Finally, at the end of *The Morning Watch*, there is a moment of space, and that moment is what gives him the courage to go out to the sand pit. He has been a timid person up to that time. He has failed, as Peter and the rest of Christ's friends failed, to identify with Christ. Finally, he achieves that identification in the last moments of his morning watch, and with that he goes out to the baptismal waters of regeneration in the sand pit. In this natural setting, he encounters a similar temptation to the supernatural one he encountered in the chapel. The waters of regeneration are also potentially the waters of drowning. He thinks about that as he clings to the rock at the bottom of the pond. It's a great temptation, something that is beautiful in his mind, something that seems to be beautiful in the life of Christ. In the end, through the communion he achieved in the chapel, it brings him round to choose as Christ did — resurrection. He surfaces and sees the snake.

The snake is a complicated symbol. I am not sure that I thoroughly understand it. The snake obviously is not the snake in the Garden of Eden, or perhaps it is, because like the snake in the Garden, his snake is beautiful and alluring; yet he destroys that snake. He smashes its head and ritualistically bathes his hands in the waters of the sand pit. In my reading of the story, I believe it is a last aggressive effort against life — a last refusal to accept what he has made his peace with when he rises to the surface. He quarrels with the beauty that he finds in life and in the flesh. It's part of his whole struggle in growing up.

In the end he has a very ambivalent response to the snake: he loves it, he hates it, he destroys it, and at the same time he wants to see it preserved. When he reaches for the symbol of the resurrection, the symbol of the ability to throw off the body and begin a new life, I think he decides in favor of the life that he has been tempted throughout the story to reject. He decides just what Holden Caulfield decides at the end of *Catcher in the Rye:* that life can be lived. So, in the end, he makes the heroic decision that all of us must make in spite of the terrible pain. One of the most beautiful things to me about this novel is how sensitive Agee is to the pain of growing up and to the pain of embracing life. Still, he overcomes that reluctance to accept pain and chooses to live.

MCDOWELL: What do you think about the imagery and description in his novel? The descriptions of objects? Of the snake? The descriptions are beautifully detailed and intricate, but there's a great bareness of description about people. Everything has to be "received" in this technique by what Richard feels. Dr. Lytle, you are so sensitive to language and to imagery. Would you consider this to be somewhat of a failure? Do you think that might make this a novella instead of a novel?

LYTLE: I would approach that by way of the structure. You have here what I call a panoramic summary, which is in the boy's mind when he is in the church, and that is reflection and thought that remain therein. Then opposed to that is this boy's world, which is the foul language and the human frailty that is always manifest in it. It's those two things that bring the whole place alive. These are real boys with the usual human frailties. The imagery is fine, and it is not limited to only the snake, and the husk on the tree, and the sand pit, and holding on at the bottom of the water. It is very concrete and absolute. It represents, in terms of the whole morning watch, the fallen condition of the world. That is, we can only approach this divine promise. We are too sunken in the flesh, in our self-indulgences and in the ego, which all these little boys manifest at this age, which is actually the thing that dies in us. What is immortal in us is the sense that man is also divine. From the moment when the dove whispered into her Ladyship the Virgin — what you have is the divine entering matter there.

MCDOWELL: Do you think, John, that we actually see these young boys? Richard, of course, comes to us by our actually getting inside his mind. But do we see him? What do you think of the depth of characterization?

REISHMAN: There is the problem of the other characters having a limited kind of reality, but I think that is offset by the intensity of Richard's own perception of them. We see the whole world through his consciousness, and this is a very powerful way of telling a story. It is the story of Richard. The world must be focused through his consciousness if Agee is to do, or to achieve, what he sets out to. I am impressed with the way in which he always keeps the consciousness of Richard in the forefront. That again says something about what Mr. Lytle was talking about: that adolescent egocentricity. That's why Holden Caulfield has to tell his own story in his own voice. That's why you couldn't have any kind of omniscient narration that would serve as a vehicle for this kind of self-examination or self-absorption which Richard does.

McDOWELL: Right. It can only be through the point of view of Richard's own consciousness. Isn't this somehow a weakness, though? Doesn't this limit its magnitude?

LYTLE: You know, the point of view is never violated, and that's the only way you can contain and restrain. You can't have too many people there. The people in *The Morning Watch* serve their purpose regarding their characters in the novel.

McDOWELL: In other words, you feel that it's a completely satisfactory work of art and novel, as it is?

LYTLE: David, only God can make it completely satisfactory. But I find it was far more successful than I thought it was on my second reading.

REISHMAN: One of the problems for me is the kind of consciousness that the boy possesses. It is, I think, a kind of consciousness that can only communicate itself to a limited kind of audience. The character of his piety may serve to eliminate a great deal of sympathy for his experience. That's why I told you of my coming to read the story. The character of my piety was so similar to Richard's, and I think it was found equally offensive by many of the people with whom I had to deal. That was the result of my formation, and I couldn't help it. Neither can Richard. That's a limitation, but that's a limitation in the audience, not in the work of the art.

LYTLE: That's a limitation of the secular world.

McDowell: Well, I've been trying to egg these gentlemen on, and I think I've succeeded. Father Martin, do you have anything?

Father Martin: I'd like to ask one question, David. Both *The Morning Watch* and *A Death in the Family* were written by a mature adult, and yet somehow he captures the feeling of a twelve-year-old in *The Morning Watch* and an even younger boy in *A Death in the Family*. I'm wondering if that's not an unusual characteristic for an author, to have such recall of his emotions as a child.

Lytle: Father Martin, everything is in the imagination. I would say these are not the feelings that he has had as a boy, but the basic feeling has gone through the imagination and he's put the artistic hand on it. Everything exists in the imagination.

Audience: Are you saying he's not really remembering what he felt as a boy? He's imagining it?

Lytle: He's taking the experiences of a little boy and by the craft of writing — this is not autobiography but a work of art that's been fashioned by the imagination.

Participants:

BRAINARD CHENEY

WARREN EYSTER

FATHER FLYE

ANDREW LYTLE

DAVID McDOWELL

DAVID MADDEN

FREDERICK MANFRED

A *Death in the Family* Panel

LYTLE: As moderator, I'm going to keep my place and put the burden of the discussion on the gentlemen to my right. It seems to me that the surest approach to any work of art is to discover what the point of view is, because the point of view controls the action. Now a piece of fiction has two kinds of action; it's what might be called the enveloping action or that universal experience of which the action of this particular book is one representation. I think that is a sure way to approach any kind of fiction.

Remember, it is always an action, and any professor who uses the word *description* makes a heinous mistake. Description is innate and dead, and action makes you see with the senses. But sight, of course, is the sovereign sense because it controls. The head controls the body and sight into the world, the vision of the artist's mind, that means by which, under the pressure of the craft, the work is done. That is, the artifact is made because the art resides in the artist.

Now the question I'm going to propose to these gentlemen is this: Point of view [in *A Death in the Family*] is not omniscient, and yet the little boy in it is not the total actor; he seems to dominate the point of view, control the action. Nevertheless, it is what it says. It is "a death in the family," and death affects various members of this family. What does death reveal in the relationship as it affects all the other members of the family?

MCDOWELL: This is a marvelous question. *A Death in the Family*, by the way, was Jim's title for this book. It was not one that I invented for the book. He had arrived at this title years ago.

EYSTER: On the situation of death affecting the various members of the family, I had always looked at the novel from three points of view. The major effect on the family: one to the mother, one to the boy, Rufus, and one part to the father himself, when he was alive as it reflects back on his death. And it seems to me that the position used, the boy's sensitivity, his awareness of what his father's death means to him and how he sometimes doesn't understand . . . well, first of all, that no one comprehends death. I think one of the powerful things about this book is that it's not taking death as something you can cope with all at the moment; that each person, especially the wife, the mother of the boy, must first get over the shock of death; second, gradually assimilate and feel for herself what it is to have the family lose the father; and then gradually come to a fuller understanding of whom she was married to. Instead of the point of view being one person, to use the technical term, this would be limited omniscience, that is, from the boy's point of view through most of the book. But, again, about one-fourth of the book deals with the wife, with the mother of the family as to how she feels about the father's death.

I wasn't really prepared for this question. There's a part of the book that's always my favorite, that to me comes to a larger question: that not only the family has to learn what it is to lose a father and a husband but also what the whole thing is, what a person means in time. I was very impressed by Agee's sense of generations, that the grandfather, the great-grandmother, the father, the son, and even future children are all part of the same heritage. And so a death in the family not only means something immediate. It also is something that gives continuity out of the past and ties into the future.

And tied in with this is, what is it when a person dies? Not only what does it mean in life but what is this heritage, if you want to call it that? It seems to me the book struggles with this: "What is the relation between the living and immortality?" There's a little passage very late in the book that deals with a butterfly. I've always been so impressed with the simple things — in my case, a curious incident that gave special value to the thing. I had a friend from Mexico who was visiting me in the United States. He did not read English very well, and I was reading him this passage of the butterfly scene very near the end of the book, and this is just simply the passage that I will read:

"If anything ever makes me believe in God," his uncle said.

Rufus looked up at him quickly. He was still looking straight ahead, and he still looked angry but his voice was not angry. "Or life after death," his uncle said.

They were working and breathing rather hard, for they were walking westward up the steep hill towards Fort Sanders. The sky ahead of them was bright and they walked among the bright, moving shadows of trees.

"It'll be what happened this afternoon."

Rufus looked up at him carefully.

"There were a lot of clouds," his uncle said, and continued to look straight before him, "but they were blowing fast, so there was a lot of sunshine too. Right when they began to lower your father into the ground, into his grave, a cloud came over and there was a shadow just like iron, and a perfectly magnificent butterfly settled on the — coffin, just rested there, right over the breast, and stayed there, just barely making his wings breathe, like a heart."

Andrew stopped and for the first time looked at Rufus. His eyes were desperate. "He stayed there all the way down, Rufus," he said. "He never stirred, except just to move his wings that way, until it grated against the bottom like a — rowboat. And just when it did the sun came out just dazzling bright and he flew up out of that — hole in the ground, straight up into the sky, so high I couldn't even see him any more." He began to climb the hill again, and Rufus worked hard again to stay abreast of him. "Don't you think that's wonderful, Rufus?" he said, again looking straight and despairingly before him.

"Yes," Rufus said, now that his uncle really was asking him. "Yes," he was sure was not enough, but it was all he could say.

I'm trying to get across that what makes something strongly meaningful for you is what you put into it. I'd always liked the passage before, or I wouldn't have read it. But as I was reading it, I was sitting beside a big oak tree, and a butterfly came and sat on the ground right near us . . . if you've ever seen how they spiral . . . just at about the time as I was reading this, when we both were aware of the butterfly, it went up toward the light, and I had for one moment that powerful sense of a real image . . . I was seeing it in front of me. I had been given what Agee was always struggling for — the picture, the reality, and the meaning. I think that's all.

LYTLE: Okay. Mr. Cheney, you're fresh on this panel. You can begin any way you like.

CHENEY: I'd like to begin by taking issue with you. Is that okay?

LYTLE: Yes. That's a good way.

CHENEY: Well, you said it was an action, and, of course, I'm not going to really take issue with you on that. But you only had to be here last night to see the movie to see how remote it is from that sort of action. I like to think of it as really a celebration of a living memory that he carried from early childhood into maturity. I guess you'd call it a spatial novel and a radical example of a spatial novel.

LYTLE: What do you mean by a *spatial novel*?

CHENEY: Well, it may be more seeming than fact, but you use the term *vital voice*. The time element here is so inconsequential, as such, that some of the passages of the earlier experience of our protagonist, Rufus, are distributed throughout the event, the introduction and death of the father, all of which occurred in three days, and Rufus's childhood, his fear of the dark. That beautiful introductory passage . . . it is a prelude and gives us a mood, in some sense the viewpoint of the novel, and this very intricate complex viewpoint implied here. "*We are talking now of summer evenings in Knoxville, Tennessee, in the time that I lived there so successfully disguised to myself as a child.*" I think this essentially states the viewpoint of Rufus. What you have there is Rufus the poet . . . the sensorium of Rufus was that of the poet. He has this sense of identity and unity as he regards himself upon maturity, which gives it both complexity and density, but the dimension I would like to talk about in this book is family devotion. I think that's what you'd call the dimension; it's a steady piece otherwise. You have there not sex; you have there normal family affection done in a completely whole design, as Warren has pointed out, in generations — the love of father and husband and wife and father and son — and this all is realized to give the book a measure of devotion, the emptying of it all through the death of the father, which gives the true dimension of the novel.

LYTLE: Mr. Manfred, would you say that the father is the only death in the family? I'm not speaking only of the grave, you understand.

MANFRED: I hadn't given that much thought. I really ought to have a day to think that over. Maybe if I start from another angle. It occurred to me that I was hearing another tone or an overtone in the book; something your earlier remark about point of view brought to a head, and that was something like this. I'm sure that all of you have been in some kind of baseball game or tennis game or basketball game in which you had some kind of terrific battle with the opposition and you lost by one point. In baseball, for example, if the ball had landed just one inch over the line, it would have been a hit, and you would have had the winning run and won. Then you go home thinking about that — if the ball had landed again and again — and you finally begin to fantasize about it. You replay the game until you have that ball land fair and win the game, and you do that so often and so thoroughly and with such disturbed eagerness that it finally becomes a real fantasy and in your mind you really do win the game. If something like that happened to you, you almost have to run head-on into somebody driving to remind you that you're here on this earth and you lost the game.

I think there is something like this going on in this book. Mr. Agee was not only trying to put this down as a remembrance and tell us about the celebration, in a somber sense, and to have this all brought to life again, but there was something else going on in his mind. I think this loss of his father was such an agony to him, such a terrible loss to him, that very often he fantasized in his mind that if the driving in the night had gone some other way, some little inch to the right or to the left so that it didn't happen, that the act of writing this was a way of having it not happen. And it's that high tone of fantasy that creeps into this and gives it a double echo; it's like a trill that you hear when the Sioux sing their war song off in the distance on some hillock, while the ladies of the tribe would stand on their mound and sing the trills, and it's something that quivers over the top of the rest and gives you that extra gift in the work of art, something that the author himself didn't calculate to get into it. I think this is not only a celebration but a very high form of fantasy, to have it not happen, to have it not be true. Now in that sense there is more than one death.

LYTLE: Would you like to speak to the point about the family gathering after they know he's dead? In other words, if this is a story about the intrusion of death into life, taking for granted the fact that we don't all die sudden deaths, are there degrees of death in the various members of the family — the grandfather and the grandmother and the aunt, and so forth — as a kind of choral effect?

MANFRED: That go along with the death itself?

LYTLE: Yes. What, for example, is wrong with the grandfather in terms of the supernatural and beyond death?

MANFRED: You mean whether or not he believes it?

LYTLE: What happens to a man who can't believe? Would he be in any way dead?

MANFRED: Yes, he would be. He has a short life, and not the one that Jim was dreaming for, in the fantasy that I like to speak of.

LYTLE: What about the grandmother? She's deprived of the second basic sense, which is hearing. And what does that do to life there? What effect does that have on life, that is, on the people who have gathered in the room to sympathize with her?

MANFRED: It cuts her off.

LYTLE: Yes, it cuts her off and intrudes. I think that is the kind of thing we can't help but notice.

MANFRED: Yes. I remember that at first when she'd be breaking in apropos of nothing, I thought that was a kind of intrusion. Then after a while I thought, no, this is very effective, this is wonderful; he's breaking up where you think it should go, but it's really going over here. Jim was revealing an aspect that ordinarily doesn't show up. I have to think about all that.

LYTLE: Well, I want you to talk about what you want to talk about.

EYSTER: Excuse me, I think I never made clear why I read that particular passage. I think it relates to something that you were just talking to. The reason I read the passage about the butterfly is that

I feel that behind the whole book, there's a very strong, a very hard decision of wanting to believe very, very strongly that there was immortality, of wanting to believe that all the family continuity had meaning. But in order for death to mean anything, in order for all the people to mean something for each other, he had to have this final belief that there was immortality. And there's an essential doubt, such as the butterfly passage, the business of when you die —

LYTLE: May I interrupt you there? What does the butterfly stand for?

EYSTER: To me, a supreme attempt on the smallest possible physical evidence to believe in the spiritual existence.

LYTLE: Yes, but it's a symbol for what?

EYSTER: For immortality, for eternity.

LYTLE: Well, the soul. It's not just an idle symbol when it lands on the coffin.

EYSTER: Oh, no. And when it goes up, it is an affirmation, but it is based on tremendous faith and tremendously small evidence.

LYTLE: Let's come back to simpler things, if we may. What's the old country expression, you're not dead till you're what?

CHENEY: Till you're buried.

LYTLE: Yes, and he's buried and his soul is perched on the coffin. Let me ask Mr. Madden here. May I ask a question?

MADDEN: I wanted to pick up on what you said before and then ask a question. I'm very interested in the point of view in the novel. I think that what Mr. Lytle said is absolutely true. Until you really get comfortable with the point of view in the novel, you're not going to be able to respond as fully to it as I think is possible. The way I've come to see it . . . I was at first bothered . . . I think I talked about it last night after the movie . . . by shifting from one point of view to another, but I was really talking out my past experience with the novel. After I've had a chance to look it over again, I think that really it is one of the most brilliant uses of point of view that I know of, helped enormously by the addition in the front by the "Knoxville: Summer 1915." Because there you have the first-person voice of the narrator, and let's forget that it's an autobiographical novel for a while and just think of the character, Rufus, made up by James Agee. Here Agee the author is letting his character Rufus speak directly to the reader in the manner of a godlike narrator. "*We are talking now of summer evenings in Knoxville, Tennessee, in the time that I lived there so successfully disguised to myself as a child."* That line also suggests that he's never really been a child; he's always been an older person in terms of his vision. He was trapped in the body of a child; he was trapped in the enforced attitudes toward life that society teaches a child to have; he always had this keenly intuitive sense of the total reality of life and death. What makes your reference to the grandmother so interesting is that the grandmother is both life and death in the midst of all these people gathered together by virtue of the fact that she can't hear what is going on as it pertains to the ongoingness of life and as it pertains to the dead person. She is a living example of life and death going on simultaneously.

Therefore, I don't feel that from the point of view of the narrator, Rufus, a created intelligence, that there is an intrusion of death upon life. I think that the attitude is that life and death are one unbroken process and that what holds the point of view of the whole novel together is "awe," the awe that a child has more than the adult, the awe that this child, as he became Agee the author, never lost. So that he is writing this book not out of celebration, not out of grief, so much as out of an awe that never left him. The whole novel is full of this wide-eyed look of "what is this?" You know, "this is fascinating, this is marvelous." So that the point of view, it seems to me, is that when he goes into the minds of other people, he remains almost like a first-person narrator. In other words, that is not James Agee going into the mind of the mother and father; that is Rufus the character becoming a third-person godlike narrator.

I like to think of writers — and I think this is a good example of it — as "God's spies." A writer is a spy for God — this is Robert Browning's idea and not mine — but I think it is a great way of looking at the writer. He is a spy for God, not to go back and carry messages, but he is an alien among normal, everyday people. He is seeing much more; he is reacting much more fully; he is taking an entirely different attitude toward life and death. He does not make the separation that they make; he does not judge in the way that other people do. At the same time, there's a kind of arrogance; there's a kind of Lucifer-like quality about the writer, a kind of Icarian quality like Icarus who flew too close to the sun and whose wings melted and he fell to earth again in attempting to be like God, to create. This is a novel in which I really feel this quality of the writer, that he is trying to be a creator almost in competition with God; events went in such and such a way, and he goes back and resurrects all that and re-creates it in his own manner. I think that, in a sense, the novel doesn't just celebrate life and death, but finally there's a kind of resurrection that occurs in the act of writing this novel. My experience in reading it is to experience the gradual resurrection of this life, not only of the father but of everything else, because when you talk about death, from the point of view of the author, in a sense everything else has died including—I thought you were going to talk about the death of innocence, but in a way he never was that innocent. He knew too much.

LYTLE: Let me just add a little to what you said. We've been speaking of the creative act for years; I've been speaking of it. I want to ask if it's not so that God can create and we imitate. We imitate God's acts in multifarious ways to create.

FATHER FLYE: Yes, I assume we do that.

CHENEY: Some of us may imitate the devil.

LYTLE: I'm speaking of artists, now, that have to create both good and bad, and that's what you're speaking of. Let me add this: I agree with you thoroughly that in the boy's mind is this intuitive sense, very mysterious, which is a kind of sense of life and learning that he doesn't quite understand. But at the same time, wouldn't you say that first he uses the innocent eye of the child, which sees more visibly and acutely than an older person? Years later, he's using the innocent eye but with the knowledge of an adult man.

EYSTER: Doesn't death make all of them innocent, though? Doesn't death disarm all the other people in the story and make them all differently innocent than the boy? The boy has the fullest innocence. Isn't the wife's trip suddenly to have to start all over again?

LYTLE: You think that restores her innocence?

EYSTER: It shakes up everything that's gone before. They suddenly have to make a completely new adjustment that is almost an innocence.

LYTLE: Well, I don't know about that. No, I don't think so, because she couldn't possibly have been innocent and borne two children.

MADDEN: The movie makes more of a point about that than the book does, I think, because the movie ends with the mother becoming childlike or surrendering to the child's—

FATHER FLYE: That's a contradiction of the movie.

LYTLE: Don't confuse the forms.

MADDEN: What I talked about last night, you see that I made an absolute distinction between the forms.

LYTLE: In line with this, as we're moving along — this relates, finally, to all that's been said here in a way. We're dealing with death as it intrudes with life, and it's inevitable that it will; it's the only sure thing we know in the world. And this brings up the matter of the supernatural and life after death. You've mentioned that in the butterfly scene. Earlier in the action, the little boy is asleep and here his mind, the rational mind — how rational a child can be — is allayed, and into that mind comes all kinds of things of darkness, which is, you remember, the struggle between the appeal of the darkness, the loss into it, and sublimation, if you want to say, or else the annihilation. But he's drawn into life through his father, and he cries out and asks his father to come, and his father does come —

CHENEY: Protector against the powers of darkness —

LYTLE: Yes, so that you get the whole thing here. He's almost willing himself into the world of darkness, but his father, who is his life and love, you see, comes, and, mind it, adults don't want the father to go. The mother wants to go, and he says no. He recognizes his cry as a pre-vision leading to his own death. He goes in, and the boy clings to him — he doesn't want to lose him — and he makes him sing songs, and these are the songs that contain the various meanings of experience and life. It seems to me that's in line with what you're saying.

MADDEN: Except I still don't think death is an intrusion from the point of view of the narrator as he is writing the novel. It was then when he was a child, but I think what he has come to see —

CHENEY: This is in the character of it being a celebration, a ritual.

MADDEN: I don't really deny that it's a celebration; I'm just putting a different emphasis on it.

CHENEY: My emphasis, I said.

EYSTER: Andrew, I think this is a profoundly religious book. It concerns salvation, the survival of this man's spirit, his soul —

LYTLE: *Caritas*, too.

EYSTER: That's right. There's a little judgment going on here from the point of view of that half-innocent, half-objective eye of the boy, that at the funeral that boy is busy rating various ones, how far are they toward salvation, and in that sense . . . there are other deaths besides the father's death.

LYTLE: That's what I think, too. And I just wondered if that is not part of the enveloping action. In life, even, there is continuous death, but the final death is in the grave, and in that there is a kind of mystery.

EYSTER: I think there are two poles in this. One of them is represented at the time of the accident. I was always struck by two points: the cotterpin, which always reminded me — I can't help but remember that Agee was so strong on Stephen Crane, "The Open Boat" sort of thing, where that point of view is that the world is sheer accident. The natural world is not against you. It's not for you. Things just happen. It isn't even whether you're strong or you're weak. It isn't even the survival of the fittest. It just happens, like the cotterpin. If the cotterpin hadn't fallen out, the accident wouldn't have happened and the man wouldn't have died. This is completely nonspiritual.

Then thrown into it is the great mystery of death with a blue point on the chin. If he hadn't landed on exactly that point. Remember, I'm talking of that section, what he's using as a motif almost, and why he hit exactly on the point, instantaneous death, that sheer freak accident. To go from that point, from almost as un-Christian, certainly as un-immortal a view as you can have, where life is sheer accident, to go from that not only to a complete affirmation, not only of immortality, but of family in life, with generations as being a part of that, which I think then relates to the celebration you were talking of, that this is the outside scope of it and the boy is a medium to that.

LYTLE: We're told that every sparrow that falls to the ground God knows about. Isn't the same thing true with the cotterpin?

FATHER FLYE: That view of God, with God as the great exponent of chance, is defensible. As a matter of fact, I sometimes feel that way about Him myself.

EYSTER: No, I wasn't concerned about how I feel about Him. I feel that that was where he started from and that the whole book is a struggle to say that isn't the way the world works, in spite of the fact. That isn't what the world is about, even if it works that way.

LYTLE: The only trouble with that one is it leaves out too much.

I think now we better ask the students to tell us where we've been obscure and, indeed, where they need further enlightenment.

AUDIENCE: Why do you think that James Agee put the ghost of the father in the novel?

LYTLE: Well, we're dealing with the supernatural world, aren't we? That's the final thing, after life ends, and that brings up the question: "Do the dead come back in a ghostly form?" You remember the place where he comes?

AUDIENCE: Just after the reunion, I think.

LYTLE: As they're sitting in there, the first time, he comes in there visibly. Well, if you believe in the divine order of the universe that there is such a thing as life after death, ghosts can possibly come back. At least that's one of the superstitions. We don't know. They can't come back in their bodies.

CHENEY: If we want to be sociological, as a social phenomenon, that's certainly part of the circumstances of death. It's part of our mores.

AUDIENCE: But why did he include it in the novel?

FATHER FLYE: Remember, he included it through the people. They felt the presence of it.

LYTLE: It's an action, don't you see? It's a part of the action. They are dealing with death, life and death, and certainly the ghost is beyond life, isn't he?

EYSTER: I would like to say on that particular point I think that he was including spiritualism as one of the human efforts — valid or invalid, you have to judge for yourself based on the book — of the attempt to bring life and death and immortality . . . to understand what happens after life . . . that he does it through the people, through the characters.

AUDIENCE: I'd like to know how fictionalized the novel was.

LYTLE: Well, I think I can answer that. He was six years old when his father died, so he couldn't have been there. He couldn't have overheard this talk. The artist himself, by his art and his craft, does it, you see.

AUDIENCE: I'd like to know how fictionalized he was in the account of his father's death.

LYTLE: I've just answered it. This is not fictionalized autobiography. This is not autobiography.

AUDIENCE: I would like to know whether details like the cotter-pin and things of that nature are exactly what happened.

LYTLE: It doesn't matter whether it happened or not. It's in the imagination.

FATHER FLYE: Let me say this. As Mr. Lytle just said, it doesn't matter. This is a fiction and should be regarded as such, but if you want to know, those are the identical circumstances under which James Agee's father died. Although the stipulation about the cotter-pin, I don't know, but the circumstances of his death were identical.

LYTLE: Just a minute. Let me try to clarify it. You're introducing a common confusion as to whether something actually happened. The book is made through the imagination, and the real events are used by the imagination, so you have to distinguish between biography and fiction. Lucius himself is not Agee. He uses the real event in writing of the child. It's not about Rufus. It's a book about a death in the family, I think. It's a book about a married couple, too. It's a family novel, about a grandmother, too.

FATHER FLYE: What is presented there at the end of the prologue is a family, there on the grass, on a summer evening, and it's magical and wonderful.

McDOWELL: Let's get back to this autobiographical thing and pull together what we've been talking about. You know that marvel-ous scene after the death of the father when they are all talking to-gether in the room, and the grandmother is deaf, and she can't hear and keeps misunderstanding? Now this is not, of course, autobio-graphical, as Andrew pointed out. He was only six years old. Some-one might have mentioned some of these things, and he remembered them as a family. That is all. It has nothing to do with an autobio-graphical sketch.

LYTLE: This matter of autobiography. There is no such thing. No man knows himself so well. Only God knows you that well. So what you have here is what you have in common with other people.

AUDIENCE: What do you think of the deaf grandmother's role in *A Death in the Family*?

MADDEN: That was my comment picking up on Mr. Lytle's. What I meant was that, since she couldn't hear what was going on with all these people gathered together, she was dead to the life going on around her, although of course she had an inner life. But a good part of the novel is about the life in the family, and since the grandmother is so old and is near death herself, she embodies both of these qualities simultaneously. A presence of life and death in one, kind of a bridge between the dead son and the living family.

LYTLE: May I add to that? You see, there's a convention to try to put the platitudes of life before the reality of grief and sorrow. If you reconstruct the way her mind works and the way she speaks, it's the convention without the heart.

MADDEN: The first words that I utter, in my pontifical way, in creative writing workshop, when we have our first meeting, are, "In the beginning was the word." And I think it would be good if we end with the words of James Agee, and I'd like to read a passage to illustrate my own point about the emphasis on the word *awe*.

LYTLE: You forgot to mention the word *flesh*, too.

MADDEN: Yes, that's what I'm trying to get at. That's what the writer does. I hope you will listen to this passage from "Knoxville: Summer 1915": "*We all lie there, my mother, my father, my uncle, my aunt, and I too am lying there.*" He's not giving it to us because it happened or trying to "tell" us something, but because he is profoundly in awe of the fact that they are sitting down and lying down, and I am, too, as a writer, which is why I wanted to become a writer, not necessarily to do with life and death and all these other things we've been talking about, but just the sheer experience:

> On the rough wet grass of the back yard my father and mother have spread quilts. We all lie there, my mother, my father, my uncle, my aunt, and I too am lying there. First we were sitting up, then one of us lay down, and then we all lay down, on our stomachs, or on our sides, or on our backs, and they have kept on talking. They are not talking much, and the talk is quiet, of nothing in particular, of nothing at all in particular, of nothing at all. The stars are wide and alive, they seem each like a smile of great sweetness, and they seem very near. All my people are larger bodies than mine, quiet, with voices gentle and meaningless like the voices of sleeping birds. One is an artist, he is living at home. One is a musician, she is living at home. One is my mother who is good to me. One is my father who is good to me. By some chance, here they are, all on this earth; and who shall ever tell the sorrow of being on this earth, lying, on quilts, on the grass, in a summer evening, among the sounds of night. May God bless my people,

my uncle, my aunt, my mother, my good father, oh, remember them kindly in their time of trouble; and in the hour of their taking away.

After a little I am taken in and put to bed. Sleep, soft smiling, draws me unto her: and those receive me, who quietly treat me, as one familiar and well-beloved in that home: but will not, oh, will not, not now, not ever; but will not ever tell me who I am.

LYTLE: Thank you, Mr. Madden. If there are no more questions, I think our time is up. Thank you all.

V

Later Remembrances

"I See Him . . ."

It's all to the good that so many of you now know James Agee's writing — his novels, his criticism, his poetry. (In a sense it was all poetry.) I wish that you could also have known Jim himself.

Let me begin by describing him physically. He was about six-two and heavy but neither muscular nor fat — a mountaineer's body. His hair was dark brown, his eyes blue, and his skin pale. His hands were big and slablike in their thickness. He was very strong, and except for one occasion, which I only heard about, when he stove a *Time* editor against the wall, he was always gentle toward his fellow humans with that kind of gentleness usually reserved for plants and animals.

His clothes were dark and shiny. I can't imagine him in a new suit. Black shoes scuffed grey, wrinkled collar, a button off his shirt and a raveled tie — he wore clothes to be warm and decent. Jim's elegance was inward. I doubt whether he had any idea of what he looked like or whether he ever looked in a mirror except to shave. Vanity wasn't in him.

He held his body in very slight regard altogether, feeding it with whatever was at hand, allowing it to go to sleep when there was nothing else for it to do, begrudging it anything beneficial such as medicine when he was sick. On the other hand, he was a chain-smoker and a bottle-a-night man.

You who didn't actually know Jim might wish that he had taken better care of himself and lived longer to write more novels and screenplays . . . more poetry. But we who did know him recognize the fact that his body's destruction was implicit in his makeup, and we thank heaven that it was strong enough to withstand for so many years the constant assaults he leveled on it.

I was with Jim at the time of his first heart attack, and while he did obey the doctors' orders over a period of weeks — out of respect for their profession — and never asked any of his friends to get him a drink or even give him a drag off a cigarette, he let it be clearly understood that once the crisis was past he intended to resume the habits of life that had led up to it. I can hear myself uttering some nonsense about doing things in moderation, like sleeping eight hours every night and smoking, say, half a pack of cigarettes a day and only having a drink or two before dinner. Jim nodded his head in mute agreement with everything I said, or if not agreement, sympathy. And he went on nodding until I faltered and finished. Then he smiled his gentle smile and, after a decent interval, changed the subject.

His regard for other people's feelings was unique in my experience. I don't believe it was because he was afraid of hurting them, and certainly it had nothing to do with gaining in anyone's estimation. It was simply that his soul rejoiced when he could say yes and mean it to something someone else believed in.

He never attempted to win anyone to his way of thinking, far less to try to prove anyone mistaken or in the wrong. He would take a contrary opinion — regardless of how foolish it was — and hold it up to the light and turn it this way and that, examining its facets as though it were a gem of great worth, and if it turned out to be a piece of cracked glass, why then he, Jim, must have misunderstood — the other fellow had meant something else, hadn't he. . . . *this*, perhaps?

And sure enough Jim would come up with some variation of the opinion that would make it flawless as a specimen jewel. And the other fellow would be very proud of having meant precisely that, and they would go on from there.

I can see him sitting on the edge of a chair, bunched forward, elbows on knees, arms upraised, the fingers of one of the slablike hands pointing at those of the other and working as if they are trying to untie a knot. His forehead is furrowed and his mouth is twisted in concentration. His head is nodding in sympathy and understanding. He is smiling. Gaps show between his teeth. (Jim only went to the dentist to have a tooth pulled, never fixed.)

He is smiling. It stops raining all over the world. A great discovery has been made. He and another are in complete agreement. We who beheld that smile will never forget it.

Florence Homolka

Jim's Many Gestures

Jim had a deep sympathy for the poor of this world — for those who were materially poor in terms of this world's goods, certainly, but most especially for those who were at a loss in life, whose minds were inadequate, whose feelings were of little account to anyone. In movies, which he liked so much and took so seriously, he would often point out nameless members of the cast with appreciation.

He always used his hands a great deal in talking. He searched so carefully, and at the same time so violently and at such length, for the exact way to express himself that it amounted almost to inarticulacy. He had great persistence: he would never give up trying to explain something he had set out to clarify, and his struggle for communication often took the form of reading out loud from his own works or those of others. He studied hard and long and sincerely, and it is sad that his end came just as he was finding ways of telling what he had to tell, not only through the printed page but also through film, which had become such a close part of his vision and consciousness. He was awarded the Pulitzer Prize more than a year after he died in a taxi that was taking him to his doctor for a heart examination. In his ironical way, he would have enjoyed this circumstance. He would have made a long embroidered anecdote out of it, telling it with his slight lisp and many gestures.

WHITTAKER CHAMBERS

Agee

There is always a certain presumption in publicly claiming close friendship with someone whom we have long felt to be greater than ourselves, especially when the world, or a part of it, has belatedly discovered that there was greatness in him, and when he is no longer here to say of us: Yes, that is how it was; or: No, I felt about it a little differently. I am speaking about James Agee, who died in 1955 of a heart attack. I want you to know that I recognize the presumption and I shall risk it anyway. . . . What I shall say is my tribute to my friend, whose grave on his quiet farm I have not seen, and may not get to see, but approach in this way.

In fact, life had separated us for several years before. I was engaged in certain well-known events. Later, I was confined about two years, writing a book. Jim was in Hollywood, working with John Huston. Then came two heart attacks in quick succession. From his sick-room came, too, seven- and eight-page letters, penciled in the minute, slantwise, beautiful script which was a personal cipher that took hours to decode. In the spring of 1952, we both happened to be in New York. Jim came unexpectedly to my hotel, and we walked down Fifth Avenue together—very slowly, he could only inch along now, so that I saw that he was taking his last walks. He stopped before a show window in which cruelly elegant mannequins in exaggerated posture swam in a sickly lavender light. He stared at them for awhile. Then, "It's a pansy's world," he said, looking at them and at the city around us. We laughed. It was a summing up. Later, I bought two chocolate Easter eggs for his little girls. And that is how we parted. It is my last vivid memory of the living man. A few months later, I was in a hospital with a heart attack of my own. At Christmas, Jim sent me a dwarfed pear tree, which somebody planted for me. When I could get about, I helped it to live under some adverse conditions. Those days all run together in weakness to form a blur. In that blur Jim died, and his death became part of the blur.

> Multas per gentes et multa per aequora vectus,
> Venio, frater, ad has inferias.

> (Carried through many people and over many waters,
> I come, my brother, to these [sad] rites of death.)
> —Catullus

For me the blur passed into an upland spell and then again into blur. In the autumn of 1955 I was unloading a truckload of hay bales—the last load of the year's last cutting of alfalfa. It was a foolish thing to do. But the day is what the day is: we do what needs doing. Before half the load was off, a heart attack.

Then the long weeks in bed while the cold came, the earth hardened, it was winter, and at last a new year. During those long silent days I read a good first novel, *Your Own Beloved Sons* by Thomas Anderson. It was about the Korean War. There was the usual misery of the front line in winter—a hardened landscape of snow not too different from that outside my window. There were familiar types, too. There was the sensitive, callow, bookish soldier named Littlejohn and, by a stroke, nicknamed Little John. There was the crude non-com. Little John was cooking and the non-com. grabbed his book. Little John tried to get it back. The book was James Agee's *The Morning Watch*. The non-com. tormented Little John by suggesting that it was sex stuff. Little John felt this as a violation. He tried to explain. It did not make sense. But then he said it: "It's about religion, but it's not a religious book." Yes, that was it, that was absolutely it.

I laid the book on the bed. It seemed to me that, for the first time in years, Jim came walking toward me across a frozen field. I could see him as we can so seldom wholly visualize the dead. And, as we met, the little nod of the head, casual but so oddly reserved, and the hands clutched against the stomach in a gesture of pain, and on the face a grimace of pain — a mocking grimace. Anybody who knew Jim well knew that gesture and that grimace.

A heart attack sets the mind to living naturally with the possibility of a sudden end. As the swift and unexpected image passed, I smiled. Its place was taken by another, humorous and rather solemn one. It was an image of myself at the Judgment, with God the Father bending a little to press a little grimly, and asking me: "Will anyone speak for this man?" Then from the seraphic sidelines Jim would step out — unshaved as nearly always, work shirt, workmen's shoes, corduroy trousers, as usual — and stand in silence beside me. And God the Father would half smile with the little gesture of the hand that means: "What can you do?" As we step back into the crowd, from the vault and from the depths, the choirs would sing in those pure tones. In all that throng, Jim, I thought, would be the only one who did not know that they were singing about him.

A sick man's thoughts about a dead man? Yes. Of course. Jim drank too much — in the end he largely drank himself to death. He was savagely unconventional and, in most practical matters of life, belligerently irresponsible. Certain things — rudeness, in particular — moved him to violence. He once drove his fist through the door of a Fifth Avenue bus, which its driver had insolently refused to open for him. He was not a religious man, not in most senses understood by the Westminster Confession, which was Jim's. But he was, among all men I have known — telling them over carefully in my mind — the one who was most "about religion."

MIA AGEE, WITH GERALD LOCKLIN

Faint Lines in a Drawing of Jim

The difficulty in composing a memoir such as this is that I know it can't be done. There is no possible way for me to evaluate or select specific telling instances that reveal anything of significance in relation to as complex a personality as James Agee's. The person closely involved in randomly selecting and relating such happenings must surely know how fragile such an eclectic process is. My memories have been carefully walled off, and I know what a dangerous endeavor it is to suddenly open such doors. I am also unable to relate everyday events in a modulated tone of voice and with the kind of distance that the passage of time is supposed to provide. So why am I in these pages at all? I agree that I probably shouldn't be, but I also felt like joining a personal memorial without really facing in any detail the realities that this would involve for me.

There has been much written about James Agee and his work since his death, and I have nothing but appreciation for most of it.

I am, however, struck by how often his critics talk about his having "wasted his time and diffused his talent." The justification given normally cites the many years he worked for *Fortune, Time,* and the *Nation.* To these are added all the many months he worked in Hollywood doing scripts for movies that saw production or a few that didn't. In addition, there are those innumerable commentaries that had to be written for foreign films, mostly documentaries. It is true that he had to work very hard at all these jobs and whatever writing he could do of his own had to be squeezed into off-hours, and there were never enough of them. However, the question still remains whether in fact this was a waste of time. I am not convinced of it. It is true he may have stayed with some of these jobs too long, but would it really have been any less wasteful had he spent his days in an advertising agency, or driving a New York cab, or becoming a dirt farmer in the Tennessee mountains? What do writers do when they have to make a living? Is it really assumed today that a writer writes because he has a private income, or is it assumed that he teaches at a college and that teaching is less a waste of time or perhaps less time-consuming, or is it simply more intellectually acceptable? Personally I see very little difference in writing for a magazine, which at least uses some of the skills a writer is most interested in developing. I know that to some extent Jim felt challenged by the idea of having to write within a set format, but working at all times against that format, creating a kind of tension, and seeing just how far he could go. I know for a fact that he enjoyed having to write long mechanical process captions as he did for *Fortune,* such as how a certain fabric was loomed or how glass was formed or how arbitrage works. These tasks had some of the intriguing characteristics of certain games and puzzles, and in Jim's hands they became small poems. Henry R. Luce wanted to send him to the Harvard Business School because he wanted to see that kind of writing applied to a corporation story (then *Fortune*'s major journalistic invention). Luce couldn't really see why Jim declined this offer. I must say I would have been interested to see such a corporation story, though I doubt that *Fortune* would ever have printed it.

Jim tried, of course, other ways of making money. He worked on *Let Us Now Praise Famous Men* for more than two years after he left *Fortune* without any personal reserves and an advance from the publisher of something around $500 — an advance the book in fact never made back. Of course, he had to have a regular job again, and he went back to *Time* to write book reviews. Since he was a slow reader and never wanted to be a speedy one, he moved into movies, and as a movie reviewer he opened up a new field for himself, though a field with which he had always been in love. He stayed on as a film critic for roughly eight years, and every few years he would try to break out of the bind by applying for grants, awards, etc., but he never made it. He finally did get out by committing himself to do some freelance articles for *Life* only to discover that, despite the fact that the articles were well paid, they consumed infinitely more time than his regular jobs did and so in effect paid him less.

Add to this the fact that Jim was a married man for most of his adult life and that for a large part of it he had children to support, and it seems surprising how much of his own work he did get done. He was a very hard and constant worker. He was at all times at work on one or more projects of his own and was always dissatisfied with himself for not getting more of his own work done. So the waste of talent is perhaps not so much a real waste (i.e., not having done enough writing) but a discrepancy between the talent and the tasks to which it was put. That, too, I think is largely debatable. One could argue that Jim's employment resulted in some very fine writing. His film criticisms are considered classics — his serious treatment of what were then called movies and now called films was far ahead of its time. *Let Us Now Praise Famous Men*, though eventually rejected by *Fortune*, did germinate from a journalistic assignment. His screenplays are a part of every film enthusiast's library, and many of his most powerful attitudes derived from his journalistic exposure to the ideas and realities of his time.

Jim worked better in some places than in others and better under some conditions than others. The best environment for him to work in was, without a doubt, the country. This was particularly true of our place in Hillsdale. The old farmhouse is about six miles from the nearest town; it lies on the outskirts of the Berkshire mountains, and the house sits on top of a hill with woods all around it and no other place in sight. There was no electricity and only an old gravity water system that broke down most of the time so that the water had to be pumped or carried. But the place has an indescribable stillness, tranquillity, and peacefulness. This is where Jim could work best. This is where he wrote his first film script, *The Blue Hotel*, a Stephen Crane story; he did it in four days, and it was a kind of tour de force. This was the place where he could recharge his psychic batteries and where he would arise early and start his work about six or seven in the morning. He would get to sleep when it got dark and he would feel in tune and happy. He would often go there by himself when he had a lot of work to do, and the children and I would stay in the city busy with our own things. On weekends and vacations we would all go there, and every one of us developed a particular affection for the place.

Jim had many friends in the city and he valued his friendships highly, but he was not in love with the city itself, and it was basically a hard place for him to do his own writing. He loved many of the stimulations and possibilities New York offered, and because he was by nature a gregarious person, much of the stimulation involved people and parties and music. He never needed much outside pressure to turn into a night person, and he would often try to work after the party was over and know that probably all he was good for by that time was writing some letters he needed to write and which he knew he didn't have to mail the next day if he didn't like them. Serious work during the night he could do only if he had worked straight through. He was extremely musical and played the piano well and with a powerful style of his own. Aside from a large classical repertoire that included everything from chamber music to opera, he also loved jazz and blues. He had a great collection of old jazz records, Bessie Smith, Louis Armstrong, etc., but he always felt that his jazz improvisations on the piano were not very good. He had a real affection for old church hymns and felt that it would be fun to write a history of the United States in terms of the popularity of church hymns and the faiths they represented. It was one of the things I could not share with him since, aside from the fact that I knew very little about them, I didn't like what I did know of them. He was extremely careful with his selection of hymns for some of the movie scripts he worked on, and both *The African Queen* and *The Night of the Hunter* made dramatic use of his selections.

Jim had the ability to give himself totally to whatever he was doing at the moment, much as a child does. It made little difference whether this was writing, playing tennis or piano, or talking to someone. He was a good listener, but he was a better talker. He could get involved in a meaningful conversation with absolutely anyone, and people tended to be dazzled by it. This did not always work in his favor. There is the story of his going to meet a publisher who was interested in one of his manuscripts (I think it was *The Morning Watch*); after spending a couple of hours with him, Jim left and the publisher turned down the manuscript without reading it because he was totally convinced that a man who could talk that way obviously couldn't write. I guess it must be unusual to be able to excel at both talking and writing.

In some ways he was an old-fashioned man. He was a man who took pride in *all* his writing; he never tossed off anything in his life, and he was incapable of a hack job. To honor verbal agreements was more important to him than legal ones. For example, he made a verbal agreement with a Filipino actor, Emmanuel Conde, to direct a film for and with him in the Philippines. While Jim was waiting in New York for Conde to contact him and finishing some previous work commitments, John Huston came to town ready to get started on their long-planned project of *Moby-Dick,* a book both Huston and Jim had talked of doing together for years and a story they both had very special feelings for. This also involved an invitation to go to Europe (Ireland and the south of France) for a year, a prospect that made me drool and that Jim would have loved to do. To my utter dismay, Jim, who was excited about both the trip and the script, told Huston that he couldn't do it at this time because of his previous agreement with Conde. Huston thought the decision insane and found another scriptwriter. Nobody knows what happened to Mr. Conde or his project since nobody ever heard from him again. Huston did direct *Moby-Dick* with Ray Bradbury as his writer, but Jim never saw the film.

I'm sometimes asked in what direction I think Jim would have gone in his career if he had had another five, ten, or twenty years to live. Of course, he wanted to direct films, and I am sure he would have done so. As early as his Harvard years he set forth one summer on a quixotic trip to Hollywood, an abortive hitchhiking trip that ended in the Midwest harvesting. Had he arrived there, I am not at all sure he would ever have returned to Harvard. He had a passion for movies. Today this is true of many young people, but in Jim's generation it was unusual for a young man with his education and talent to consider movies as a significant new art form and not simply as entertainment.

To speculate about what he might have done as a writer had he lived seems futile, since so little is left of notebooks and manuscripts. Most of his papers were stolen while in storage in his sister's house. He had done some preliminary work on a novel about modern marriage. He wanted very much to get back to poetry, and he was planning an original film script. That is all I know.

Jim had a great sense of humor and always wanted to do more humorous writing. He could be a wicked satirist, and some of his oldest friendships were based on a shared style of humor and satire — Wilder Hobson, for example, and Dwight Macdonald. When meeting at parties they would set each other off into imitations, parodies, and puns and outdo each other in spontaneous inventions.

The role of father both attracted and terrified him. Not really a contradiction but simply a characteristic double feeling about important matters, taken very seriously. He had an appreciation of babies, probably relating to their mute expressiveness and their wide-open potential. It seems that other poets such as Byron shared this fascination. When I was working for *Fortune* and wanted to go to Europe for a three-month assignment, I planned to make special provisions for the care of the children, but he insisted that he wanted to take care of them himself. My misgivings were misplaced, and they all enjoyed being on their own.

He was a magnificent, warm, sensitive, contradictory, passionate, compassionate human being, but he was psychologically incapable of moderation, even during the period of his last illness. His motto was "a little bit too much is just enough for me." I am asked, was he self-destructive? Obviously in a sense he was, and since he was a romantic, he was strongly disinclined to let himself be programmed by necessities and external realities. He was always full of good intentions for reform and discipline in the wake of a severe setback, but his reforms never lasted very long. He had a very strong physique and so was always able to count on his body doing what he wanted it to do.

Possibly, as part of his religious upbringing as well as a strong poetic sensibility, he had an alive religious nerve of some kind and he conceived life as basically tragic. His tendency toward self-pity was more a pity for humanity, which happened to include himself. He had a strongly developed sense of guilt, a sense of guilt that at times could paralyze him and that at the same time formed a very basic part of his character. He said that I had pointed out to him that

his greatest weakness was self-pity, where he had always felt that it was a weakness of will. I am not so sure that they are not essentially the same.

He was never ill until his first heart attack in 1951. As a result he was constitutionally an unlikely candidate for the role of invalid or even the role of a man who has to budget his physical strength, has to be careful about what he eats, drinks, smokes, etc. All his instincts worked along an absolute assumption of physical well-being and the ability to be careless about physical strength. He loved to play tennis, hadn't played it in New York for many years, and was delighted to start playing again when he came to California. He ignored the fact that he was out of training, that his life had been largely sedentary, and that he was no longer twenty-five years old. He started playing singles at seven o'clock in the morning, after having worked all night writing, with an enthusiasm that was best and most accurately described as a bull charging on red cloth. This produced his first heart attack, and that was the reason he wasn't able to go to Africa for the filming of *The African Queen*, a trip he had been very much looking forward to.

I have been asked to what extent I think of Jim as being southern. Naturally I don't think of him as the stereotypical Southern Gentleman but, yes, I do think of him as being southern. A certain kind of sensitivity and gentleness and true courteousness to me are part of this. I think I associate those qualities most perhaps with his father's Tennessee mountain background. I myself have a feeling for the South that has nothing to do with any contemporary clichés, and to this day I find that people in the South establish a simpler, more immediate human contact with me. Traveling through the South, I can stop for coffee at a little roadside place and come away a half an hour later feeling that I have been in some simple communication, recognized as another human being rather than as a traveling android.

Jim had an enormous empathy with people. No doubt this was due in part to his imagination, but it was also a function of his essential humanness. He saw other people's dilemmas and seemed always able to respond. This, of course, was time-consuming. He was a generous man, both with money and time. He had fluctuated between having no money, having little money, and having occasionally a fair amount of money. He never became accustomed to those various levels. Even

when he had money, setting out on a trip, he would pull into a gaso-
line station and ask for a dollar's worth of gas (a Depression habit).
Contrarily, at a critical time he would buy me three evening gowns
to cheer me up, though I never used evening gowns, but they were
very pretty. He hated to have to think about money, and he didn't do
much of it except in extremities. One day I got a call from the cleaner
to whom Jim had taken his suit to be pressed, and he told me he had
found $450 in Jim's pants pocket. Jim had just cashed a paycheck,
changed his suit, and never missed it.

I have tried to follow a sequence of questions about Jim that have
been put to me, and I hope I have at least partially answered them,
but what does it all add up to? Maybe the best thing would be not to
try to add anything up but simply to let it go as faint lines in a drawing
that may eventually form a pattern but that so far is indistinguishable
as a portrait.

Saturday Panel: Reminiscences

McDOWELL: I'm going to simply ask you a little bit about your individual relationships with James Agee. We will make some comment on his work as well as his life. We're not going into any deep criticism, because we've been doing that all week on the panels: *The Morning Watch* and *A Death in the Family*; *Let Us Now Praise Famous Men*; his film criticism, and we've shown films; and we've had a special panel on his poetry. All among us on this panel knew Agee and his work. Father Flye, of course, knew him from the time that he was a small boy. Father, would you like to make just a brief recollection of your first encounter with him? Give us your reaction to Jim before he went to Exeter.

FATHER FLYE: In the summer of 1918, Rufus Agee's mother with her two children, Rufus and his younger sister, Emma, came to the mountains here at St. Andrew's, having known of the place and perhaps met or known some of the members of the Order. They spent the summer here. The following summer, she was more attracted by the atmosphere of this place. She was not a solemn woman but a deeply religious woman with a lovely sense of humor. She was a charming and a dear person.

I had a parish down in Milledgeville, Georgia, after graduating from seminary, and my wife and I were there. Father Harrison had been down to see me and asked if I would consider coming up here to teach. I'd taught some before I went to seminary, and I said I would. So, in the fall of 1918, I came and began my teaching here.

I stayed through the next summer doing some work on the house. It was the summer of 1919. Mrs. Agee and the two children had come for their second summer, and it was my first summer at St. Andrew's. The school was closed, and some boys were staying here, and here was Mrs. Agee and the two children, and we all got acquainted. So I met Rufus, as we called him then, using his middle name, which he afterwards came to dislike and dropped, and his little sister, Emma. I got to know them very well, and he was a charming little boy, not quite ten years old. I just loved him. He was dear and warm and intelligent and very trustworthy, and he read quite a bit. He had a good mind, and we talked a bit of the reading he'd done, a bit about science and natural history and pets and the woods and fossils, and we had a lovely fellow companionship. It was a lovely family.

At the end of that summer, Mrs. Agee decided, instead of going back to Knoxville, she'd stay around in a little cottage that was available and let the children go to school, and so they did. He was here for four years. He spent one year in Knoxville High School, and after that he went to Exeter. Those are the circumstances under which I got to know him from his childhood. I wasn't with him all the time, but we had a dear and understanding friendship, and the friendship continued as long as he lived.

McDOWELL: Did Agee show very early interest in, and intelligence about, creative writing?

FATHER FLYE: I would say not at all, as far as I knew, as long as he was at St. Andrew's. These were his earlier years, and he left here when he was about fourteen. I can't entirely answer that. I was not his English teacher, and I don't know what he may have done in papers for English, but I've known boys who were interested in writing when they were young. I've had a little boy come up to me at twelve years old and hand me a poem that he had written, and I would certainly encourage him and say, "By all means, if you feel like writing, do it, even if it's not good. You're not competing with anyone. It's what you can do and develop it." I tried to encourage him, and sometimes they would be very good poems. I never had anything like that from Jim, not a word of poetry. He wrote good papers for my history classes, well expressed, but nothing of genius. That's what came a little later.

McDowell: When did he first express interest in film to you? That struck him very early, I understand.

Father Flye: As a child. I can't say how early, but certainly when he was ten or eleven years old. He was interested in movies, not as a boy might be, but he would say, "Oh, yes, look what the director did. Look how he put that together. Look at the camera work." He was highly interested in movies.

McDowell: Dwight, you first got to know him through a friend. You were at Exeter when Jim got there. Is that correct?

Macdonald: I graduated in 1924, and he came in the fall of 1925. We had an English professor, Mr. Williams, in common.

McDowell: So you started corresponding about 1927?

Macdonald: Yes, the first letter was in 1927.

McDowell: Was the nature of your correspondence with him more about film than about writing?

Macdonald: It began about writing. I think Jim really became a writer at Exeter. I know I did. I think that's when he really came alive.

Father Flye: His first published letter is dated September 1925, and at that time he was getting some things into magazines. He then began writing poetry.

Macdonald: Exeter was the place for writers. It had a marvelous English department. The Lantern Club was a rather sophisticated literary club. I think it became clear to us very early that we were both interested in movies. This is unusual for then. Now there is nothing to it. Every kid is interested in movies. They make their own movies! In those days, to be interested in movies as serious art was unusual, and that was really the basis of our correspondence and of our relationship. Then I went to *Fortune*, and Jim was writing to me from Harvard. He desperately needed a job, and I got him a job. I was a writer on *Fortune*, and I had no trouble getting him a job, as I had no trouble getting myself a job, because we were both very good writers. We knew how to write.

McDOWELL: You hear a lot of talk about Agee having sold himself to the Luce publications. You must keep in mind, all of you, that this was 1932, the absolute depths of the Depression. There were plenty of people with great talent at that time who couldn't find jobs. He not only wanted a "job," as he said, but he wanted a job writing. I want to get this across to everybody because too much is made of it. He wrote to Mr. Macdonald and said that he was with eyes uplifted and his stomach empty, and he was very grateful to have a job.

MACDONALD: Being a writer in the early Depression was a great thing, because that was one of the few places where there were still a lot of jobs. It was very hard. If he sold himself to Luce, then I did, too. However, I do think that it was a great mistake that he kept on so long. He should have stayed there much less time. I think I stayed there six years; that was two years too long.

McDOWELL: You got to know him at Harvard. Is that right, Mr. Fitzgerald?

FITZGERALD: I got to know him as a freshman. Jim was one class ahead of me. The class we had in common was in versification, with Dr. Robert Hillyer. There were very few fellows in this class, perhaps six or seven. Jim sat in the front row, one desk ahead of me on my right in the entirety of every class. He was a very impressive figure, even then. I especially remember, and have written about, his being asked to read in class. He was reading from Donne. He read with great internal pressure. His reading during the years I knew him was always very, very impressive. It was low-pitched, very grave, and under enormous control. He was calibrated as to pitch and accent and tempo and rhythm. Of course, he loved to read things aloud. That was marvelous. He loved to try out his own work on his friends. I remember *Ulysses* class. You really didn't understand the book until you heard somebody like Jim read it.

McDOWELL: His reading was not in any way stagey or arty.

FITZGERALD: No, it was underkey. He did share with Joyce a marvelous ear. Music was almost as important to him as books were.

McDOWELL: It's simply astonishing. He had so many interests: movies, books, his own writing. He could very well have been a professional musician. He was talented at it. Did he at any time think about being a musician?

FATHER FLYE: Yes, I think so. He took piano lessons, when he was at St. Andrew's, over at Sewanee. He liked this. His Aunt Paula, whom I still see occasionally, taught music in New York City. I don't know how often he saw her, but I remember her saying that he was a pretty good musician. He would have liked to compose. He wrote me in one of his letters that he could have been a musician. Perhaps he was, though not one of the professional, creative ones.

McDOWELL: Joyce could have been a musician, too. In fact, he had a beautiful voice, and his wife once said, "Why do you insist upon writing? Why don't you be another John McCormick?" Robert, you were in Europe for a year near the end of Jim's life.

FITZGERALD: Regrettably in that way. I saw nothing of him that year. When I got back the following year, I would hear a word occasionally about how he was working in a skyscraper, as he was, in the Chrysler Building. He was working mostly at writing, and I think it was in those years that he worked out that great trick of trimming on the vine, getting his ears close to the language.

McDOWELL: He was a slow reader, and he didn't skim. He felt he had a duty to read each thing carefully. He had such respect for the written word and for anyone who was trying to achieve it.

MACDONALD: One thing about Jim and the movies — the first letter I ever got was remarkable, I think in 1927. I quoted it in a thing I did for *Film Heritage*. First, he knew that he wanted to go to movies, and that was unusual; second, he formulated a perfectly viable aesthetic of film work. I don't think that I could have done that at that age; he really developed the asset very early.

McDOWELL: Once he began to review movies, he was much happier. I remember when he and Mr. Chambers were doing the book reviews. After he dropped that, he began to be a regular movie critic for *Time*. Later on, he also did a monthly column for the *Nation*, in which he had more space to write.

FATHER FLYE: These articles were signed, also. The ones in *Time* were not.

McDOWELL: I suppose that this was an age where the movies occupied the minds of the young more, and as Dwight points out, the beginning of that was about the time that Agee was reviewing movies for *Time* and the *Nation*. The people began to think of movies as a serious art form, as Agee had done at the beginning.

MACDONALD: I don't think that it was anywhere near as early as that. I would say that movies were not taken seriously as an art form until about 1960. One thing that struck me about Jim was that I think he was ill-fated. I think his stars were crossed. When he reviewed movies, from 1945 to 1952, right after the war, that time happened to have been the almost low point of movies after the silent era, and he died almost a year before the great Bergman revival and the New Wave. That's another reason, by the way, that movies were so admired in the last ten or fifteen years, because they were so much better. Jim died just before that.

McDOWELL: Andrew Lytle, when did you first encounter Jim's work?

LYTLE: Unlike these other gentlemen, I encountered Jim through his work. The only time I met him was at a party at David McDowell's house, and he dropped me off in the Village later in the evening. As we rode in the cab, I was impressed by his brilliant, almost titanic energy and goodwill and good humor.

McDOWELL: We've had some marvelous talk about *A Death in the Family* in previous panels here and about *The Morning Watch*. A great deal of the burden of that was getting into whether *A Death in the Family* was an autobiographical novel, what was really true in it and what was not, and everyone decided, especially Father Flye and Dr. Lytle, that it didn't make any difference. Would you like to rattle on about that for a moment, Andrew?

LYTLE: *The Odyssey* is a book about history, and you can find truth in it. But it has nothing in the world to do with fiction. The biographical material that goes into a novel where man uses his day-to-day life is transformed by the mystery of the craft that is going through the imagination. It's just a part of the material that he is using to explain himself in the book. It's after the fact. He uses the past information and fits in an action, which is really fiction.

McDOWELL: Walker Percy, would you like to add something to that?

PERCY: I never knew Agee. I wish I had. I can only speak about his influence on me as a writer. I suppose I can best describe this as being technical. I think of him not with southern writers but rather with Englishmen and Irishmen, Hopkins and Joyce — the early Joyce. Agee's main influence has been technical, simply in the way that he crafts an English sentence and his use of poetic devices, of metaphors, and the structure of a sentence within a paragraph. Maybe someone who knew Agee could tell me how close he was to Hopkins and how much store he set by him, especially when Agee is writing about nature and his use of metaphors. He reminds me very much of Hopkins's nature journal. Somebody should write a book about the relationship between Hopkins's philosophy of inscape, the idea of seizing a concrete thing by way of a metaphor, and the way Agee did it, too. To me, they are very close together. So that would be the summary of Agee's influence on me.

MCDOWELL: Robert, you could tell us. Did you and he talk very much about Hopkins?

FITZGERALD: That's a very interesting point, one that I don't believe that I have ever heard mentioned, at least in print. In my own memoir of Jim, I remember quoting a long passage from one of his notebooks on surf coming in at Anna Maria Key, which is one of the islands off the West Coast of Florida. He lived on it six months when he was twenty-five or twenty-six. I likened it there, precisely, to a passage from Hopkins's journal. No one has picked this up or has done anything about it. All I could say as to Jim's familiarity with Hopkins is this: he and I both took I. A. Richards's course in modern English literature in 1932. For two weeks out of the ten or twelve that Richards lectured, we were hearing him recite and read great poems of Hopkins. At that point, if not before, Jim Agee's ear, you know, was delighted and amazed by such things as Earnest, Earth's, Equal, Atunable, Voluminous, Stupendous, Evening, Strained, and other marvelous metaphors and precisions that came in, so that from that time forward, I do not remember Jim speaking very much of Hopkins. It was taken for granted between him and me that we both looked up to and respected him a great deal.

MCDOWELL: Robert Daniel knows an enormous amount about poetry. It's his specialty. What do you think about that Hopkins allusion? Do you feel it this way that Robert and Walker do? By the way, all of this is covered in Robert Fitzgerald's introduction to *The Collected Short Prose of James Agee*; the memoir prefacing that is the best thing that I've read on Agee. It's a short thing. It doesn't go into deep scholarly pursuit, but as a memoir and an introduction to his work, it is invaluable. Let me get back to you, Robert.

DANIEL: I was thinking of going back a step or two. I never had the privilege of knowing James Agee, but I did live in Knoxville for twelve years while I was teaching there. I think the city became very possessive of him, particularly around the university, perhaps more so than any other southern writer. If you read *A Death in the Family,* which is so saturated with the atmosphere of the place in theory — no, the book is supposed to contain, when you really come down to it, the artist. If you have a close familiarity with the place where it is supposed to be happening, it reads in a way that is theoretically illegitimate.

McDOWELL: David Madden, the distinguished novelist, who has been here with us all week and who was once a pupil of yours, resented *A Death in the Family* a little bit as a Knoxville boy. When he encountered Agee, he seemed to feel that Agee was somehow on his territory. He appropriated a few things that he wanted to use himself — before he read Agee, that is. Would you like to add anything about your reaction to his book yourself?

MADDEN: I just feel the connection between Agee and Hopkins. I don't think of any specific parallel.

McDOWELL: [To Daniel] When did you first read Agee? When did you encounter his work?

DANIEL: I think it was while I was in Knoxville. There was so much talk about him among the students; they were writing theses about him.

McDOWELL: There are a good many of those being done. All of these panels, incidentally, all this will be kept not only recorded but on videotape, and they will be very useful to scholars. Father, when did he begin to send poems to you?

FATHER FLYE: I think that was the next step. That was in his senior year at Exeter. In a letter to me, he might include some poetry. He would sometimes copy poems that he liked very much, and he would say, "Isn't this wonderful?" Going back over his letters through the years, noticing the poems that he had sent to me, I can't say, but I think that it was in the senior year at Exeter.

McDOWELL: In other words, when he was here at St. Andrew's, he never showed you any poems, or do you recall?

FATHER FLYE: They say in logic that it is impossible to prove a negative, and I can't say that he never wrote a poem when he was here, but I doubt that he ever did. He certainly never showed me any, or I had no reason to think that he did. I'm sorry that I cannot verify that. His mother would have known.

MACDONALD: I suppose that he began writing poetry at Exeter.

McDowell: Did you discuss poetry as much as you did movies?

Macdonald: I have several very long letters about Whitman and other poetry he was reading, and Chaplin, a great interest of mine.

McDowell: [To Percy] You said that Agee had an influence on you. Were you interested in the prose itself, or in the structure, or the kind of characterization he did, and in which part of Agee's structure were you most interested or most influenced?

Percy: Something that has already been suggested, something that, I suppose, you would call poetic prose. His poems are not particularly impressive to me. But there's something going on in his prose. Maybe this is a development of the novel. Something has happened to the novel in the last sixty years. The novelist poeticizes. I think some of the best poetry is in the novels. I think Agee was one of the first to do it.

Macdonald: I think that his poetry was the only part where he comes forth a little old-fashioned, the only old-fashioned, romantic thing that even by 1925 was pretty much played out. He was the best prose writer of my generation in the sense of having the most complete command of the medium and versatility. He could handle all kinds of different styles, and he always put his mark on it. He could be expository, funny, eloquent, etc.

McDowell: He could do the most beautiful kind of things, some of the most concrete descriptions that I have ever read, something like that passage on the overalls in *Let Us Now Praise Famous Men*. It's bare. Its not really poetic at all. Its poetic sense is great, but it does not have any kind of fancy writing about it. He could shift gears from that into something else completely.

Macdonald: You and Robert have both commented on what a marvelous mimic he was. Joyce was, too. He had dozens of styles that he could command. He has a voice like in *Ulysses*, and he shifts styles all the time. Agee was like this but in a slightly smaller light.

Daniel: There's an aspect in the book *A Death in the Family* that we haven't mentioned. The dialogue. I think that's one of the most marvelous things about it. He's absolutely true to life. It goes back to that good ear he had, but it's even more than that. It's just fine.

Lytle: It's connected too, though, Robert. I remember, rereading it this time. It's just fine. We repeat ourselves in the accidents of words so very much. Agee was selective.

Macdonald: What do you mean by selective?

LYTLE: Some select, and some select better than others.

MCDOWELL: This point came up when you [Fitzgerald] were making the collection [*The Collected Poems of James Agee*]. It was hard to decide what to put in. This calls for the most serious kind of thought. I was faced with the same sort of problem with *A Death in the Family*. What I put in is a sort of prologue. "Knoxville: Summer 1915" was not a part of that book. I would have been his editor, had he lived. It was one of the best things he ever did, and it fits in perfectly there; it sets a tone and a rhythm. Anyway, that was a serious decision to put that there. And Robert, you were confronted with much the same problem when you were collecting his poems.

FITZGERALD: I never have been able to say to myself very certainly whether or not Jim would resent and dislike my having included so much documentary criteria, which was so often his, whether he would agree to it, because no doubt a great deal of the verse that I put in wasn't very good verse. You know it as well as I.

FATHER FLYE: "Knoxville: Summer 1915" was written during the period when he was at Anna Maria Island in 1936. He read to me, when he got back from that trip, a number of things that he had written at that time, and this was one of them.

MCDOWELL: I don't know of any short piece of prose myself that is so brilliantly sustained as that, so packed.

FITZGERALD: I think, speaking of Jim as a poet, maybe he was a poet who did his best poetry in prose. Some of his best poetry is in *Let Us Now Praise Famous Men*.

MCDOWELL: He was, essentially, a poet.

FITZGERALD: I don't like his rhythmical poems as much as I like his prose.

MACDONALD: That first part, "Knoxville: Summer 1915," was there at your suggestion?

MCDOWELL: Yes, I put it there. He didn't put it there. But I would have urged him to put it there. I saw him, on Friday the thirteenth, three days before he died. He had hoped — at that time he was working on lyrics for *Candide* — and he expected to go up to his farm in Hillsdale, New York, to finish it [*A Death in the Family*]. He hoped to finish up in a month or so, as he felt by the end of the summer that he might be able to complete it. The problem when he died was what to do with this manuscript. There were certain parts of it that needed to be fitted in somehow. There are two time schemes, as you already know. I added nothing to it whatsoever. The only thing that I did, and I think it was the most important editorial decision I ever made, was to put in that beautiful piece, "Knoxville: Summer 1915," which seemed to belong there. It was not written for *A Death in the Family*, but I would have urged him to put it there. Other than that, there were no editorial changes; the manuscript is as it was written. It is sort of ironic. Shortly before the publication of the book, I came down to Tennessee. My son was a student here at that time, and I came through Knoxville. This was two months before the publication of the novel. And I called up the managing editors of the two papers and said, "We're bringing out a book called *A Death in the Family* by a Knoxville boy, and it deals with Knoxville." Neither one of them cared enough to see me. When I got into Nashville, I found that not a single one of his books was in the Tennessee State Library. He was not at that time considered to be a Tennessee writer. How things have changed. Now he is one of the glories of Tennessee letters.

AUDIENCE: [unintelligible]

MACDONALD: I would say that Agee was probably the best American film critic. For one thing, he had a very good background. Not only was he a creative writer, but he was unlike Thomas Wolfe, say, in having a brain; he really could discuss ideas. He was an intellectual as well as a very talented prose writer. He brought to his film criticism much knowledge of movies as well as books, as well as a very sound education at Exeter and Harvard. This intellectual quality in Agee added depth to his film criticism. That is, he brought a knowledge of Italian nonwar times to his criticism of films from Italy right after the war.

AUDIENCE: [unintelligible]

McDOWELL: Mr. Percy's book was called *The Moviegoer*, and it won the National Book Award, so he is most qualified to comment.

PERCY: I'd like to speculate on the relationship between Agee's moviegoing and his film criticism. It caused a political reaction. Agee was radicalized by *Fortune*, according to Dwight Macdonald. That may be true. I think he was radicalized by the movies he had to see between 1945 and 1950. They were the worst movies I can remember. He had to see them all because he was the reviewer. I think that there was only one good movie the whole time. That was *The Treasure of the Sierra Madre*.

MACDONALD: One thing, though. I did the same thing for *Esquire* for six years. I'm lucky, unlike him. For one thing, I'm still alive. I'm lucky because I began in 1960, and that was just when the whole New Wave of movies was opening up, and it wasn't that bad at all for those six years. I never did it on a regular basis, though. One thing that might have preserved Agee when he was doing film reviews for the *Nation* was one of the characteristics of his mind. He's a romantic critic, and I'm a classic critic. The classicist looks at the thing as a whole; the romantic has no sense of the structure as a whole but looks at details. Agee would see one thing in an hour-and-a-half movie and would magnify it and that would color his whole view of the movie. I would say terrible, and he would say that it was neat. He wouldn't suffer as much at a bad movie as I would.

AUDIENCE: Would you comment on Agee's importance as a poet?

MACDONALD: I really don't know. I didn't think so much of the poetry, but then I really don't know. The collection [*The Collected Poems of James Agee*] has just been put out.

AUDIENCE: [unintelligible]

McDOWELL: He welcomed criticism more than any writer I've ever known, and I've been working with them most of my life. He loved to read whatever he was working on to friends or any other group. He was as open as anyone I've ever known to criticism.

MACDONALD: The only other person I know who is equally open to criticism is Norman Mailer.

FITZGERALD: Both were probably secure. Jim was secure in that he knew that he was a decent writer. He could listen to the worst criticism and hear it. It was so easy for him to accept criticism, and he was generous and open about it. After all, what he was about was making something good. Whether this came about in the untouched singular of his own effort or whether it came about with a few touches of assistance doesn't matter at all. The thing was to get it right—to get the words in the right order. He was selfless in this area in many instances. What he wanted was wonderful writing. If it was his, that was fine, but if it was yours, equally fine, in fact even better.

FATHER FLYE: If you see manuscripts of his, you see that he revised quite a bit as he wrote. And so he would commonly welcome suggestions from someone else, which he would certainly consider.

McDOWELL: As an amateur writer, working with writers, I always find out what the writer is trying to accomplish and, if possible, try to aid him in that. Not to rewrite it. I wouldn't say, "Why don't you make the man a woman, or why don't you set it in Paris instead of where you were originally trying and planning to set it?" Many editors are, unfortunately, like that and would try to mess around with somebody's work.

MACDONALD: I remember one instance when Agee's literary talents failed him, when Henry Luce discovered that Agee had for three years been writing for *Fortune* what we called beautiful writing. He used to write articles about the most precious jewels in the world and kinds of orchids, and he never wrote the corporation stuff. *Fortune* was about business. Luce decided that he should also have to write about business. He assigned Agee the topic of the price of steel rails, and Luce would be the editor on that piece. He tried to explain to Agee why this was an interesting subject. The price of steel rails was the same from 1893 until 1933. Agee simply could not get with it, and Luce then had the audacity to give me the article.

FITZGERALD: I suppose in many cases when factual material was needed —

McDOWELL: The insistence was that you had to make him observant.

MACDONALD: If you have as big a mind as Agee, you have to be big enough to swallow the world.

McDOWELL: I think we can all testify that he put on a mighty good show with his pyrotechnics and mimicking and gesticulating. But he didn't mind being interrupted. Generally, he was so good that most of the other people just sat back and watched.

MACDONALD: He really gave of himself too much. I think that's one of the reasons that he died so early. He simply wore himself out.

FITZGERALD: Jim's power of attention of any other human soul was endless. He had the power to sympathize with and understand others.

FATHER FLYE: Some say he was a drunk, an alcoholic. This was not true. I know him too well and know that was not true.

McDOWELL: The one thing that you have to have with a heart condition is rest, and if you don't get it, your chances for recovery drop rapidly — even worse than smoking. It goes without saying that he didn't get that rest!

Robert Fitzgerald

"What Was Pure and Immediate": James Agee Memorial Library Dedication

Dear hosts, dear guests, please do not look forward to an address which I found myself programmed for. I'm incapable of an address! I might, perhaps, say a few words. An address, no! Let's keep that for the State of the Union and things like that. I have put down — it's always such a problem, you know. What should one do, anyway?

The rehearsed words, the prepared words, may or may not be suitable to the occasion. Nevertheless, one in all decency should prepare a few words, put one's mind on it, and I did, and whether or not something sensible might be said. And so, now, not even remembering quite what these words were, I have them in my pocket and will put them on the podium now. And if, in any way, they seem to be ridiculous, I will raise my hand and say, "I'm sorry," you know, or some other suitable apologetic remark.

As you know, Agee, with difficulty, reconciled himself to institutions in general, to educational and religious ones in particular, because the aspect of them that struck him and aroused him was their often deadening and muffling power over what was pure and immediate in perception, in thought, and in art. Truth took on falsity as it went from hand to hand — "radium into lead," as he once put it. Given his irritated sense of this aspect, he was sensitive to the complacency or pretense, detectable at any time, in what these institutions might claim for themselves, either openly or by implication. His skin crawled at any manifestation that seemed phony. And this became a great word with Jim. This, of course, made matters worse in the case of institutions that, by their very nature, must claim for themselves, at least implicitly, a great deal. Not that he was unaware of institutional virtues, disinterestedness, for example, and the honorable custody of good things. Oh no! He was aware of these. But he was just terribly alive to institutional defects.

I begin with these reflections because we have come here to see a library dedicated in Agee's name, at an institution that he attended. And we have to face, inevitably, such questions as how he would like this and what would he think of it. I think that the whole occasion, or in fact any such occasion, would have brought out in him that state of conflicting attitudes that he called a "split" or ambivalence. Any such occasion would have been aggravated to quite a pitch by the fact that he himself and his work are the objects of our piety.

At Houghton in Boston, they still remember a meeting that Paul Brooks, an editor there, had with Agee and Evans to talk over the format in which they were going to publish *Let Us Now Praise Famous Men*. When they came to the kind of paper it should be printed on, Agee said he thought the best thing would be newsprint. Brooks took this in and said mildly: "But Jim, newsprint! In fifty years newsprint will crumble away to dust." And Agee said, "That's what I mean!"

I could not speak for him to the point of knowing what attitude he might finally take toward the present occasion. But I can say, and it's high time I did, that the institution of St. Andrew's comes off pretty well in my own view of the matter. It is not that St. Andrew's has accepted Agee and, as we say, honored Agee. That would have been easy. And in a sense one has no choice — one has no choice.

But St. Andrew's has not only named its new library for him but has given a big place in it to his work, his films, everything that could be found and accumulated and stored and given respect, as will be shown to you now, as this afternoon some wonderful things were shown to me. So that's serious! And has not only honored him but deliberately, with public ceremony, as a school, as a community, has paid attention for a week to what he said.

Anybody who does this knows that along with profound pleasure, he has met both a chastening and a challenge. And as every institution breaks down into persons, there are a number of persons here to whom that chastening and that challenge have come home by virtue of this institutional occasion.

So what else or what more could Agee expect or desire? He wanted, above all, to make what he had seen visible to other people. He wanted to make what he felt apprehensible to other people. He went to great lengths, took exquisite pains that this should occur. Not very many of us will be up to the full range of what he registered. I am not. But to the extent that each of us can take it in, he will know that his own mind and senses have been enlarged and alerted, and his life will be slightly changed.

Suppose Agee had not gone to work in New York. Suppose he had never taken the direction that led to the Alabama book or to cinema. Suppose he had accepted the art of fiction as capacious enough for him for life and had settled into it with all his heart. Just suppose. That very likely would entail a somewhat different Agee. But let us make the supposition just the same, or the hypothesis, because the consequences would have so clearly been very interesting. Imagine a series of fictional works beginning thirty-five years ago and still in progress; works in which the experience of a variety of Americans would be embodied, full of their own truth, as he conceived the task when he thought of it in his twenties — in situations worked up by an imagination of perfect courage, concern for the deepest meaning, as well as the most dramatic and musical form. Our landscape in narrative literature would have one more long vista, marked by eminence. Not long ago a writer in the *London Times Literary Supplement* touched on this only partly realized possibility. He said that through Agee, a positive creative attitude could well have established its own tradition in this country, and that was everybody's loss that the American novel had, in effect, waved good-bye to everything Agee represented. And he went on to say that Agee was not bored by virtue but could see what was interesting about normality, and that "when he went down he took three or four decades of ordinary American life with him."

That's very penetrating in a way, and at the same time oversimplified, overdramatized, to put it in those terms. In England, they may be too aware of our sensational fiction, of our rough stuff, and not aware enough of the very beautiful work done here in those very decades for ordinary American life — done, a lot of it, by writers in the South — by some who have been here, in fact. My characterization of Agee somewhat misses, too. He was not bored by virtue, that's true. But he was not bored by anything. It was not so much that he could see what was interesting about normality but that he saw no such thing. He did not see, let us say, a small boy's normal fear of the dark. He saw with measured, grave, intrepid precision, a specific soul, alone, with specific powers of darkness. (I'm thinking of some great pages in *A Death in the Family.*) Allowed to have seen this, to have seen this and to have had the means of putting it down were both, in Agee, tokens of what I should call high culture — a culture of mind and memory embracing the religious — not just the religious interest but the religious consciousness. It is high culture that he would have brought to the American novel. And we have needed all we could get of that in these decades amid so many examples of mere brilliance, mere fantasy, mere savagery, mere cheapness. At the height of his bent, Agee did not present ordinary American life but American life transfigured by the attitudes he saw it under. This is true of the grand passages of the tenant farmer book and the two novels. If he had devoted himself to fiction from the start — this is my hypothesis — would there not be a great deal more of this? A great deal more, too, in the way of invented form?

Now, last point, the high culture of which I speak. How did Agee come by it? He was apt for it, yes. But where did it come from? I think the answer is unavoidable: that he found it in the very institutions against whose failings he could flare up. When all is said and done, through St. Andrew's and Exeter and Harvard and the Church, he had the access to living traditions — venerable, but still fresh, because glimpsing them through all that betrays and obscures them, superior in quality, picking them out in their harsh difficulty and their tenuous delicacy and holding onto them strictly for what they were worth; he did not, because in honesty he could not regard certain values as shown up or superseded. He explored them and he brought them to bear, for the compunction and the elevation of Americans.

Chronology

1909 November 27
      James Rufus Agee born in Knoxville, Tennessee.
1916 May 18
      Agee's father, Hugh James Agee, killed in automobile
      accident.
1919 Autumn
      Enters St. Andrew's, a boarding school for boys. Meets Father
      Flye and his wife, who live on school grounds.
1924 Agee's mother marries Father Erskine Wright, bursar at St. An-
      drew's; they move to Rockland, Maine.
1925 Summer
      Visits France and England with Father Flye.
      Autumn

Enters Phillips Exeter Academy, Exeter, New Hampshire. Corresponds with Dwight Macdonald.

1927 Elected editor of *Exeter Monthly* and president of Lantern Club (literary club).

1928 Autumn
Enters Harvard University; Robert Saudek is his roommate.

1929 Summer
Works in Nebraska and Kansas.

1930 Robert Fitzgerald is his classmate in Robert Hillyer's and I. A. Richards's classes.

1931 Agee is president of *Harvard Advocate*.
May
"The Truce," a short story, published in *Harvard Advocate*.

1932 Spring
Graduates from Harvard, and as a result of a parody issue of *Time* and of Dwight Macdonald's efforts, is engaged as a cub reporter, then as a regular staff writer for *Fortune* in Chrysler Building.

1933 January 28
Marries Olivia Saunders.

1934 October
Permit Me Voyage published in Yale Series of Younger Poets, with foreword by Archibald MacLeish.

1935 November to May 1936
Leave of absence from *Fortune*; lives and writes in Anna Maria, Florida.

1936 Spring
Attends David McDowell's commencement at St. Andrew's while visiting Father Flye.
Summer
Spends eight weeks with Walker Evans in Alabama, interviewing and photographing tenant families for a series of *Fortune* articles.

1938 Spring
Moves to 27 Second Street, Frenchtown, New Jersey.
Marries Alma Mailman.

1939 Summer
Delivers manuscript of *Three Tenant Families* to Harper.
Begins reviewing books for *Time* with Whittaker Chambers.
Robert Fitzgerald works with Agee at *Time*.
T. S. Matthews is Agee's editor at *Time*.

1939 Moves to Saint James Place, Brooklyn, New York.

1940 March 20
First son, Joel, born. Agee moves to West 15th Street.
Robert Fitzgerald leaves *Time*.

1941 Autumn
Let Us Now Praise Famous Men published by Houghton
Mifflin.
October
Begins reviewing films for *Time*.
Moves to Bleeker Street.
Robert Fitzgerald returns to *Time*.

1942 December to September 1948
Writes signed column on films for the *Nation*.

1943 May
Robert Fitzgerald joins navy.

1945 *In the Street*, a short, lyrical documentary film, directed and
photographed by Helen Levitt, Janice Loeb, and James Agee.
Autumn
Begins writing special feature stories for *Time*. Marries Mia
Fritsch.

1946 November 7
First daughter, Julia Teresa, is born.
Robert Fitzgerald returns to New York.

1948 Leaves *Time*. Under contract to Huntington Hartford, writes
film scripts based on "The Blue Hotel" and "The Bride

Comes to Yellow Sky" by Stephen Crane.

Writes commentary for Helen Levitt's film *The Quiet One*.

World premier of *Knoxville: Summer of 1915* for soprano and orchestra, music by Samuel Barber, words by Agee, with Eleanor Steber singing and Serge Koussevitzsky conducting the Boston Symphony Orchestra (recorded 1950; later recorded with Leontyne Price).

1949 September 3

"Comedy's Greatest Era," a study of silent film comedians, published in *Life*.

1950 May 15

His second daughter, Andrea Maria, born.

Spring

Robert Fitzgerald sees Agee for the last time.

Louis Kronenberger sees Agee for the last time.

Autumn

Goes to California to work with John Huston on a script for *The African Queen*, based on C. S. Forester's novel.

September 18

"Undirectable Director," a portrait of John Huston, is published in *Life*.

1951 January

Has first heart attack, in California.

April

The Morning Watch published by Houghton Mifflin.

1952 Writes script on the life of Lincoln, commissioned by the Ford Foundation for television (*Omnibus*, Robert Saudek, producer).

Whittaker Chambers sees Agee for the last time.

July

"A Mother's Tale" published in *Harper's Bazaar*.

1953 Writes script for *Noa Noa*, based on Paul Gauguin's diary.

1954 Writes script for *The Night of the Hunter*, based on a novel by
Davis Grubb.

Father Flye leaves St. Andrew's after the death of his wife in
January.

September 6

His second son, John Alexander, born.

1955 May 16

Dies of a heart attack while riding in a taxicab in New York
City.

Father Flye comes from Wichita to conduct funeral service;
Agee is buried in Hillsdale, New York.

1957 *A Death in the Family* published posthumously by McDowell-
Obolensky, edited by David McDowell.

1958 *A Death in the Family* wins Pulitzer Prize.

Agee on Film, published by McDowell-Obolensky.

1959 Father Flye moves to New York City.

1960 Second volume of *Agee on Film* published by McDowell-
Obolensky, with foreword by John Huston.

Let Us Now Praise Famous Men reprinted by Houghton Mifflin, with new preface by Walker Evans.

November 30

All the Way Home, stage adaptation of *A Death in the Family*,
opens. Wins Pulitzer Prize and Drama Critics Award.

1961 *Letters of James Agee to Father Flye* published by George Bra-
ziller, Inc., with essay by Robert Phelps.

1963 *All the Way Home*, screen adaptation of the play and novel
appears.

1965 *A Way of Seeing*, photographs of Spanish Harlem by Helen
Levitt, with an essay by James Agee, published by Viking.

1966 *Agee*, by Peter H. Ohlin, published by Obolensky.

Agee's mother dies.

1967 Autumn

Film Heritage publishes special Agee issue.

1968 *The Collected Poems of James Agee*, edited with an introduction by Robert Fitzgerald, published by Houghton Mifflin.

1969 *The Collected Short Prose of James Agee*, with "Memoir" by Robert Fitzgerald, published by Houghton Mifflin.

1971 *James Agee: A Portrait* released by Caedmon records, with Agee speaking "a letter to a friend" and reading from his work (1953), and Father Flye reminiscing and reading from Agee's work.

Second edition of *Letters of James Agee to Father Flye*, with a new preface by Father Flye and previously unpublished letters, introduction by Robert Phelps, published by Houghton Mifflin.

1972 Spring

Harvard Advocate publishes commemorative issue on James Agee.

October

Agee Week Conference and dedication of Memorial Library at St. Andrew's School in Tennessee.

1974 *Remembering James Agee*, edited by David Madden, published by Louisiana State University Press.

1979 *Agee*. Film by Ross Spears produced by the James Agee Film Project.

1981 *Twelve Years: An American Boyhood in East Germany*, by Joel Agee, published by Farrar.

1984 *James Agee: A Life*, full-length biography by Laurence Bergreen, published by Dutton.

1989 Agee Legacy Symposium at University of Tennessee, Knoxville.

1992 *James Agee: Reconsiderations*, edited by Michael A. Lofaro, published by the University of Tennessee Press.

Contributors

MIA AGEE was born in Vienna, Austria, and came to the United States in the late thirties. She was a *Fortune* researcher when she met Agee. The mother of three of Agee's four children, she worked after Agee's death at the University of California, San Diego. Her memoir is based on an interview Gerald Locklin conducted with her in the winter of 1974.

CHARLES ANGERMEYER is a graduate of St. Andrew's School. He produced the documentary *School on a Hill*, which was screened at the Agee Week Conference in 1972.

SCOTT BATES taught in the theater department at the University of the South. He has published extensively on Apollinaire and contributed essays and poems to many national publications.

EDWARD CARLOS served as a member of the Department of Fine Arts at the University of the South at the time of the Agee Week Conference.

WHITTAKER CHAMBERS was born in 1901 in Philadelphia. He attended Columbia from 1920 to 1922. As book reviewer, writer, and editor at *Time* beginning in 1938, he was a close associate of Agee. He was a contributor to *Life's Pictorial History of Western Civilization* (1947) and wrote two autobiographical books, *Witness* (1952) and the posthumously published *Cold Friday* (1964).

ARTHUR BEN CHITTY has served in administrative posts at the University of the South, including director of public relations from 1946 to 1965.

BRAINARD CHENEY was a novelist and a journalist with several Nashville newspapers.

ROBERT DANIEL was born in Memphis in 1915. He graduated from the University of the South and earned his Ph.D. from Yale University in 1939. He taught at various universities before coming to Kenyon College in 1960.

WALKER EVANS was born in 1903 in St. Louis. He began taking photographs in 1928 after returning from studies at the Sorbonne in Paris. He met Agee in Greenwich Village in 1936 and went with him to Alabama to research and take photographs for *Let Us Now Praise Famous Men*. His photographs are collected in three other volumes: *American Photographs* (1938), *Many Are Called* (1966), and *Message from the Interior* (1966). The Museum of Modern Art held a retrospective of his work in 1971. He taught at Yale before his death in 1975.

WARREN EYSTER taught at Louisiana State University, where he directed the creative writing program. He is the author of many works of fiction.

ROBERT FITZGERALD, poet, critic, translator, was born in Geneva, New York, in 1910 and grew up in Springfield, Illinois. One year behind Agee at Harvard, he was a member of the *Harvard Advocate*. He wrote for the *New York Herald Tribune* (1933–1935) and *Time* (1936–1949); and he taught at Sarah Lawrence (1946–1953) and Princeton (1950–1952); he also served as Boylston Professor of Rhetoric at Harvard. His volumes of poetry are *Poems* (1935), *A Wreath for the Sea* (1943), *In the Rose of Time* (1956), and *Spring Shade* (1971). For his translation of *The Odyssey* he received the Bollingen Award in 1961. For many years until his death in 1985, his permanent residence was in Perugia, Italy.

FATHER JAMES HAROLD FLYE was a history teacher at St. Andrew's for almost forty years (1918–1954). He later held posts in Wichita, Kansas, and New York City. Agee's teacher and friend, he edited *Letters of James Agee to Father Flye*, first and second editions.

JEFFREY J. FOLKS has degrees from Reed College and Indiana University, where he received his Ph.D. in 1977. He has taught at Tennessee Wesleyan College and in Macedonia and Bulgaria on Fulbright lectureships. His book *Southern Writers and the Machine: Faulkner to Percy* appeared in 1993. With James A. Perkins he edited *Southern Writers at Century's End*. He is professor of literature at Miyazaki International College in Japan.

FLORENCE HOMOLKA inspired the following comment by the editor of *Focus on Art: Photography and Notes by Florence Homolka*: "She is a photographer's photographer. An artist in her own right she has moved with quietude and humility through life, and she has photographed extraordinary people under extraordinary conditions — in their homes. Certainly Mrs. Homolka could never have done so had she not received their regard and friendship in return." She died in 1962.

JOHN HUSTON was born in 1906 in Missouri. Included among the works of this highly individual director, writer, and occasional actor are *The Maltese Falcon* (1941), *Treasure of the Sierra Madre* (1947), *The Asphalt Jungle* (1950), *The Red Badge of Courage* (1951), *The African Queen* (1952), the script for which was written predominantly by Agee, *Moby-Dick* (1956), an experiment in color, *Reflections in a*

Golden Eye (1967), and *The Man Who Would Be King* (1975). Mr. Huston lived in Ireland until his death in 1987.

LOUIS KRONENBERGER was born in Cincinnati in 1904. After serving as an editor for Boni & Liveright and Alfred A. Knopf (1926–1935) and as board member of *Fortune* (1936–1939), he became drama critic for *Time* (1938–1961). From 1952 until retiring in 1970, he was professor of theater arts at Brandeis; between 1950 and 1968 he was a visiting professor at Columbia, City College of New York, Harvard, Stanford, and Berkeley; he also gave lectures at Oxford and the Christian Gauss seminars at Princeton. He was a member of the National Institute of Arts and Letters and of the American Academy of Arts and Sciences. Mr. Kronenberger was the author of *Kings and Desperate Men* (1942), *Company Manners* (1954), *Marlborough's Duchess* (1958), *The Cart and the Horse* (1964), *No Whippings, No Gold Watches* (1970), and *The Extraordinary Mr. Wilkes* (1974). He adapted Jean Anouilh's *Colombe* for Broadway (1954) and edited numerous books, including the Burns Mantle *Best Plays* (1953–1961), and he was general editor of the Great Letters series and the Masters of World Literature series.

JAMES WARD LEE, a member of the Department of English at the University of North Texas, edited the scholarly journal *Studies in the Novel* and published extensively on American fiction, including books on J. D. Salinger, William Humphrey, and John Braine.

HELEN LEVITT was born in New York City. With James Agee and Janice Loe, she made *In the Street* (1945), an award-winning documentary set in the upper East Side of Manhattan. Agee wrote the commentary and dialogue for *The Quiet One* (1948), a feature documentary to which she contributed some camera work; first-prize winner at the Venice Film Festival, it is narrated by Gary Merrill. Her photographs have appeared in exhibits at the Museum of Modern Art and the Chicago Institute of Design. Her book of photographs, *A Way of Seeing*, with an essay by Agee, appeared in 1964.

GERALD LOCKLIN was born in Rochester, New York, in 1941. He has been teaching literature at California State in Long Beach since

1966 and has written fiction and several volumes of poetry; two of his essays appear in *Nathanael West: The Cheaters and the Cheated.*

ANDREW LYTLE is one of this century's foremost southern writers. His novel *The Velvet Horn* has been frequently reprinted, and his nonfiction includes *The Hero with the Private Parts* and a family memoir, *A Wake for the Living.*

DWIGHT MACDONALD was born in New York City in 1906. He began corresponding with Agee soon after his graduation from Phillips Exeter Academy in 1924. After graduation from Yale in 1928, he became a staff writer for *Fortune* (1929–1936). He was an editor of *Partisan Review* (1938–1943), editor and publisher of *Politics* (1944–1949), and advisory editor of *Encounter* (1956–1957). He was a movie reviewer for *Esquire* and a staff writer for the *New Yorker* in the fifties and sixties. Among his books are *Henry Wallace, the Man and Myth* (1948), *Memoirs of a Revolutionist* (1957), *Against the American Grain* (1962), and *Dwight Macdonald on Movies* (1969). He was also editor of *Parodies* (1960). A collection of his essays, *Discriminations,* was published in 1972 by Grossman. Macdonald died in 1982.

DAVID MCDOWELL was born in 1918. From 1931 to 1936, he attended St. Andrew's, where he first met Agee. He was an editor for New Directions, Random House, and the *Saturday Evening Post.* He was editor and publisher of *A Death in the Family* and *Agee on Film,* volumes 1 and 2. Custodian of the James Agee Trust, he was also a senior editor at Crown Publishers. At the time of his death in 1985, Mr. McDowell was writing a biography of Agee and editing Agee's letters.

DAVID MADDEN was writer-in-residence at Louisiana State University from 1968 to 1992; he directed the creative writing program from 1992 to 1994. He also created and became director of the United States Civil War Center at LSU in 1992. Born and raised in Knoxville, Tennessee, he has published seven novels, including *Bijou, Cassandra Singing, The Suicide's Wife,* and *Sharpshooter,* a novel of the Civil War. He has also published books on Wright Morris, James M. Cain, and Nathanael West.

FREDERICK MANFRED has enjoyed a long career as one of America's foremost western novelists. Born in Iowa in 1912, Mr. Manfred has published many novels, including *The Chokecherry Tree, Lord Grizzly, Riders of Judgment,* and *King of Spades.*

FATHER FRANKLIN MARTIN was headmaster of St. Andrew's School at the time of the Agee Week Conference.

T. S. MATTHEWS was born in Cincinnati in 1901. Having graduated from Princeton in 1922 and from Oxford in 1924, he worked for the *New Republic* from 1925 to 1929, when he began writing for *Time*; he was managing editor of *Time* from 1943 until 1950; Agee wrote many articles under his editorship. His books include *To the Gallows I Must Go* (1931); *The Sugar Pill* (1959); *Name and Address* (1960), an autobiography; *O My America!* (1962); and *Great Tom* (1974), a biography of T. S. Eliot. He lived in Suffolk, England, until his death in 1991.

CYNTHIA O'FLAHERTY was a member of the English Department at St. Andrew's School at the time of the Agee Week Conference.

WALKER PERCY was one of the most influential American novelists and social critics. His novel *The Moviegoer* was awarded the National Book Award in 1965. His other books included *The Last Gentleman, Lancelot,* and *The Second Coming.* Percy also published several influential works of nonfiction, including *The Message in the Bottle.*

JOHN REISHMAN is dean and director of summer school at the University of the South.

ROBERT SAUDEK was born in Pittsburgh in 1911. He was Agee's roommate at Harvard. A television and film producer, he has won four Peabody and twelve Emmy Awards. He produced *Omnibus*, which presented Agee's series on Lincoln and the award-winning series *Profiles in Courage*, based on John F. Kennedy's book. He was also a visiting lecturer in visual studies at Harvard.

Edwin M. Stirling taught in the Department of English at the University of the South for many years.

William Stott is professor of American studies at the University of Texas. His pioneering work on American documentary writing includes the book *Documentary Expression and Thirties America*.

Agee, James Rufus (*continued*)
xiii, xxix, 24, 113, 115, 244; and failure,
xv, xxviii, 81, 113, 117, 128, 167, 182, 221,
222; and his father, xvi, 92, 172, 189–
90, 198, 205, 206 (see also *Death in the
Family, A*); as film critic, xiii, xxix, 82,
150–51, 222, 239; and love of film, 81,
85, 180, 222, 231; and filmmaking, 84,
150, 180; longing for freedom, xiv, 60,
61, 79–80, 121, 169, 184, 221, 222 (*see
also* Guggenheim Fellowship); generosity of, 92, 96; gestures of, 98, 215,
219; and Harvard Glee Club, 13, 45;
health of, 52, 91, 180; humor of, 174,
225; and innocence, 42, 137, 146, 153,
160, 202; as innovator and precursor,
xii, xiii, xxix, xxx, 24, 222; integrity of,
xxiv, 96, 121, 183, 223, 224; and journalism, xii, xviii, xxix, 53, 84, 111, 183; as
listener, 13, 90; marriages of, 65, 71,
77, 80, 86, 126, 174, 175, 198, 225 (*see
also* Fritsch, Mia; Mailman, Alma;
Saunders, Olivia); as mimic, 63, 237,
241; morality of, xiv, xvii, xix, 117, 173;
and musical influence, 61, 137, 140,
172, 180, 223, 232; as musician, 74, 223,
233; and night, 48, 98–99, 131, 223;
overreaching by, xxviii, 30, 48, 72;
parodies by, 62, 63; physical appearance of, 11, 40, 52, 73, 74, 91, 97, 98,
211–12, 213, 219; as poet, xiii, 22–34,
85, 171, 172, 185, 211, 238; poetic prose
of, xii, 31, 92, 180, 237, 238; and politics, xiv, xvi, 39, 58, 84, 151, 181, 182,
239; quest for identity by, xv, xvi, 96;
reading aloud by, 14, 66, 69, 90, 92,
215, 232, 238, 240; and rebellion, xv,
99, 177; and reception of his work,
167, 181, 182; and religion, xxviii, 8, 9,
47, 51, 54, 55, 62, 83, 84, 99, 128, 134,
178, 182, 187, 190, 196, 203, 204, 219,
223, 225, 245; and screenwriting, xii–
xiii, 82, 180, 222; self-criticism by, xiii,
29, 30, 57, 85, 222; self-destructive personality of, xviii, xxviii, 13, 178, 179,
180, 212, 219, 223, 225, 241; selflessness

of, xvi, 80; and sensitivity toward others, 9, 42, 99, 103, 110, 119, 125, 129, 145,
166, 191, 211, 212, 227, 241; and sentimentality (*see* Sentimentality); and
sexuality, 103, 104; spirituality of, xiv,
99, 104, 106, 196; and truth, xiii, 56,
57, 62, 84, 140, 142, 149, 150, 151, 181,
183, 244; value of the human being by,
xiii, xiv, 116, 119, 245; voice of, xxvi, 97
WORKS BY:
— *The African Queen*, xxii, 86, 108, 146,
148, 153, 154–60, 178, 180, 223, 227;
Agee on Film, 108; "Ann Garner," 41;
"The Bride Comes to Yellow Sky"
(Agee's adaptation of), xxvi, 178; "Chorale," 54, 55; *The Collected Poems of
James Agee*, 47, 85, 238, 240; *The Collected Short Prose of James Agee*, 235;
A Death in the Family (*see under main
entry title*); "Dedication," 9, 54, 55;
"Delinquent," 33; "Epithalamium,"
16, 41; "The Great American Roadside," xiv, 58; "Knoxville: Summer
1915," xxv, 92, 173, 200, 207, 238, 239;
Let Us Now Praise Famous Men (*see
under main entry title*); "A Lullaby,"
33, 34; "A Mother's Tale," 167, 177, 184;
The Morning Watch (*see under main
entry title*); *The Night of the Hunter*,
xxii, 153, 178, 223; "Night Piece,"
("Theme with Variations"), 49; "Notes
for a Moving Picture: The House," 82;
Permit Me Voyage, 31, 53, 54, 65, 177,
181; "Six Days at Sea," 64; "Sleep,
Child," 85; "Songs on the Economy
of Abundance," 65; "Sunday: Out-
skirts of Knoxville," 65; "They That
Sow in Sorrow Shall Reap," 87; "The
Truce," 44, 45; introduction to *A Way
of Seeing*, 63; writing habits of, 14, 43–
44, 48, 72, 74, 98–99, 131, 223
Agee, Joel, 74, 78
Agee, John, xxvi
Agee, Mia. *See* Fritsch, Mia
Agee, Teresa, 85
Agee on Film, 108

Index   263